MONOGRAPHS OF THE
SOCIETY FOR RESEARCH IN
CHILD DEVELOPMENT

Serial No. 263, Vol. 65, No. 4, 2000

PARAMETERS OF REMEMBERING AND FORGETTING IN THE TRANSITION FROM INFANCY TO EARLY CHILDHOOD

Patricia J. Bauer
Jennifer A. Wenner
Patricia L. Dropik
Sandi S. Wewerka

WITH COMMENTARY BY
Mark L. Howe

MONOGRAPHS OF THE SOCIETY FOR RESEARCH IN CHILD DEVELOPMENT
Serial No. 263, Vol. 65, No. 4, 2000

CONTENTS

ABSTRACT

BAUER, PATRICIA J.; WENNER, JENNIFER A.; DROPIK, PATRICIA L.; and WEWERKA, SANDI S. Parameters of Remembering and Forgetting in the Transition from Infancy to Early Childhood. With Commentary by MARK L. HOWE. *Monographs of the Society for Research in Child Development*, 2000, **65** (4, Serial No. 263).

The ability to recall is something that most intact adults take for granted. For much of the last century, this feature of mental life was not considered to extend to very young children. There now is evidence that 1- to 2-year-olds are able to recall specific events after delays of several months. Over the short term, 1- to 2-year-olds' recall is affected by the same factors that affect older children's recall; it is not clear whether similar effects are apparent over the long term. Moreover, although age-related increases in long-term recall are assumed, there have been few empirical tests of the question.

We examined recall by 14- to 32-month-olds for events experienced at 13 to 20 months. Using elicited imitation of novel multistep event sequences we examined effects of (a) delay length, (b) age at the time of experience, (c) temporal structure of events, (d) mode of experience of events, and (e) availability of verbal reminders, on long-term recall. Participants were 360 children enrolled at 13 (n = 90), 16 (n = 180), and 20 (n = 90) months. All of the 13-month-olds and half of the 16-month-olds were tested on 3-step event sequences; all of the 20-month-olds and half of the 16-month-olds were tested on 4-step event sequences. Within each age and step-length group, equal numbers of children were tested after intervals of 1, 3, 6, 9, and 12 months (n = 18 per cell). Children were tested on a variety of sequence types. For half of the events, imitation was permitted prior to the delay; for the other half, children were not permitted imitation. At delayed testing, children experienced a recall period during which they were cued by the event-related props alone, followed by a period in which recall was cued both by the event-related props and by verbal labels for the event sequences.

Within step-length groups, the length of time for which older and younger children showed evidence of memory did not differ. Nevertheless, when the children were prompted by the event-related props alone, there were age-related differences in the robustness of children's memories (as indexed by higher levels of recall for older children relative to younger children). When the children were prompted by the props and by verbal labels for the event sequences, at the longer retention intervals, there were age-related differences in the robustness of children's memories and in the reliability with which recall was evidenced (as indexed by the larger numbers of older children evincing recall). Age-related effects were particularly apparent on children's ordered recall. Across the entire age range, the children were similarly affected by the variables of sequence type, opportunity for imitation, and verbal reminding.

I. INTRODUCTION

The ability to form, retain, and later retrieve memories of both mundane, everyday events and unique experiences is something that most intact adults take for granted. Whereas we might at times marvel at the apparently random chains of events that bring to mind memories presumed long since forgotten, we do not take particular note of the fact that such experiences occur. In contrast, for most of the last century, researchers and theoreticians subscribed, either explicitly or implicitly, to the view that infants and very young children do not share this feature of mental life. Quite the contrary—it was widely assumed that the young of our species did not, and, furthermore, could not, recall previous experiences. The past 2 decades have seen challenges to this assumption. Current theory ascribes to infants and young children explicit representational ability (e.g., Mandler, 1998); there is mounting empirical evidence that by the second half of the 1st year of life, children are able to recall specific events (e.g., Barr, Dowden, & Hayne, 1996; Carver & Bauer, 1999; Meltzoff, 1988b). What remains uncharted are the parameters of remembering and forgetting during the period of transition from infancy to early childhood, the age range during which recall abilities consolidate and become reliable. In this *Monograph*, we report the results of a large-scale investigation of mnemonic performance by children aged 13 to 20 months at the time of experience of events and 14 to 32 months at the time of recall of them. In it we examined effects of (a) age at the time of experience of events, (b) the length of the delay interval over which recall was tested, (c) the nature of to-be-remembered events, (d) the mode of experience of events, and (e) the availability of reminders of events, on long-term recall.

TRADITIONAL CONCEPTUALIZATIONS OF YOUNG CHILDREN'S MNEMONIC COMPETENCE

For much of the period of history of cognitive and developmental science, it was widely assumed that infants and very young children were

1

unable to form memories of specific events that would endure and be accessible over time. The assumption was apparent both in general theories of cognitive development and in theories of memory phenomena. It was particularly prominent in theories designed to account for the phenomenon of infantile or childhood amnesia—the relative paucity among adults of memories of events that happened before their 3rd or 4th birthday (e.g., Rubin, 1982; Sheingold & Tenney, 1982; West & Bauer, 1999; Winograd & Killinger, 1983; although see Eacott & Crawley, 1998, and Usher & Neisser, 1993, for adults' reports of events from the age of 2 years). Freud referred to the absence among adults of recollections of unique events experienced in the first years of life as the "remarkable amnesia of childhood ... the forgetting which veils our earliest youth from us and makes us strangers to it" (1916/1966, p. 326). A variety of explanations for the amnesia were advanced. Most shared the perspective that over the course of development, recall processes change qualitatively. For example, in addition to his more widely known explanation of infantile amnesia, namely, that memories of early childhood exist, but are repressed (Freud, 1916/1966), Freud also proposed that the memories created by very young children are qualitatively different from those formed later in life. Early in development, children were thought to retain traces, fragments, or images of events, but not to retain coherent representations of past experiences (Freud, 1905/1953). Freud suggested that childhood amnesia exists because adults failed to reconstruct or "translate" these fragments into a coherent narrative (see Pillemer & White, 1989, for further discussion of this and related proposals).

Predictions of qualitative change in what information is encoded, in how it is encoded, or both, also serve as the centerpiece of more contemporary social (e.g., Neisser, 1967, 1988; Schachtel, 1947) and cognitive (e.g., Wetzler & Sweeney, 1986; White & Pillemer, 1979) accounts of the dearth of memories from infancy and early childhood. Although these accounts differ widely in their attributions, they have in common the notion that cognitive structures change qualitatively over time. After the change, children are thought capable of forming memories of specific events or episodes that they later are able to recall. Before the qualitative change, they either cannot form such memories (e.g., Piaget, 1952), or early memories become inaccessible over the course of development (e.g., Bower, 1981; Neisser, 1962, 1988).

Until surprisingly recently, largely absent from the scene of speculation as to the source (or sources) of infantile amnesia were any data that bore on the issues of whether children actually are able to form and retain accessible memories of the events that they experience. As a result, theories developed to explain the "remarkable amnesia of childhood"

(Freud, 1916/1966) were uninformed with respect to a critical point, namely, whether their charge was to account for why memories of events from early in life are not formed, or why they later seemingly become inaccessible. The past 20 years have been witness to a correction to this oversight in the form of a virtual explosion of research on memory by children as young as preschool age. The findings have been strikingly consistent: Young children are able to verbally recall events from the recent as well as the distant past (see Fivush, 1997, for a review). The first reports of early mnemonic competence began "leaking out" in 1980, largely in the form of diary studies and naturalistic observations (e.g., Ratner, 1980; Todd & Perlmutter, 1980). On their heels was Nelson and Gruendel's 1981 publication of their research showing that children as young as 3 years of age already have well-organized representations of familiar events, such as going to McDonald's. The 1986 publication of Katherine Nelson's edited volume *Event Knowledge: Structure and Function in Development* brought additional evidence of preschoolers' mnemonic prowess (e.g., Hudson, 1986; Nelson & Gruendel, 1986; Slackman, Hudson, & Fivush, 1986; see K. Nelson, 1997, for further discussion of early developments in the study of young children's memory). These findings not only provided the impetus for further examination of questions as to the fate of children's earliest autobiographical memories (e.g., Fivush, Gray, & Fromhoff, 1987; Hamond & Fivush, 1991) but also for work on basic mnemonic processes in children younger than age 3: If 3-year-olds already evidence coherent memories of past events, the capacity to construct them must have developed earlier. It is on developments in the fundamental ability to recall the past in children younger than 3 on which the present report is focused.

METHODOLOGICAL ISSUES

The study of event memory in children younger than the preschool years presents a major methodological challenge: Because they are largely pre- or early-verbal, children younger than 3 cannot adequately be tested with the paradigm of choice for memory researchers, namely, verbal report. Even from preschoolers, verbal reports are elicited only with prompting and directed questioning by adults (Fivush et al., 1987; Fivush & Hamond, 1990). In Hamond and Fivush (1991), for example, 78% of the information provided by 3- to 5-year-olds in a structured interview was elicited by prompts and directed questions from the adult interviewer. Moreover, compared with nonverbal measures of recall memory (described below), verbal measures underestimate the mnemonic competence of children as old as 6 years of age (Fivush, Kuebli, & Clubb, 1992; Price & Goodman, 1990; Smith, Ratner, & Hobart, 1987). For example, in Goodman, Rudy, Bottoms, and Aman (1990), 5-year-olds recalled twice as much information when they were asked to act out an event than when asked to provide a verbal report of it.

By necessity, researchers have looked to nonverbal behaviors for evidence of memory in preverbal children. Use of such methods has revealed that, from very early in life, infants are capable of some amazing mnemonic feats. At only a few days old, they demonstrate recognition memory (e.g., Slater, 1995). For some stimuli (e.g., faces), recognition takes place after delays of as long as 2 weeks (see Fagan, 1990, for discussion). Rovee-Collier and her colleagues have shown that by 2 months of age infants are able to retain conditioned responses for up to 3 days (Greco, Rovee-Collier, Hayne, Griesler, & Earley, 1986); by 6 months, the retention interval increases to 14 days (Hill, Borovsky, & Rovee-Collier, 1988), and can be extended to 28 days by a brief reinstating experience (i.e., exposure to some component of the original test event) (Rovee-Collier & Fagen, 1981; see Rovee-Collier & Gerhardstein, 1997, for a review). Recent research indicates that some experiences may have even longer lasting effects: Myers, Perris, and Speaker (1994) provided evidence that experiences in the 1st year of life still may influence behavior at the age of 5 years. Thus, virtually from birth, infants are affected by experiences, the influences of which may be revealed even after a long time has elapsed. In fact, DeCasper and Spence (1986) suggest that even prenatal experiences later may manifest themselves in changes in behavior toward stimuli.

Use of nonverbal methods has yielded ample evidence of facilitated processing of previously encountered information, even by very young infants. However, because these demonstrations are not necessarily indicative of recall, they cannot inform questions regarding the development of that particular mnemonic function. Recall entails retrieving a cognitive structure, established on the basis of past experience, in the absence of ongoing perceptual support for that experience (Mandler, 1986). Recall is, by definition, a conscious product. When an adult provides a verbal report of a past experience it is clear that the remembered material has been made accessible to the conscious mind. Because the subjects of research on memory for experiences early in life are preverbal or barely verbal, we are unable to query them to ensure their awareness that their behaviors result from some previous experience. There is ambiguity then as to whether the basis on which we infer memory, namely, a change in nonverbal behavior, results from conscious recollection or unconscious influence. Because nonverbal methods of testing memory were used in the present research, we review the relevant arguments.

4

Distinguishing Declarative and Nondeclarative Memory

The distinction between a mnemonic behavior based on conscious recollection versus one resulting from an unconscious influence is fundamental. Although some have cautioned that application of the criterion of conscious awareness to preverbal and nonverbal organisms may not be reasonable, due to our inability to query them regarding their level of awareness (see, for example, C. A. Nelson, 1997, and Rovee-Collier, 1997), the distinction figures prominently in the memory literature in general and in particular, in the literature describing different types and subtypes of memory. Researchers have proposed a variety of classification schemes to capture the phenomena reflective of different mnemonic processes, including, but not limited to, distinctions between explicit and implicit (Schacter, 1987), declarative and procedural (Cohen & Squire, 1980; Mandler, 1984), and declarative and nondeclarative (Zola-Morgan & Squire, 1990) memory. The precise distinctions captured by these classifications are not identical. Nevertheless, they overlap to a large extent and they have in common a view that memory is best conceived not as a unitary trait, but as comprised of different systems or processes, which serve distinct functions, and are characterized by fundamentally different rules of operation (e.g., Sherry & Schacter, 1987; Squire, 1992; Tulving, 1985). For ease of exposition, throughout this *Monograph*, we use the terms "declarative" and "nondeclarative" to indicate the relevant distinctions.

Declarative memory captures most of what we think of when we refer to "memory" or "remembering" (Zola-Morgan & Squire, 1993). It involves the capacity for explicit recognition or recall of names, places, dates, events, and so on. In contrast, nondeclarative memory represents a variety of nonconscious abilities, including the capacity for learning habits and skills, priming, and some forms of classical conditioning (see Parkin, 1997, for a review). A defining feature of nondeclarative memory is that the impact of experience is made evident through a change in behavior or performance, but that the experience leading to the change is not consciously accessible (Zola-Morgan & Squire, 1993). Declarative memory is characterized as fast (e.g., supporting one-trial learning), fallible (e.g., memory traces degrade, retrieval failures occur), and flexible (i.e., not tied to a specific modality or context). Nondeclarative memory is characterized as slow (i.e., with the exception of priming, it results from gradual or incremental learning), reliable, and inflexible (Sherry & Schacter, 1987; Squire, Knowlton, & Musen, 1993). What tasks tapping declarative memory have in common is that they require recollection of a specific episode. In contrast, what tasks tapping nondeclarative memory have in common is that recollection of a specific episode is not required, and in most cases (priming being an exception), learning proceeds gradually, as a result of repeated practice.

In order to study development of the ability to recall the past, what is needed is a nonverbal analogue to verbal recall: The mnemonic behavior must be derived from a task that engages the same cognitive processes as those involved in verbal recall, yet does not require a verbal response. Because many of the behaviors infants can perform, such as looking for a longer period of time, or kicking more vigorously, cannot with confidence be attributed to the function of recall memory or even necessarily to declarative memory (C. A. Nelson, 1995), tasks based on them do not represent particularly viable candidates. In contrast, deferred imitation of actions (Meltzoff, 1990b, 1995) and elicited imitation of actions and action sequences (e.g., Bauer, 1995, 1997; Mandler, 1990; Mandler & McDonough, 1995; McDonough, Mandler, McKee, & Squire, 1995; Squire et al., 1993) increasingly are recognized as acceptable analogues. Because we used the imitation paradigm in the present research, we first describe the task and then review in some detail the argument that it affords a test of recall.

Elicited Imitation

In elicited imitation, props are used to demonstrate a specific action or action sequence. Either immediately after demonstration, after some delay, or both, the child is allowed to imitate the actions that the model produced. In our laboratory, before the event is modeled, the props are given to the children for a baseline period, during which spontaneous production of the target actions and sequences is assessed (in other laboratories, a between-subjects manipulation is used to obtain an uninstructed baseline: e.g., Meltzoff, 1988a). After baseline, experimenters label the event to be produced, and then narrate their actions as they use the props to produce the event. In situations in which immediate imitation is assessed, after modeling, the experimenter returns the props to the child, who is invited to imitate. To test retention of information over time, the child returns to the laboratory after an appointed delay. The props then are given to the child, with no instruction and no modeling. Procedurally, the delayed assessment period is identical to baseline. To the extent that production of target actions and sequences after exposure to the model differs from baseline, either immediately or after the delay, we infer memory for the event. A comparison of performance immediately after exposure to the model with that after the delay affords a test of the amount of information retained over the interval.

In some applications of the imitation task, the opportunity to imitate is deferred for a period of hours (e.g., Meltzoff, 1988a) to months (e.g., Meltzoff, 1995). That is, children are not permitted to imitate prior to imposition of a delay. Whereas, conceptually, elicited-imitation protocols that permit imitation prior to imposition of a delay and those that do not (i.e., deferred-imitation protocols) might be thought to test different underlying abilities (Piaget, 1952, 1962), empirically, it appears that they do not. Data relevant to this summary statement are described below. Because the term "elicited imitation" characterizes both protocols that require deferral of imitation and those that do not, unless the distinction between protocol types is relevant, for the balance of this *Monograph*, we will use the more generic term to refer to the task.

Elicited Imitation as a Nonverbal Measure of Recall

With elicited imitation, aspects of original learning and later testing of memory contraindicate suggestions that the infant's or child's behavior is mediated by a mechanism other than recall. First, it is unlikely that elicited imitation evidences acquisition of a nondeclarative procedural or sensorimotor memory. Gradual or incremental learning is characteristic of procedural or sensorimotor acquisition (Bachevalier, 1992; Mandler, 1988, 1990; Schacter & Moscovitch, 1984). Whereas procedural tasks such as serial reaction time require 200 to 400 interactive trials to be learned (Knopman & Nissen, 1987), in the elicited-imitation paradigm, children are provided as few as one to three exposures to novel, to-be-remembered events. The opportunity for reproduction of the events occurs only after they have been demonstrated; there is no opportunity for practice during exposure to the events. Furthermore, the opportunity to reproduce the test events prior to imposition of a delay is not necessary for later reproduction (e.g., Bauer, Hertsgaard, & Wewerka, 1995; Mandler & McDonough, 1995; Meltzoff, 1988a). These conditions are not conducive to procedural or sensorimotor acquisition (Mandler, 1990; Meltzoff, 1990b; Schacter & Moscovitch, 1984).

It also is unlikely that the infant's or child's behavior in elicited imitation evidences unconscious priming or reactivation, processes by which previously experienced information becomes activated in memory without awareness that it has been encountered before, and without deliberate search (e.g., Graf, Squire, & Mandler, 1984). It has been demonstrated that these processes are highly dependent on specific features of the stimuli: Changes across, as well as within, modality diminish the influence of prior experience (thus, one source of the characterization of nondeclarative memory as "inflexible") (Schacter, 1990). In adults, for example, word fragment priming effects decrease when target words are presented in the visual modality, but are tested auditorily (Jackson & Morton, 1984). Even within the visual modality, priming effects decrease when, for example, target words are presented in script, but at test are presented in typed form (Roediger & Blaxton, 1987). Similar levels of specificity are required to reactivate previously conditioned responses in infants. For example, in the conjugate reinforcement paradigm, unless they are trained on a variety of exemplars, if even a single feature of the design on the liner of the crib in which 6-month-old infants are trained is changed (e.g., the shape of the figures is changed from a square to a circle), the infants respond as if they have had no previous training (Rovee-Collier & Shyi, 1992).

In contrast, performance on the elicited-imitation task, like that on commonly used tests of declarative memory, is less affected by changes across or within modality. In fact, Meltzoff (1990b) has argued that the elicited-imitation task is a cross-modal one: The model is observed visually and later matched with the child's own actions. Imitation occurs even when the target action has been demonstrated by a televised model. For example, in Meltzoff (1988c), 14-month-olds visually perceived a black and white, two-dimensional model and later matched the behavior with their own actions using three-dimensional props. Nine-month-olds are able to use still photographs of events to facilitate long-term memory for them (Carver & Bauer, 1999). Moreover, within a modality, children generalize recall across manipulations of the specific features of the stimuli. For example, in Bauer and Dow (1994), 16- and 20-month-olds were tested for reproduction of target sequences immediately and after a 1-week interval. At delayed testing, the props for some of the sequences were changed. The new props could be used to produce events that were structurally identical to the originals (e.g., both versions of the event might involve pretending to put a character to bed), but with different surface instantiations (i.e., in one version, a large bear might be put into a large wooden bed, whereas in another version, a small dog might be put into a plastic crib). Although there was some decrement in children's production of the individual actions of the event sequences, (a) the children nevertheless used the new props to produce the individual target actions of the event sequences (see Barnat, Klein, & Meltzoff, 1996, for similar results on children's production of single object-specific actions), and (b) the prop-change manipulation had no effect on children's ordered recall. In sum, the circumstances of the elicited-imitation task contraindicate the possibility that performance on it could be supported by some form of nondeclarative memory. Consistent with this argument is the finding that adult humans suffering from amnesia (in whom declarative memory processes are disrupted) are unable to perform an age-appropriate version of the task (McDonough et al., 1995).

Finally, not only is performance on the elicited-imitation task indicative of declarative memory, it also can be differentiated from other demonstrations of declarative memory, such as are evidenced in some recognition tasks. The available props do provide perceptual support or cues to recall. However, this is not a critical distinction because all recall is cued, either by an external prompt (e.g., "Tell me what you remember about X"), or by an internal association (Spear, 1978). Moreover, in the case of imitation of multistep sequences, critical information about the order in which the event should unfold is not even perceptually cued: Once the model is gone, so are cues to temporal order. To reproduce previously modeled actions and action sequences then, information about what is to be performed, and in what order, must be encoded during demonstration and later retrieved from a representation of the event, in the absence of ongoing perceptual support. The circumstances of elicited imitation thus closely mimic those of standard verbal recall paradigms (Mandler, 1990), and the behaviors derived from it meet the definition of recall (see Bauer, 1995; Bauer, Hertsgaard, & Dow, 1994; Bauer & Mandler, 1992; Mandler, 1990; and Meltzoff, 1990b, for further discussion).

RECALL OF EVENTS BY INFANTS AND VERY YOUNG CHILDREN

There now exist sizeable literatures on infants' and young children's successes on a number of memory tasks (e.g., habituation, preferential looking, acquisition of conditioned responses). However, because, as discussed above, it is not clear that they assess recall ability, we do not include discussion of findings from these tasks in the review to follow. Moreover, although elicited imitation and other re-enactment paradigms have been used with children throughout the preschool years (e.g., Fivush et al., 1992), we restrict our review to studies conducted with children who, at the time of experience of the to-be-remembered event, were age 24 months and younger. We do so in order to focus specifically on issues most relevant to development of recall ability in children in the target age range, namely, the 2nd year of life. We have targeted the 2nd year of life because it is during that time that recall abilities consolidate and become reliable. The bases for this argument are outlined below.

The Neural Correlates of Long-Term Recall

There is increasing speculation and evidence that in human infants, the neural substrate necessary for long-term recall undergoes significant development during the second half of the 1st year of life. The capacity to recall an event that happened in the past is thought to depend upon a specific neural substrate, namely, a cortico-limbic-diencephalic circuit involving medial temporal lobe structures (e.g., the amygdala and hippocampus and surrounding cortices) as well as higher cortical association areas (Mishkin & Appenzeller, 1987; Squire & Zola-Morgan, 1991), including the prefrontal cortex and sensory association areas. Medial temporal lobe structures are necessary for consolidation of new memories (i.e., those

9

established within days or weeks) (e.g., Squire, 1992; Zola-Morgan & Squire, 1990); neocortical association areas serve as the storage sites for long-term memories (Squire, 1992; Zola-Morgan & Squire, 1993); prefrontal cortex most likely serves the function of retrieval of representations (Tulving et al., 1994). Thus, the establishment and maintenance of specific event memories that can be recalled after long delays requires the functioning of medial temporal lobe structures, neocortical association areas, and the prefrontal cortex, as well as the reciprocal connections between these areas (Bachevalier & Mishkin, 1994). As a consequence, the time course of development of this neural circuit establishes an absolute lower limit on the capacity for long-term recall of the past.

Although there is not unanimous agreement as to when the medial temporal lobe components of the declarative memory system becomes fully mature, behavioral data indicate that with some exceptions (e.g., dentate: C. A. Nelson, 1997), they may be functional at an early age: Human infants and nonhuman primates perform tasks that require their integrity (e.g., visual paired comparison: Bachevalier, 1990; Fagan, 1970; see also McKee & Squire, 1993, for data from adults with amnesia tested on paradigms typically used with infants; see C. A. Nelson, 1995, for discussion). In contrast, the neocortical components and the reciprocal connections between the medial temporal lobe structures and the neocortex appear to develop more slowly (Bachevalier, 1992; Bachevalier, Brickson, & Hagger, 1993; Bachevalier & Mishkin, 1994; Webster, Ungerleider, & Bachevalier, 1991). In human infants, a variety of practical and ethical concerns preclude the type of research necessary to pinpoint the precise time course of development of these connections. Convergence of behavioral, neurobiological, and neuroanatomical evidence allows for a best estimate of sufficient functional maturity of the system by between 6 and 12 months of age (C. A. Nelson, 1995). Assuming relative accuracy of this estimate, we would expect the capacity for long-term recall to become evident during the second half of the 1st year of life.

Long-Term Recall in the 1st Year of Life

Use of elicited imitation tasks with infants younger than 1 year has yielded a small body of data consistent with the suggestion that the onset of the capacity to recall the past occurs in the second half of the 1st year of life: Infants aged 6, 9, and 11 months have been shown to recall material immediately as well as after a relatively short delay. Barr et al. (1996) tested the ability of infants as young as 6 months of age to reproduce a three-step sequence involving removing a mitten from a puppet, shaking the mitten (which had a bell inside), and replacing the mitten on the puppet. Seventy-five percent of the infants imitated one action of the sequence (i.e., removing the mitten) after a delay of 24 hours. This level of production was observed even though the infants had been required to defer imitation over the delay. Meltzoff (1988b) and McDonough (1991) tested the ability of infants 9 and 11 months of age, respectively, to defer imitation of single object-specific actions for 24 hours. In the case of the 9-month-olds, the modeled actions were novel (e.g., depressing a recessed button in a box, causing it to "beep"); in the case of the 11-month-olds, some of the actions were novel (e.g., pulling two pieces of pipe apart to reveal a hidden toy), whereas others would be considered to be more familiar (e.g., "feeding" a stuffed bear using a schematic bottle). In both age groups, of the three actions demonstrated, half of the infants produced none or one of them, and half produced two or all three of them. In contrast, 81% of children in naive control groups produced no or one target action and only 19% of them produced two or all three of them. Heimann and Meltzoff (1996) reported a replication of this finding using a 10-min, rather than 24-hr, delay. The 11-month-olds in McDonough (1991) also reproduced single object-specific actions immediately and after a 24-hour delay (see also Bauer & Mandler, 1992, and Mandler & McDonough, 1995, for additional evidence of recall ability in 11-month-old infants). Results from elicited-imitation tasks are consistent with reports from diary studies (e.g., Ashmead & Perlmutter, 1980) and object hiding and retrieval paradigms (e.g., Diamond, 1985), which are suggestive of developments in recall memory during the second half of the 1st year of life (see Fox, Kagan, & Weiskopf, 1979; Kagan & Hamburg, 1981; and Schacter & Moscovitch, 1984, for earlier suggestions of this time frame).

Evidence that by early in the 2nd year of life the ability to recall has further consolidated and become more reliable also is available. In Heimann and Meltzoff (1996), at 9 months of age, 48% of infants reproduced no or only one target action after the 10 min delay, whereas the other 52% reproduced two or all three of the actions. When the same infants were tested for recall of different actions 5 months later, at the age of 14 to 15 months, fully 70% of them produced two or all three of the target actions and only 30% produced none or only one of the actions. Thus, variability in the sample reduced considerably with age. By the time they are 13 to 14 months of age, variability in samples tested for recall of single object-specific actions (e.g., Meltzoff, 1988a) and of multi-step sequences (e.g., Bauer & Hertsgaard, 1993; Bauer et al., 1995) is the exception, rather than the rule. That by early in the 2nd year of life the ability to recall after a delay is relatively robust supports our selection of the 2nd year as a period of particular interest in which to observe developments in long-term recall ability.

Recall by Children in the 2nd Year of Life

Studies from a number of laboratories employing variants on the elicited imitation and other, similar enactment paradigms have revealed that children in the 2nd year of life have well-developed abilities to recall after short to intermediate length delays of days to weeks. There also is a proportionally smaller body of literature suggesting recall over more substantial delays of 8 months and longer. We review the evidence of each in turn.

Recall Over Days and Weeks

Children 12 months of age have been shown to recall single object-specific actions after delays of 3 min, 1 week, and 4 weeks (Klein & Meltzoff, 1999). In children of this age and older (i.e., 14 months: Meltzoff, 1985, 1988a), the ability to imitate such actions is quite robust. For example, in Meltzoff (1988c), 14-month-olds evidenced both immediate and 24-hour deferred imitation of actions that they had seen demonstrated only on television. Moreover, they generalize imitation across changes in context: In their homes, after a 48-hour delay, young children imitated actions seen demonstrated by a peer in a laboratory or day care setting (Hanna & Meltzoff, 1993; see also Barnat et al., 1996). Evidence of generalization across changes in context recently has been demonstrated in 12-month-olds, even after a delay of as long as 4 weeks (Klein & Meltzoff, 1999).

Children of roughly the same ages as those tested for recall of single object-specific actions also imitate multistep event sequences. For example, Bauer and Hertsgaard (1993) demonstrated recall of both two- and three-step event sequences by children 13 and 16 months both immediately and after a 1-week delay. On both two-step and three-step events, relative to performance immediately after modeling, children produced fewer of the possible pairs of actions after the delay: On two-step events, for which there is one possible correctly ordered pair of actions (i.e., Step 1 followed by Step 2), correct production fell from approximately 80% to approximately 60%; on three-step events, for which there are two possible correctly ordered pairs (i.e., Step 1 followed by Step 2, Step 2 followed by Step 3), it fell from 50% to approximately 40%. Nevertheless, even after the delay, the children produced correctly ordered sequences of action. This demonstrates that children not only are able to remember the individual actions of events, but also the order of multistep event sequences, thereby demonstrating organized recall, even after some forgetting.

Findings of recall after short to intermediate delays have been replicated a number of times over. Indeed, with delay intervals of as many as 8 weeks, the ability to recall is quite well documented in children 14 months of age (Bauer et al., 1995; Meltzoff, 1990a), 16 months of age

(Bauer & Dow, 1994; Bauer, Hertsgaard, Dropik, & Daly, 1998; Bauer & Mandler, 1989), and 18 to 23 months of age (Barr & Hayne, 1996; Bauer & Dow, 1994; Bauer & Mandler, 1989; Bauer & Shore, 1987; Boyer & Farrar, 1994, as cited in Boyer, Barron, & Farrar, 1994; Hudson & Sheffield, 1998).

Recall Over More Substantial Intervals

To date, the longest retention interval over which young children have been tested for recall of specific novel multistep event sequences is 8 months. Bauer et al. (1994) tested children 21, 24, and 29 months of age for their recall of events that they experienced 8 months previously, as 13-, 16-, and 20-month-olds. The children originally participated in experiments requiring two visits to the laboratory, spaced 1 week apart. At Session 1, they had a baseline period, after which the experimenter modeled the specific sequences. The props then were returned to the children, and they were allowed to imitate (i.e., immediate recall). After 1 week, the children were tested for delayed recall. After the delayed recall period, the sequences were modeled again, and the children were allowed to imitate. Thus, by the end of their second visit to the laboratory, the children had been exposed to the event two times, and they had had three opportunities to produce each sequence (immediate, delay, and after remodeling; see Bauer & Hertsgaard, 1993, and Bauer & Dow, 1994, for details). To evaluate memory after the long delay, performance of the experienced children was compared to that of age- and gender-matched control children who never before had seen the test events (naive controls). Although the naive children spontaneously produced some of the target actions and sequences in all three age groups, the experienced children produced more of the actions in the correct temporal order than did the naive controls (Bauer et al., 1994). Thus, even the youngest children showed evidence of memory for the novel events over the 8-month delay.

Although representing the longest interval over which nonverbal measures have been used to test recall of multistep event sequences, Bauer et al. (1994) does not stand alone in suggesting very long-term recall by children in the 1- to 2-year age range. Additional nonverbal evidence of long-term recall is available in Meltzoff (1995) who observed recall by 18- and 20-month-olds of single, novel object-specific actions that they had experienced 4 months previously, as 14- and 16-month-olds. Hudson and Sheffield (1998) observed recall after 6 months of activities that children originally had experienced at 18 months of age. McDonough and Mandler (1994) reported that 63% of 23-month-olds reproduced one of four single object-specific actions (i.e., "feeding" a schematic bottle to a stuffed bear) that they had experienced 12 months previously, when they were

13

only 11 months of age. Only 17% of matched naive control children produced the same action. Suggestively, Myers et al. (1994) reported that 32-month-olds who had last been exposed to a unique toy 18 months earlier, at the age of 14 months, "rediscovered" for themselves how to operate it; naive control children only operated the toy after receiving adult instruction. Whereas this body of research is not large, the data from it suggest that by late in the 1st year and early in the 2nd year of life, children have the capacity for nonverbal recall of specific events after long periods of time.

In addition to being able to show that they remember the past, children are able to provide verbal evidence of long-term recall of events experienced prior to 24 months of age. For example, Fivush et al. (1987) interviewed 29- and 35-month-old children and found that they were able to report on events that happened 6 months to 2 years earlier. Nelson and Ross (1980) reported instances in which 21- to 27-month-old children verbalized about events or objects they had experienced 6 to 12 months previously. Myers, Clifton, and Clarkson (1987) included a report of a 32-month-old who correctly verbally identified as a "whale" the subject of a hidden picture last seen at the age of 10 months. Finally, Peterson and Rideout (1998) reported that although children who were 18 months of age and younger at the time they visited an emergency room for treatment of injuries later were unable to verbally recall their experiences, children who were 20 to 25 months at the time of their injuries were able to recall them as many as 6 months later. Together, the results of studies examining nonverbal and verbal indices of memory demonstrate impressive abilities on the part of children 24 months and younger to remember over the long term.

QUESTIONS THAT REMAIN

Particularly in light of the stage against which the studies just reviewed were set, namely, one dominated by expectations of mnemonic incompetence on the part of children younger than age 2 to 3, the "yield" from the studies is impressive indeed. There remain, however, a number of questions about children's long-term recall ability. Chief among these are questions as to whether the length of the interval over which children are able to remember events increases systematically with age and whether factors known to affect immediate recall and recall over the relatively short term also affect recall over longer retention intervals. We discuss each of these major issues in turn. We do so in the context of data derived from nonverbal measures of recall memory. The number of studies of children's verbal reports of memories for experiences in the second year of life is limited; the variables most relevant to the issues at hand have not been the focus of the research. Moreover, in most cases, because the events on which children were asked to report were naturally occurring, the available degree of experimental control would not permit address of them.

Age-Related Changes in Long-Term Recall Ability

The existing literature contains tests of recall by children of various ages throughout the period of infancy to early childhood, over retention intervals of 10 min to 18 months. It thus would seem to afford address of a question of long-standing interest as well as practical and theoretical significance: Does the length of time over which material can be recalled increase with age? In a 1985 publication, Brainerd and colleagues identified this question as one of the most significant in the memory development literature and, ironically, as one of the issues about which we know the least (Brainerd, Kingma, & Howe, 1985). A full decade later, in a 1995 publication, Brainerd and Reyna were still calling for research on the issue. By many, there is assumed to be a steady increase in the length of time over which material can be remembered (e.g., Brainerd & Reyna, 1995; Hartshorn et al., 1998; Howe & Courage, 1997a; Hudson & Sheffield, 1998). In children of preschool age and older, the question has been put to empirical tests: The length of time over which material can be recalled seems to increase with age (see Howe & O'Sullivan, 1997, for a review). However, whether this developmental trend extends to children younger than preschool age, and what the shape of retention functions look like prior to the preschool years, are questions that cannot be addressed by the existing literature.

First, the existing literature contains contradictory findings. Some studies with children younger than 2 have reported retention over equivalent intervals by children of different ages. For example, in Bauer et al. (1994), children 13, 16, and 20 months of age all evidenced memory for the temporal order of event sequences after an 8-month retention interval. Similarly, in Meltzoff (1995), there were no age differences in recall by 14- and 16-month-olds over intervals of 2 and 4 months. In contrast, Sheffield and Hudson (1994) reported longer retention by 18-month-olds (10 weeks) than by 14-month-olds (8 weeks). Likewise, Howe and Courage (1997b) reported that over a 3-month delay, 15-month-olds evidenced more forgetting than 18-month-olds (Experiment 1) and 12-month-olds evidenced more forgetting than 15-month-olds (Experiment 2). Thus, the data on age differences in retention are not definitive. Second, studies have shown retention by very young children over intervals longer than those seemingly tolerated by children much older. For example, McDonough and Mandler

(1994) reported retention over 12 months of at least one specific action by children who had been only 11 months at the time of exposure; Sheffield and Hudson (1994) reported forgetting after 10 weeks by children 18 months at the time of exposure (see also Mandler & McDonough, 1995).

Third, to date, the scales of investigations have been small. In most cases (Meltzoff, 1995, and Myers et al., 1994, being exceptions), the studies that have tested recall over long retention intervals were not originally designed for that purpose (e.g., Bauer et al., 1994; Boyer et al., 1994; McDonough & Mandler, 1994). As a result, the number of children available for inclusion in the samples has been limited, requiring in some cases that researchers go so far as to "collapse" across cells of their original designs in order to provide sufficient cell frequencies (e.g., Boyer et al., 1994). Moreover, it typically has been the case that no more than two age groups have been compared in any single experiment. Equally important, direct comparisons of the same age group over different retention intervals are the exception. Indeed, only studies by Meltzoff (1995) and Myers et al. (1994) were designed to permit such comparisons. In Meltzoff (1995), relative to at immediate testing, levels of recall after 2- and 4-month delays had declined for both 14- and 16-month-olds; performance after 2 and 4 months did not differ. In Myers et al. (1994), the opportunities afforded by the design could not be actualized because clear examples of recall were relatively rare.

Finally, the existing literature precludes a valid test of whether the length of time over which material can be recalled increases with age because of a number of differences across studies. A partial list of the features on which they vary includes: (a) whether or not children were permitted to perform the target actions or events prior to imposition of the delay (e.g., Bauer & Hertsgaard, 1993, permitted imitation whereas Meltzoff, 1988a, did not), (b) the length and complexity of the to-be-remembered material (e.g., McDonough & Mandler, 1994, tested one-step events; Bauer et al., 1994, tested two- and three-step events; Boyer et al., 1994, tested nine-step events), (c) the number of exposures that children had to the events (e.g., Meltzoff, 1995, permitted one; Bauer et al., 1994, permitted two; Bauer et al., 1995, permitted three), (d) the timing of potentially reinstating subsequent exposures to the events (e.g., compare Bauer et al., 1994, and Hudson & Sheffield, 1998), (e) the relative novelty of the events tested (e.g., the long-term recall data from Mandler & McDonough, 1994, are for "familiar" events, whereas the events in Bauer et al., 1994, were novel at the time of experience), and (f) the availability of verbal reminders of the to-be-remembered events (e.g., in Meltzoff, 1995, children were provided no specific verbal cues to the events, whereas in Bauer et al., 1994, children were verbally reminded of them). This brief review makes clear the current impediments to evaluation of the important question of whether there are age-related changes in the length of time over which material can be recalled. Accordingly, one purpose of the research reported here was to provide data relevant to the question of age-related changes in long-term recall. Our goal was not to establish "growth chart"–type functions that would describe the definitive retention curves for children in the second year of life. It is reasonable to expect that the functions would vary for different paradigms, different types of to-be-remembered materials, and so forth. The value of our endeavor is not in establishment of such functions but, rather, in address of the general question of whether there are systematic changes in the level of children's recall as a function of age and the length of the retention interval. In the present research, children ranged in age from 13 to 20 months at the time of exposure to to-be-recalled material; recall was tested at intervals of between 1 and 12 months.

Determinants of Long-Term Recall

The second major question on which the existing literature is largely silent is whether factors known to affect recall over the short and intermediate terms of hours to weeks also affect recall over longer retention intervals. A review of the literature reveals four major determinants of young children's event recall: At least over the short and intermediate terms, the nature of the temporal relations inherent in events, the number of experiences of events, active participation in events, and the availability of cues or reminders of to-be-remembered events all affect recall memory in children in the target age range.

Nature of the Temporal Relations in Events

Younger children, as well as older children and adults, show superior ordered recall of events characterized by enabling relations, compared with events that are arbitrarily ordered. Enabling relations are said to exist when, for a given end-state or goal, one action in a sequence is both temporally prior to and necessary for a second action in the same sequence. For example, in making a milk shake, physical law dictates that the ingredients be put into the blender before the lid is put on. Likewise, to avoid losing the ingredients to the counters or walls of the kitchen, the lid must be put on the blender before the motor is turned on. In contrast, actions in an event are said to be arbitrarily ordered when there are no inherent constraints on their temporal position in a sequence. To continue the example, in making a milk shake, whether the ice cream or the chocolate sauce is put in first is a matter of personal preference alone: it has no consequences for the outcome of the event.

That enabling relations facilitate recall in older children is readily apparent in the literature (e.g., Hudson & Nelson, 1986; Price & Goodman, 1990; Slackman et al., 1986). Preschool-age and older children show a consistent pattern of superior ordered recall of events characterized by enabling relations, compared with events that lack such relations, and thus, are arbitrarily ordered (e.g., Hudson & Nelson, 1986; Price & Goodman, 1990; Ratner, Smith, & Dion, 1986; Slackman et al., 1986; Slackman & Nelson, 1984). It also is apparent that enabling relations facilitate recall in very young children. In several studies researchers have contrasted recall of novel events containing enabling relations (such as *making a rattle* of two nesting cups and a rubber ball: put the ball into one cup, cover it with the other cup, shake the cups to make a rattle) with that of novel arbitrarily ordered events (such as *making a party hat*: put a pompom on the top of a cone-shaped base, attach a sticker to the front of the cone, attach a colored band around the base of the cone) (e.g., Barr & Hayne, 1996; Bauer & Dow, 1994; Bauer & Hertsgaard, 1993; Bauer & Travis, 1993; Mandler & McDonough, 1995). The findings from these studies are remarkably consistent.

First, children typically produce an equivalent number of individual actions on events with and without enabling relations. This suggests that they find the two event types equally interesting. Moreover, it precludes the possibility that differences in ordered recall are an artifact of a larger number of opportunities to produce ordered pairs (i.e., production of individual actions and production of pairs of actions are not independent). Second, although children produce an equivalent number of individual actions, they do not produce an equivalent number of ordered pairs of actions: Children's ordered recall of events with enabling relations consistently is greater than that of arbitrarily ordered ones. The advantage is apparent both at immediate testing (e.g., Bauer, 1992; Bauer & Thal, 1990; Bauer & Travis, 1993) and after short delays (e.g., Barr & Hayne, 1996; Bauer & Dow, 1994; Bauer & Hertsgaard, 1993; Bauer, Hertsgaard, et al., 1998; Bauer et al., 1995; Bauer & Mandler, 1989; Mandler & McDonough, 1995). It also is apparent even after several experiences of arbitrarily ordered events in an invariant temporal order (Bauer & Travis, 1993) (see Bauer, 1995, for a review; see Bauer, 1992, 1995, and Bauer & Travis, 1993, for discussion of the means by which enabling relations in events may influence ordered recall). Whether it is apparent after longer delays is an open question. Only one investigation to date has permitted a test of the effects of enabling relations on recall over the extended term. The results from it were not definitive: After an 8-month delay, children's recall of two-step event sequences was not affected by the nature of the temporal relations inherent in the event; their recall of three-step event sequences was affected (Bauer et al., 1994).

Moreover, it also is possible that there would be an interaction between age and the effects of the structure of to-be-remembered material on recall over extended intervals. From as young as they have been tested, children demonstrate the ability to recall specific event sequences, the orders of which are constrained by enabling relations (e.g., Carver & Bauer, 1999; Mandler & McDonough, 1995). In contrast, children's ability to accurately recall arbitrarily ordered events develops slowly, throughout the second and early part of the 3rd year of life. Specifically, in Bauer, Hertsgaard, et al. (1998), we found that on the basis of a single experience, 16-month-olds, the youngest children tested, did not reliably reproduce arbitrarily ordered events, either immediately or after a 2-week delay. Children 22 months of age reproduced the events immediately after seeing them modeled, but they did not maintain order information over the 2-week delay, whereas 28-month-olds, the oldest age group included in the research, reliably reproduced the events immediately and also after the delay (see Wenner & Bauer, 1999, for additional data on the time course of development of reliable immediate recall of arbitrarily ordered event sequences). Critically, lack of inherent organization apparently can be overcome: In Bauer, Hertsgaard, et al. (1998), after three experiences, 16-month-olds recalled arbitrarily ordered events after the 2-week delay, at least when they were reminded of them. Over the course of the 2nd year of life, children's developing facility with arbitrarily ordered material could be expected to result in differential patterns of long-term recall of events with and without temporal constraints. In order to test this suggestion, in the present research, we presented children with multistep event sequences that were completely constrained by enabling relations, event sequences that lacked enabling relations and thus, were arbitrarily ordered, and event sequences that contained a mixture of enabling and arbitrary temporal relations.

Number of Experiences of Events

It is almost trivial to say that what is remembered is dependent upon what was encoded in the first place: Material to which one has had more exposures is better recalled, relative to material to which one has had fewer exposures. For older children, although repeated experience is not necessary for accurate recall (e.g., Hudson, 1986; Smith et al., 1987), it aids memory both in terms of (a) the amount of information that is remembered (e.g., Fivush, 1984; Hudson, 1986, 1990), and (b) the length of time over which events can be recalled (Fivush & Hamond, 1989). For example, Fivush and Hamond (1989) found that when asked to reenact test events after a 3-month delay, 24- and 29-month-old children who had experienced the events two times recalled more about them than children

19

who had experienced them only once. Moreover, children with repeated experience recalled as much after the 3-month retention interval as they had after only 2 weeks.

Similar facilitating effects of repeated experience have been observed in children in the second year of life. For children aged 13 and 15 months, repeated experience is not necessary for recall of events over the short term: After 1 week, 13- and 15-month-olds recall both the individual target actions and the temporal order of actions of novel events experienced only once (Bauer & Hertsgaard, 1993; Bauer et al., 1995). Nevertheless, particularly over the longer term, repeated experience clearly facilitates recall. For example, in Bauer et al. (1995), for events experienced only once, relative to performance after a 1-week delay, performance after 1 month fell off precipitously. In contrast, events experienced three times before imposition of a 1-month delay were well recalled. Notably, recall after 1 month of events experienced three times was comparable to that after 1 week of events experienced only once (Bauer et al., 1995). In the present research, in order to ensure adequate encoding of the to-be-remembered material, prior to imposition of the delay, children were provided three experiences with the target event sequences.

Active Participation in Events

Active participation in an event leads to better recall in older (e.g., Baker-Ward, Hess, & Flannagan, 1990) as well as younger children. In Bauer et al. (1995, Experiment 3), 14-month-old children either were allowed to imitate events before imposition of a 1-month delay, or they only were allowed to watch the events being modeled. The children who merely watched the events modeled remembered them over the delay (see Barr & Hayne, 1996; Carver & Bauer, 1999; and Meltzoff, 1995, for additional evidence that imitation is not necessary to ensure long-term recall). Nevertheless, effects of the opportunity to imitate were clear: Children in the imitation group recalled more accurately than children in the watch-only group. Meltzoff (1990a) reported similar effects over a 24-hour delay for children of the same age. In contrast, over longer delays, effects of active participation seem to be less apparent: In Meltzoff (1995), recall after 2 and 4 months was comparable for children who were and were not allowed to imitate prior to imposition of the delays. Thus, over the short term, there seems to be an effect of the opportunity to imitate; over the long term, the effect may dissipate. In the present research, in order to test the effects on long-term recall of mode of participation in an event, children were tested on some events that they were permitted to imitate and some events that they only watched.

Availability of Verbal Reminders of Events

Cues or reminders of previously experienced events facilitate retrieval after a delay. Preschool-age children report more information when, at test, they are provided with specific cues or otherwise reminded of to-be-remembered events (e.g., Fivush, 1984; Fivush & Hamond, 1990; Fivush, Hudson, & Nelson, 1984; Hudson, 1990; Hudson & Fivush, 1991). Although verbal rehearsal alone may not be effective in preserving young children's memory for events (Hudson, 1993), verbal reminders provided at the time of retrieval facilitate recall even in very young children. For example, in Bauer et al. (1995), in addition to the props used to produce the event (which always are present when recall is tested, and thus serve as one type of reminder), at delayed testing, the experimenter also provided a verbal reminder of the event in the form of a label for it. For example, on *Make a rattle*, the experimenter presented the props and said "You can use this stuff to make a rattle. Show me how you make a rattle." Following provision of the verbal information, the children were given the opportunity to produce the events.

After a short delay (i.e., 1 week), verbal reminding had a small yet significant facilitating effect on 15-month-olds' performance: Children reminded of the events showed no significant decrement in performance over the delay; children not reminded exhibited a significant decrease in ordered recall. Over a longer delay of 1 month, the effects of verbal reminding were more pronounced. Children remembered events of which they were not verbally reminded; they recalled significantly more of events of which they were reminded (Bauer et al., 1995). In fact, with reminding, performance after 1 month was roughly equivalent to that after 1 week.

That memories can be triggered by verbal reminders is particularly important to recall after long periods of time: Over significant delays, regardless of age, little that is not reminded is retrieved (e.g., Hudson & Fivush, 1991). However, there are reasons to expect age-related changes in the efficacy of verbal reminding. First, reminding seems to work to ameliorate forgetting of events the representations of which are well organized. For 14-month-olds, verbal reminding has been shown to be effective in aiding children in recall of the temporal order of events constrained by enabling relations, but not of arbitrarily ordered events (Bauer et al., 1995, Experiment 1). This does not mean that the effects of verbal reminding are event-type specific: At 28 months, when children demonstrate the ability to construct and maintain temporally ordered representations of arbitrarily ordered events, they also are affected by verbal reminders of them (Bauer, Hertsgaard, et al., 1998). Moreover, after treatment designed to enhance organization of representations of arbitrarily ordered events (i.e., repeated experience), 14-month-old children's recall

21

also is facilitated by verbal reminders (Bauer, Hertsgaard, et al., 1998). Thus, it appears that within the target age range, the efficacy of verbal reminding is not age or event-type specific, but rather, is related to the strength of the organization of the representation of the to-be-remembered material. This finding has implications not only for expectations as to the effects of verbal reminding on different event types, but for expectations about the efficacy of verbal reminding over various delay intervals as well: As delay intervals increase and memory traces decay, the efficacy of verbal reminders would be expected to diminish.

A second reason to expect age-related changes in the efficacy of verbal reminders is that their effects may reasonably be expected to depend upon children's level of command of language: Children with less facility with language could be expected to benefit less from the availability of verbal reminders. Given that language develops rapidly over the course of the second year of life, we might expect to see age-related changes in the strength of verbal reminding effects. In the present research, we examined the efficacy of verbal reminders as a function of delay interval, age, event sequence type, and mode of participation in the event.

PRESENT RESEARCH

The purpose of the research reported in this *Monograph* was to inform the questions of whether, during the 2nd year of life, there are systematic, age-related changes in the length of time over which information can be recalled, and whether factors known to affect immediate recall and recall over the short term also impact recall over longer retention intervals. The vehicle for the inquiry was a sample of 360 children enrolled at the ages of 13 months (90 participants), 16 months (180 participants) and 20 months (90 participants). These particular age groups were selected for two reasons. First, there are a number of studies that have been conducted with children of these specific ages (e.g., Bauer & Dow, 1994; Bauer & Hertsgaard, 1993). As a result, for these age groups we could use the literature as a guide in selection of age-appropriate materials as well as in determination of the variables to be examined in the research. Second, inclusion of three ages spaced 3 to 4 months apart provided sampling of sufficient density to permit a relatively microgenetic examination of age-related changes, while simultaneously providing groups sufficiently distant in age to permit observation of age-related differences.

Within each age group, using elicited imitation, we tested equal numbers of children for recall of specific novel multistep event sequences after intervals of 1, 3, 6, 9, and 12 months. In order to provide each age group with appropriate levels of challenge of to-be-remembered material, we tested all of the 13-month-olds and half of the 16-month-olds on event sequences that were three steps in length, and all of the 20-month-olds and the remaining half of the 16-month-olds on event sequences that were four steps in length. Two considerations entered into selection of these sequence lengths: (a) the sequences needed to be within the realm of possible acquisition at the time of exposure to them, and (b) the sequences needed to be of sufficient length to reduce the likelihood of spontaneous generation of them at the time delayed recall was tested as many as 12 months later. The first consideration led us to select three-step sequences for the 13-month-olds (based on the results of Bauer & Hertsgaard, 1993); the second consideration led us to select four-step sequences for the 20-month-olds (based on the results of Bauer, Schwade, Wewerka, & Delaney, 1999). Testing groups of 16-month-olds on both sequence lengths permitted direct age comparisons with both younger and older children.

To permit evaluation of the effects of event type on children's recall at various retention intervals, we tested them on equal numbers of event sequences completely constrained by enabling relations, those completely lacking enabling relations, and those that were a mixture of enabling and arbitrary temporal relations. The children experienced each of the event sequences at each of three exposure sessions spaced 1 week apart. Multiple exposure sessions were deemed desirable to ensure that the to-be-remembered event sequences were adequately encoded prior to imposition of the delays. There were two reasons why we elected to use a fixed number of exposures, rather than a criterion design, whereby children receive exposures until they demonstrate a predetermined level of mastery (e.g., Howe & Courage, 1997b). First, to afford evaluation of whether the opportunity to imitate prior to imposition of the delay affects long-term recall, we wanted to compare children's long-term recall on event sequences that they imitated prior to the delay and event sequences that they only watched prior to the delay. Use of a criterion design would have necessitated that we obtain measures of imitative performance on all sequences, thereby precluding this comparison. Second, a criterion design likely would have resulted in a larger number of trials to criterion for younger children compared with older children and for arbitrarily ordered event sequences compared with sequences constrained by enabling relations. Multiple opportunities to imitate could produce ambiguity as to whether the resulting mnemonic trace was reflective of declarative or nondeclarative memory. In contrast, merely watching an event sequence, even at three exposure sessions, is extremely unlikely to result in a nondeclarative memory representation: We know of no reports in the literature of implicit acquisition of a temporally ordered sequence via a limited number of observational trials alone.

23

To afford comparison of long-term recall of event sequences previously imitated and previously only watched, without raising the specter of nondeclarative acquisition, for half of the event sequences (one of each type), children were permitted to imitate the event one time before imposition of the delay; for the other half of the event sequences (one of each type), children were not permitted the opportunity for imitation. In addition to the question of effects of mode of participation, this manipulation provided a direct assessment of whether the children had encoded the to-be-remembered material prior to imposition of the delay: their level of immediate imitation could be evaluated and compared. Moreover, it permitted a direct assessment of the amount of information forgotten over time (i.e., comparison of levels of immediate and delayed recall).

To assess the efficacy of verbal reminders of previously experienced events as a function of age, event type, retention interval, and mode of participation, at the time delayed recall was tested, children first experienced a recall period during which they were prompted only by the event-related props, after which verbal reminders of the events were introduced. Both girls and boys were included in the samples. For the majority of the children, parental reports of their level of productive vocabulary development were available, thereby permitting an independent evaluation of the degree to which the various delay groups were matched to one another.

II. METHOD AND ANALYTIC STRATEGY

METHOD

Participants

Three hundred sixty children were included in the final sample. At the time of enrollment, 90 children had a mean age of 13 months 8 days (range = 12 months 20 days to 13 months 20 days), 180 children had a mean age of 16 months 7 days (range = 15 months 21 days to 16 months 21 days), and 90 children had a mean age of 20 months 9 days (range = 19 months 17 days to 20 months 21 days). Half of the 16-month-olds were randomly assigned to the four-step sequence group and half to the three-step sequence group (see below). There were 46 girls and 44 boys in the 13-month age group; 45 girls and 45 boys in the 16-month, three-step group; 49 girls and 41 boys in the 16-month, four-step group; and 45 girls and 45 boys in the 20-month group.

The participants were recruited from an existing pool of volunteer parents who had indicated interest in participating in research at the time of their children's births. Five of the children were African American, three were Asian, five were Hispanic, one was Native American, and the balance were Caucasian. The racial and ethnic composition of the sample is roughly representative of the population from which it was drawn (i.e., 4% nonmajority compares favorably with the 6% nonmajority population of the state of Minnesota). The participant pool primarily includes families of middle- to upper-middle-class status. Children were given a gift for their participation. At the final session, parents were provided a copy of their children's videotape.

An additional 67 children were enrolled in the study but not included in the final sample: (a) 15 children (four 13-month-olds, five 16-month-olds, and six 20-month-olds) completed at least one session but did not return for all four sessions (six failed to keep appointments, six were unable to continue participation because of adverse weather or medical conditions or serious scheduling conflicts, one moved, and two explicitly withdrew from participation in the study); (b) 4 children (two 13-month-olds, one 16-month-old, and one 20-month-old) were unable to complete one or more testing sessions (due to fatigue or fussiness); (c) 22 children (seven 13-month-olds, twelve 16-month-olds, and three 20-month-olds) were excluded due to technical failure or procedural error (e.g., recording equipment or recording medium failure, failure to administer all test sequences); (d) 9 children (three 13-month-olds and six 16-month-olds) were excluded because of experimenter-related scheduling conflicts that prevented completion of one or more sessions within the designated time window; and (e) 17 children (two 13-month-olds, nine 16-month-olds, and six 20-month-olds) who had completed all four sessions nevertheless were excluded in order to provide equal frequencies across all cells of the design. Eight of the 17 children were selected for exclusion because they were missing one or more data points; nine children with complete protocols were excluded on a pseudorandom basis (i.e., within the constraints of approximate gender balance).

Timing of Exposure and Test Sessions

All of the children were seen in the laboratory for four sessions. The first three sessions (exposure sessions) were spaced an average of 1 week apart (M delay between Sessions 1 and 2 = 6.98 days; M delay between Sessions 2 and 3 = 7.01 days); the fourth session took place an average of either 1, 3, 6, 9, or 12 months from the date of the final exposure session (M number of days between Sessions 3 and 4 = 30.9, 91.9, 181.7, 272.6, and 366.6, for the 1-, 3-, 6-, 9-, and 12-month delay conditions, respectively). Within each of the four groups (i.e., 20-month-olds, 16-month-olds on four-step sequences, 16-month-olds on three-step sequences, 13-month-olds), 18 children were randomly assigned to each of the five delay conditions. Analyses revealed that, within each group, at the time of enrollment, the mean ages of the children assigned to the various delay conditions did not differ.

To determine whether the length of the intervals between Sessions 1 and 2, Sessions 2 and 3, or both differed across groups or delay conditions, we conducted 4 (group) × 5 (delay) between-subjects analyses of variance for each between-session interval (i.e., Session 1–2, Session 2–3). There was a main effect for group in the delay between Sessions 1 and 2: $F(3,340) = 3.48$, $p < .03$, $MSE = 3.27$. A Tukey (HSD) test revealed that the 13-month-olds' between-session delay of 7.26 days was longer than that of the 16-month-olds tested on three-step event sequences ($M = 6.88$ days) and of that of the 20-month-olds ($M = 6.83$ days); the Session 1 to 2 delay for the 13-month-olds did not differ from that of the 16-month-olds tested on four-step event sequences ($M = 6.94$ days). There were no other significant differences among means. Neither the main effect of delay nor the Group × Delay interaction was reliable. The analysis for the Session 2 to 3 delay revealed no significant effects. With the exception then of an approximately 10–12 hour difference in the length of the delay between Sessions 1 and 2 for the 13-month-olds compared with the 16-month-olds tested on three-step events and the 20-month-olds, the delays between exposure sessions did not differ across groups and delay conditions.

To determine whether, across groups, the lengths of the delays between the final exposure sessions (Session 3) and the delayed recall test sessions (Session 4) were equivalent for children within a delay condition, for each delay condition, we conducted separate one-way between-subjects analyses of variance with four levels of group. In the 1-month delay condition, the effect of group was significant: $F(3,68) = 4.28$, $p < .008$, $MSE = 8.34$. A Tukey (HSD) test revealed that the length of the delay for the 13-month-olds ($M = 32.5$ days) was longer than that for either group of 16-month-olds ($Ms = 29.7$ for both the three-step and four-step groups); the delay for the 13-month-olds did not differ from that for the 20-month-olds ($M = 31.5$); the delay for the 20-month-olds did not differ from that for the 16-month-olds. In the 3- and 6-month delay conditions the delays did not differ. In the 9-month delay condition, analysis of the main effect, $F(3,68) = 5.09$, $p < .004$, $MSE = 56.45$, revealed that the average lengths of delay for the 16-month-olds tested on three-step events ($M = 275.4$) and the 13-month-olds ($M = 275.3$) were equivalent and greater than that for the 16-month-olds tested on four-step events ($M = 266.9$); the average delay for the 20-month-olds ($M = 272.8$) did not differ from that of any of the other groups. Finally, in the 12-month delay condition, the delays were equivalent.

Materials

Test Events

Children were exposed to multistep event sequences that were either three steps or four steps in length: All of the 13-month-olds and ninety 16-month-olds were exposed to three-step sequences; ninety of the 16-month-olds and all of the 20-month-olds were exposed to four-step sequences. Two different sequence lengths were included in order to provide age-appropriate levels of challenge both at the time of exposure to the test sequences and at the time of the delayed recall test.

The test sequences were of three types: those completely constrained by enabling relations (enabling), those that lacked enabling relations (arbitrary), and those that contained a mixture of enabling and arbitrary temporal relations (mixed). Enabling relations are said to exist when, for a particular outcome or goal, one action in a sequence is both temporally prior to and necessary for a subsequent action in the same sequence. In contrast, sequences are said to lack enabling relations and thus, to be arbitrarily ordered, when there are no inherent constraints on the order in which actions in the sequences occur. "Mixed" sequences are partially temporally constrained. In the case of three-step sequences, one pair of actions was joined by an enabling relation, whereas the other was not; in the case of four-step sequences, two pairs of actions were joined by enabling relations whereas the third pair of actions was not. The presence or absence of enabling relations in each event initially was evaluated by PJB and subsequently was verified by SSW, both of whom had prior experience and training in identifying enabling relations.

All of the sequences were judged to be novel at the time of children's exposure to them. Although no event is entirely "novel," events do vary on a continuum of familiarity (Fivush & Slackman, 1986). We expected that the specific sequences would not previously have been performed by the children, and that they would not have expectations about the individual components of the events, or their temporal order. Our expectations of the novelty of the sequences was verified in informal interviews with the parents of children who participated in research undertaken in part to inform the design of the present experiment (Bauer et al., 1995). A complete listing of test sequences used is provided in Appendix A (Event Sequences Used).

Vocabulary Checklist

At the time of enrollment, children's parents completed the MacArthur Communicative Development Inventory for infants (13- and 16-month-olds) or toddlers (20-month-olds). Parents were asked to indicate which words their children produced. The instrument has been externally validated through comparison with observational measures and has considerable stability with respect to its assessment of general linguistic sophistication (Fenson et al., 1994). In some cases, the parents either did not complete or did not return the language inventory. As a result, we have vocabulary data on 336 (93.3%) of the children: eighty-five 20-month-olds, eighty-three 16-month-olds tested on four-step event sequences, eighty-four 16-month-olds tested on three-step event sequences, and eighty-four 13-month-olds.

Procedure

The 1,440 sessions necessary to complete this investigation were conducted between January 11, 1993, and June 4, 1997. Two female experimenters conducted all of the sessions. During the first 2.5 years of the study, the sessions were conducted by SSW; PLD conducted the balance of the sessions. Before she began, the second experimenter underwent extensive training under the direction of the first experimenter, in order to ensure fidelity in all aspects of testing. A given child was tested by the same experimenter at each session. The first experimenter (SSW) conducted the sessions for 218 of the children: fifty-three 13-month-olds, fifty-six 16-month-olds tested on three-step event sequences, fifty-five 16-month-olds tested on four-step event sequences, and fifty-four 20-month-olds. The second experimenter (PLD) conducted the sessions for 142 of the children: thirty-seven 13-month-olds, thirty-four 16-month-olds tested on three-step event sequences, thirty-five 16-month-olds tested on four-step event sequences, and thirty-six 20-month-olds. Because the number of children tested by each experimenter differed across conditions (SSW tested the majority of children in the 9- and 12-month delay conditions; PLD tested the majority of children in the 1- and 3-month delay conditions; each experimenter tested approximately half of the children in the 6-month delay condition), potential effects on delayed recall performance of the confound between experimenter and delay condition could not be evaluated. Potential experimenter effects were, however, evaluated at both baseline and immediate testing. As fully described in Appendix B (Potential Effects on Children's Performance of Features of the Research Design: Experimenter), there were some isolated and inconsistent effects of experimenter on children's performance prior to exposure to the modeled event sequences (i.e., in the baseline assessment period), but there were no effects on imitative performance.

For each session, children were seen individually in a laboratory playroom. Testing took place with the children seated across an adult-size table from the experimenter. One of the children's parents remained in the room throughout each session. Parents were asked not to label any objects, to suggest behaviors to their children, or to otherwise assist their children in any way. The parents of the children included in the final sample complied with these requests. A schematic representation of the design of the study is provided in Figure 1.

Exposure Sessions

Children were exposed to the events at each of three sessions. To assess the influence of mode of experience of the events on long-term recall, children watched, but did not imitate, three test events (one of each sequence type). For another three events (one of each sequence type), children were allowed to imitate prior to imposition of the delay. To address concerns regarding the nature of memory tested when imitation

Session, Sequence type, and Experience condition	Testing phase		
	Pre-modeling	Demonstration	Post-modeling
Session I (Exposure)			
Enabling-imitate	A	A	—
Enabling-watch	B	B	—
Mixed-imitate	D	D	—
Mixed-watch	E	E	—
Arbitrary-imitate	G	G	—
Arbitrary-watch	H	H	—
Session II (Exposure)			
Enabling-imitate	—	A	—
Enabling-watch	—	B	—
Mixed-imitate	—	D	—
Mixed-watch	—	E	—
Arbitrary-imitate	—	G	—
Arbitrary-watch	—	H	—
Session III (Exposure and for "imitate" sequences, immediate recall test)			
Enabling-imitate	—	A	A
Enabling-watch	—	B	—
Mixed-imitate	—	D	D
Mixed-watch	—	E	—
Arbitrary-imitate	—	G	G
Arbitrary-watch	—	H	—
1-, 3-, 6-, 9-, or 12-MONTH DELAY IMPOSED			
Session IV (Delayed recall test for "imitate" and "watch" sequences; "new" sequences as within-subjects controls)			
Enabling-imitate	A	A	A
Enabling-watch	B	B	B
Enabling-new	C	C	C
Mixed-imitate	D	D	D
Mixed-watch	E	E	E
Mixed-new	F	F	F
Arbitrary-imitate	G	G	G
Arbitrary-watch	H	H	H
Arbitrary-new	I	I	I

FIGURE 1.—A schematic representation of the study design. Unique alphabetical characters designate unique event sequences (see Appendix A for a complete description of all event sequences). Event sequences and experience conditions (i.e., imitate, watch, new) were presented in counterbalanced order.

is permitted (i.e., implications of the involvement of nondeclarative memory when imitation is permitted compared with declarative memory when it is not), the children were permitted to imitate the events only once, at the third exposure session.

At the first exposure session, children and their parents were escorted to the laboratory playroom where they engaged in a few minutes of free play. During this time the experimenter reviewed with the parents the purposes and procedures to be followed and addressed any questions that they had about the study. As the children became acclimated to the surround, the experimenter initiated a routinized sequence of turn-taking games designed to encourage interaction between the children and experimenter. Once the children had "warmed up," the experimenter, child, and parent moved to the adult-sized testing table. Parents' written consent for their children's participation was obtained at that time.

Prior to testing, children were exposed to a familiarization sequence. It was designed to establish the turn-taking and prop-exchanging routines necessary for the protocol. The experimenter first gave a slinky and ball to the child and encouraged manipulation of them. The experimenter then retrieved the objects from the child and demonstrated rolling the ball and placing it on top of the slinky. The two-step sequence of actions was demonstrated two times in succession, with narration (i.e., "Roll the ball. Put it on top."). Immediately after the second demonstration, the experimenter removed the slinky and ball from the table.

The procedure for the six test sequences was identical to that for the practice sequence. For each sequence in turn, the children were given all of the event-related props and were encouraged to manipulate them (e.g., "Look at that stuff. What can you do with that stuff?"). Children's pre-modeling performance provided a baseline measure of the spontaneous occurrence of the target actions. The period was "child controlled": it ended when the child pushed the props away, or engaged in repetitive exploratory behaviors, such as banging or mouthing the objects, or engaged in other "off task" behaviors, such as throwing the props on the floor.[1] After the baseline assessment, the experimenter modeled the sequence twice in succession, with narration. After all six of the test sequences had been modeled twice, the child was dismissed from the laboratory.

---

[1]Child-controlled, rather than experimenter-controlled, response periods were used in order to permit children to, in essence, work at their own paces. In previous related research, we have found wide variability in the lengths of time that children remain engaged with the event-related props, both prior to and after exposure to the target event sequences. For example, in Bauer and Hertsgaard (1993), the lengths of the initial baseline periods ranged from 20 s to 135 s, and the lengths of the immediate recall periods ranged from 9 s to 86 s. Moreover, there are suggestions of age-related differences in the lengths of response periods. Again, in Bauer and Hertsgaard (1993), the average length of the baseline period for 13-month-olds was 79 s whereas the average length of the baseline period for 16-month-olds was 34 s. Given the wide range in age covered in the present research (i.e., 13 to 32 months), child-controlled response periods were deemed most desirable. See the section on timing of the child-controlled response periods for further discussion of this matter.

Notice that the children were not permitted imitation of any of the sequences.

At the second exposure session, all six event sequences again were modeled twice in succession; the children were not allowed to imitate any of the sequences. Moreover, unlike at the first exposure session, they were not permitted any interaction with the props used to produce the events. To increase children's tolerance for the procedure, after the modeling of each sequence, the children were allowed to manipulate an unrelated distracter toy. The distracter toys apparently were successful at reducing any irritation that might have been associated with denial of the opportunity to reproduce the events: no attrition resulted from this aspect of the procedure.

The first half of the third exposure session proceeded exactly as had the second exposure session. That is, for three of the event sequences (one sequence of each type), the experimenter modeled each sequence two times in succession. After each modeled event, children were permitted to manipulate an unrelated distracter toy. For the remaining three event sequences (one sequence of each type), immediately after the second modeling, the children were allowed to imitate. That is, the props to produce the event were given to the children and they were encouraged to "make/do X, just like I did." This provided a measure of immediate recall. The order of presentation of the watch and imitate experience conditions was fixed in order to avoid attrition: Permitting children to imitate and then denying them the opportunity to do so is a recipe for unhappy participants. In summary, by the end of the third exposure session, the children had been exposed to each sequence a total of six times (i.e., two presentations at each of three exposure sessions). They had been permitted one imitation of one sequence of each type. At the end of the third exposure session, the participants were dismissed from the laboratory, having been told that they would be asked to return after an interval of between 1 and 12 months.

Delayed Recall Test Session

After the appointed delay, the participants returned to the laboratory for a delayed recall test session. In addition to the three event sequences that they had been permitted to imitate prior to imposition of the delay (imitate sequences) and the three event sequences that they had only watched (watch sequences), they were presented with three new event sequences (new sequences), as a within-subjects control. For each sequence in turn, the experimenter delivered all of the event-related props to the children with no instruction and no modeling. After a child-controlled period of time, the experimenter provided a verbal reminder of the event sequence, in the form of the verbal label given the event each time it was modeled.[2] For example, on *Make a gong*, the experimenter said, "You can use this stuff to make a gong. Show me how you make a gong." Note that the verbal information cued the event, not the individual target actions. That is, the instruction was "make a gong," not "put up the bar." Moreover, note that the verbal information was provided for events previously experienced (i.e., imitate and watch sequences) as well as for the events that were new to the children (i.e., new sequences). For the new sequences, the verbal information served as a suggestion of plausible activities to be performed with the available props. Following the verbal reminder, the children were given another child-controlled period of time in which to interact with the props. Finally, the experimenter retrieved the props from the children and demonstrated the event sequence once, with narration, after which the children were permitted a final opportunity to imitate.

The three phases of testing of each event sequence provide three measures of performance. For the events that the children previously had experienced (i.e., imitate and watch events), the period of time between delivery of the props and provision of the verbal reminder permitted assessment of the children's level of delayed recall of the events when prompted by the props alone. The period of time before the verbal label and after the verbal label permitted assessment of the children's total production when prompted by the props and the verbal reminder. The period of time after the experimenter's demonstration of the events permitted a measure of relearning. For the events that the children had not previously experienced (i.e., the new events), the respective periods afforded assessment of baseline performance, performance after a suggestion of plausible event sequences, and a measure of immediate imitation.

---

[2] The prereminder and postreminder periods were divided by the verbal label alone; the experimenter did not retrieve the props from the child, provide the verbal label, and then return the props for the postreminder assessment. Removing and then returning the props might actually have been disruptive to children's performance, rather than facilitative of it. Had we removed and then returned the objects, the children would have been required to "start over" in their reproductions of the event sequences. This was undesirable for two reasons. First, in previous related research, we have observed a certain reluctance on children's parts to immediately reproduce their own actions on the event-related props. Second, such an intervention may have been perceived as a "correction" of children's behavior, either on the part of the children or their parents. We wanted to avoid any perception that children's pre-verbal-reminder performance was incorrect or deficient.

Counterbalancing

At the exposure sessions, the first three events presented included one sequence of each type and the second three events presented included one sequence of each type; the event sequences were presented in different serial orders at each exposure session. At the delayed recall test session, the nine test sequences (three imitate, three watch, three new) were presented in order such that sessions never began or ended with a new event sequence. This was done in order to ensure that, were they to obtain, lower levels of performance on the new sequences could not be due to warm-up or fatigue effects. Within that constraint, the test sequences of the different types (enabling, mixed, and arbitrary) and in the different mode of experience conditions (imitate, watch, and new) were interspersed with one another and each was presented in each serial position approximately equally often (with the exception of new sequences, as noted).

With the exception of the position constraints at the delayed recall test session just described, the investigation was, at the outset, completely counterbalanced across the 20 cells of the design (four groups × five delay conditions per group). However, due to unanticipated attrition, participants later excluded in order to provide equal cell frequencies, and occasional procedural errors, in the end, counterbalancing was only approximate. Nevertheless, it was the case that across mode of experience conditions (imitate, watch, new), each event sequence was tested approximately equally frequently (for four-step event sequences, M number of times tested = 135.3, range = 124–144; for three-step event sequences, M number of times tested = 134.3, range = 123–149). Moreover, each event sequence was tested in each mode of experience condition approximately equally frequently (for four-step event sequences, M number of times tested in each mode of experience condition = 45.1, range = 33–54; for three-step event sequences, M number of times tested in each mode of experience condition = 44.8, range = 32–58). For the four-step event sequences, there was one exception to the pattern of roughly equivalent representation in each mode of experience condition: Although the chi-square statistic fell below the conventional level of statistical significance ($p < .08$), the enabling event sequence *Walk the duck* was presented more often in the watch ($n = 53$) than in the imitate ($n = 33$) and new ($n = 38$) conditions (expected frequency = 41.33). For the three-step event sequences, the only exception to the pattern of roughly equivalent use in each mode of experience condition was the enabling event sequence *Make a gong*, which was presented more often in the watch ($n = 58$) and new ($n = 51$) than in the imitate ($n = 34$) conditions: $\chi^2(2) = 6.39$, $p < .05$ (expected frequency = 47.67). There were no other reliable deviations in the distributions of specific event sequences across the different mode of experience conditions, for either step-length group (all $ps > .10$).

Not only was it the case that, across mode of experience conditions, each event sequence was tested approximately equally frequently, but each event sequence also was used as a to-be-remembered event (i.e., it appeared in the imitate or watch experience condition) approximately equally frequently in each delay condition. To determine whether there were any reliable deviations in the distributions of specific event sequences across the different delay conditions, for each step-length group, we conducted chi-square analyses on the number of times that each event sequence was used as either an imitate or as a watch-only event in each delay condition. None of the analyses was significant (all $ps > .30$). Thus, although counterbalancing across all cells of the design was not perfect, with the two exceptions noted above (i.e., one sequence in each step-length group), there were not systematically differential distributions of specific event sequences either across experience conditions or across delay conditions. There was little cause for concern then that sequence-specific effects would influence the results obtained. The possibility of such effects nevertheless was evaluated formally and the null results are reported in Appendix B (Potential Effects on Children's Performance of Features of the Research Design: Item-Specific Effects).

Scoring

The first and third exposure sessions and the delayed recall test session were videotaped for later analysis. Because no measures of children's behavior or performance were obtained from it, the second session was not videotaped.

Coding

Due to the large number of sessions included in the investigation (over 1,440) and the extended period of time over which it was conducted (4.5 years), a number of individuals worked to code the videotapes of the children's performance. In each case, individuals were trained against a coding template to identify target actions. After reaching agreement of 90% or greater with the template on three successive transcripts, the coders were deemed reliable. Frequent reliability checks were made, in order to ensure against "coder drift."

Individuals coded either the first (baseline) and third (immediate recall) or the fourth (delayed recall) test session; in no case did the individual who coded a given child's performance prior to the delay also code the child's performance after the delay. Thus, coders of the delayed recall test sessions were not aware of which event sequences the children had imitated, which they had only watched, and which were new to them. For half of the sample, the coders were not explicitly aware of the age group or delay condition of the children they were coding: The information was "masked" with an elaborate participant numbering system. Moreover, the coders were not aware of the overall design of the study, or of the specific manipulations in it. The balance of the sample was coded by graduate students and staff who were aware of the design of the study and, in some cases, of the "code" for the participant numbering system. In all cases, individuals were assigned randomly generated lists of videotapes to code. The lists invariably included children from different groups and different delay conditions. Therefore, the possibility that error associated with any one individual coder might have had a significant impact on the results for an age group or delay condition is exceedingly small.

Data Reduction

For each sequence, we calculated the total number of individual target actions produced (maximum = 3 for each sequence on three-step events and 4 for each sequence on four-step events) and the total number of pairs of actions produced in the target order (maximum = 2 for each sequence on three-step events and 3 for each sequence on four-step events). For the latter measure, only the first occurrence of each target action was considered. As an example, consider a three-step sequence. If children produced all three actions in the target order, they would receive credit for three different target actions and for two ordered pairs of actions (i.e., Pair 1–2 and Pair 2–3). If children produced Target Actions 1 and 3 in that order, two points would be credited for target actions and one point would be credited for target order (i.e., Pair 1–3). However, if children produced the string of Target Actions 3–1–2–3, they would be credited with three different target actions, but with only one correctly ordered pair: 1–2. They would not be credited with the correctly ordered Pair 2–3, because they already would have been credited with production of Target Action 3; the second production of this action would not be considered. This scoring procedure reduces the likelihood that children will receive credit for pairs of actions that are correctly ordered by chance or by trial and error.

Note that the two dependent measures are not independent of one another: The number of target actions produced affects production of pairs of actions in the target order. Nevertheless, it is possible for children to earn a high score on the measure of number of different target actions and not earn a high score on the measure of pairs of actions in the target order. Thus, differences in the latter dependent measure cannot be attributed solely to differences in the former. Moreover, although it is the case that, by definition, actions joined by enabling relations must occur in an invariant temporal order, for scoring purposes, children were credited with an action regardless of the order in which it occurred. For example, in *Make a gong*, children could be credited with ringing the gong (Target Action 3) regardless of whether they had (a) put the vertical support bar in place (Target Action 1), or (b) suspended the metal plate from the bar (Target Action 2). Thus, even on events constrained by enabling relations, high levels of ordered recall cannot be attributed to physical constraints imposed by the stimuli, or their manner of combination. Even though differences in the number of pairs of actions produced in the target order cannot be attributed solely to differences in the number of individual target actions produced, in examination of children's ordered recall performance, as a supplement to analyses of variance, we conducted analyses of covariance controlling for the number of individual target actions produced.

Reliability

Reliability was checked on a regular basis throughout the period of the study. Eventually, it was evaluated on 90, or 25% of the participants (i.e., for a given participant, all three sessions that included child data, namely, Exposure Session 1, Exposure Session 3, delayed recall test session, were coded for reliability purposes). The participants on whom reliability was calculated were approximately evenly divided across all cells of the design.

Overall reliability on the number of target actions produced was 95% (range = 81–100%); overall reliability on the number of pairs of actions produced in the target order was 95% (range = 74–100%). Reliability was high both for the coders who were more aware of the purposes and procedures of the research (96% on $n = 45$ participants) and for the coders who were less aware of the purposes and procedures of the research (94% on $n = 45$ participants). For the variable of production of individual target actions, in 101 of the 108 cells of the research design [(baseline: 3 sequence types × 2 experience conditions = 6 cells) + (immediate recall: 3 sequence types × 1 experience condition = 3 cells) + (delayed recall: 3 sequence types × 3 experience conditions = 9 cells) + (relearning: 3 sequence types × 3 experience conditions = 9) × 4 groups = 108 cells], reliability was in the range of 90–100%. For the variable of production of pairs of actions in the target order, in 102 of the 108 cells of the design, reliability was in the range of 90–100%; in only one cell was reliability below 80%. Reliability was well within the acceptable range whether examined as a function of (a) group (range = 93–96% and 95–97%, for target actions and pairs of actions, respectively), (b) experience condition (95–96% and 92–97%, for target actions and pairs of actions, respectively),

37

(c) sequence type (range = 95–96% and 96–97%, for target actions and pairs of actions, respectively), or (d) recall condition (range = 93–98% and 86–99%, for target actions and pairs of actions, respectively).

Treatment of Missing Data

In a small number of cases, for a given session, for a given child, the data for a particular event sequence were missing. The modal reason for missing data was the unavailability of one or more of the materials necessary to complete the sequence (i.e., over the 1,440 testing sessions, we had a few "casualties" among our props). Missing observations were replaced by the group mean for that cell of the design. In no case did the number of missing observations exceed 1% of those potentially available.

Timing of the Child-Controlled Response Periods

Because the response periods were child controlled, rather than experimenter controlled, they could be expected to vary in length. It is possible that differences in the time allowed to manipulate the props varied systematically by age, delay, experience condition, or sequence type, and that the variability could result in differences attributed to these variables. To examine this possibility, we timed the response periods for 25% of the participants (90 children; for a given participant, all three sessions that included child data, namely, Exposure Session 1, Exposure Session 3, delayed recall test session, were timed). The sample was the same as that on which we calculated reliability of coding. As such, the participants whose sessions we timed were approximately evenly divided across all cells of the design.

Timing was done using values electronically recorded on the videotapes at the time of the sessions. Elapsed time of each response period was noted to the nearest 1/10 of a second. A response period was considered to begin when all of the props for the event sequence were placed in front of the child and the experimenter withdrew her hands from the props. A response period was considered to end either (a) when all of the individual target actions were produced (regardless of order), or (b) on trials on which the children failed to produce all of the target actions, when the experimenter removed the first of the props for a given event sequence. The results of analyses of the lengths of the response periods are provided in Appendix B (Potential Effects on Children's Performance of Features of the Research Design: Length of Response Periods). To foreshadow the results of the analyses: In no case could the patterns of performance reported in the chapters to follow be attributed to systematic differences in the lengths of the child-controlled response periods.

ANALYTIC STRATEGY

Half of the children in the present research were tested on four-step event sequences (ninety 20-month-olds and ninety 16-month-olds) and half were tested on three-step event sequences (ninety 16-month-olds and ninety 13-month-olds). Although the four-step and three-step groups were tested concurrently, we analyzed the results for each step-length group separately (i.e., one set of analyses comparing the performance of the 20-month-olds and the 16-month-olds tested on four-step event sequences, and one set of analyses comparing the performance of the 13-month-olds and the 16-month-olds tested on three-step event sequences). We adopted this approach, rather than global analyses involving all groups, because direct comparisons across sequences of different lengths would have necessitated analysis of proportion, rather than raw, scores. Analysis of proportions is somewhat problematic because it is not clear that the mnemonic act of recalling, for example, three individual target actions out of four, for a resulting proportion of .75, is, as suggested by the resulting value, "better" than recalling two individual target actions out of three, for a resulting proportion of .67. Proportions thus could be expected to introduce certain ambiguities in interpretation of the findings.

Within each step-length group, we first examined baseline levels of performance (i.e., performance prior to the first modeling of the event sequences at Session 1). This permitted determination of whether the children differed in their manipulations of the event-related props, even prior to exposure to the test events. We next examined baseline levels of performance compared with performance immediately after exposure to the test events at the third (and final) exposure session. This analysis permitted determination of whether the children learned the event sequences and whether there were systematic differences in initial learning. The analysis was carried out only on the event sequences that the children were permitted to imitate prior to imposition of the delay. On event sequences that the children only watched, no measures of immediate recall and thus, no measures of initial learning, were available.

The third phase of analysis involved comparison of children's performance at delayed recall testing on events that they previously had been permitted to imitate and previously had only watched with that on events that were new to the children at the delayed recall test session (i.e., Session 4). These comparisons afforded a direct indication of whether the children remembered the events over the delays (i.e., differences in performance on previously experienced events and on new events would be indicative of memory). They also permitted examination of whether conclusions regarding patterns of remembering and forgetting were affected by any of the other variables of interest in this research. We then proceeded to examination of

39

the factors potentially affecting children's long-term recall performance, including the length of the delay interval, age at the time of exposure to the event sequences, sequence type, mode of experience of the events, and the availability of verbal reminders of the to-be-remembered events. Next, we compared children's levels of immediate and delayed recall performance, to determine whether forgetting was in evidence (i.e., reliable differences between levels of immediate recall and levels of delayed recall would be indicative of forgetting). We then compared children's levels of performance after exposure to the test sequences at Session 4, to determine whether there was any evidence of savings in relearning. The results of each of these six analyses are presented for each step-length group in turn: the analyses of the performance of the children tested on four-step event sequences are presented in Chapter III; the analyses of the performance of the children tested on three-step event sequences are presented in Chapter IV.

As will become apparent, the critical comparisons of children's performance on event sequences that they previously experienced and event sequences that were new to them at the time of delayed recall testing suggested differences in the retention intervals tolerated by 16-month-olds tested on four-step event sequences and 16-month-olds tested on three-step event sequences. The next step in the analysis was to test a number of hypotheses regarding the source or sources of the differential patterns. These analyses are presented in Chapter V. In Chapter VI we present the results of analyses conducted to establish the proportion of variance in long-term recall performance accounted for by various potential predictor variables. In Appendix C (Potential Effects on Children's Performance of Child Language and Gender) appear the results of analyses conducted to test the possibilities that endogenous factors of child level of productive vocabulary development and child gender qualified the results obtained. The analyses are reported in an appendix, rather than in the body of the text, because the factors proved to have little substantive bearing on the major questions of the research.

In the analyses to follow, the variables delay (1, 3, 6, 9, or 12 months) and age (13, 16, or 20 months) are between-subjects; the variables mode of experience (or simply "experience": imitate, watch, new), sequence type (enabling, mixed, arbitrary), modeling condition (pre-modeling, post-modeling), and recall condition (immediate, delay) are within-subjects. Where significant, main effects involving more than two cells were further examined by Tukey (HSD) tests of significant difference among means ($p < .05$). In comparisons of performance on events previously experienced with that on events new to the children at Session 4 (i.e., maturation control events), Dunnett's tests were used to compare performance in each of the "old" event conditions (i.e., imitate and watch) to that on new event sequences ($p < .05$).

III. CHILDREN TESTED ON FOUR-STEP EVENT SEQUENCES

BASELINE LEVELS OF PERFORMANCE

Descriptive statistics on baseline levels of performance by the 20-month-olds and the 16-month-olds tested on four-step event sequences are provided in Table 1. As will become apparent, although there were some differences in levels of performance across the cells of the design, they had no consequences for children's initial mastery of the to-be-remembered event sequences (see Immediate Recall Performance), and they contributed virtually no variance in children's long-term recall (see Chapter VI: Predictions of Long-Term Mnemonic Performance). We compared children's baseline levels of production of the individual target actions of the event sequences and of pairs of actions in the target order in 5 (delay: 1 month, 3 month, 6 month, 9 month, 12 month) × 2 (age: 16 month, 20 month) × 3 (sequence type: enabling, mixed, arbitrary) × 2 (experience: imitate, watch) mixed analyses of variance for each dependent measure. The 20-month-olds ($M = 0.93$, $SD = 0.84$) produced a larger number of individual target actions relative to the 16-month-olds ($M = 0.66$, $SD = 0.73$): $F(1,170) = 21.47$, $p < .0001$, $MSE = 0.92$. The effect was, however, qualified by the four-way interaction among the variables: $F(8,340) = 2.25$, $p < .03$, $MSE = 0.58$.

To pursue the four-way interaction, we conducted separate analyses by sequence type. The effect of age was apparent on events with enabling relations, $F(1,170) = 8.54$, $p < .004$, $MSE = 0.73$ [$Ms = 0.96$ and 0.70 ($SDs = 0.91$ and 0.79) for the 20- and 16-month-olds, respectively], and on arbitrarily ordered events, $F(1,170) = 16.28$, $p < .0001$, $MSE = 0.57$ [$Ms = 0.90$ and 0.58 ($SDs = 0.83$ and 0.69) for 20- and 16-month-olds, respectively]. On mixed event sequences, analysis of the Delay × Age × Experience interaction, $F(4,170) = 4.31$, $p < .003$, $MSE = 0.45$, revealed that the age effect was apparent only on sequences that the children subsequently would be permitted to watch but not to imitate, and then only in the 1-, 3-, and 6-month delay conditions [Age × Delay interaction in the watch condition,

TABLE 1

Means and Standard Deviations for the Baseline Number of Individual
Target Actions and Pairs of Actions Produced in the Target Order
by Children Tested on Four-Step Event Sequences

Age group/ Delay condition/ Experience	Sequence type							
	Overall		Enabling		Mixed		Arbitrary	
	Mean	SD	Mean	SD	Mean	SD	Mean	SD
Number of individual target actions produced (max. = 4.0)								
20-month-olds								
1-month delay								
Imitate	1.06	0.76	1.18	0.78	0.94	0.73	1.06	0.80
Watch	1.06	0.92	1.00	0.77	1.12	0.90	1.06	1.11
3-month delay								
Imitate	0.93	0.91	1.00	0.91	0.78	0.88	1.00	0.97
Watch	0.88	0.77	0.94	1.00	1.06	0.64	0.65	0.59
6-month delay								
Imitate	0.98	0.81	0.83	0.99	0.88	0.68	1.22	0.73
Watch	0.85	0.88	0.78	1.06	1.22	0.88	0.56	0.51
9-month delay								
Imitate	1.02	0.88	1.28	1.07	1.11	0.76	0.67	0.69
Watch	0.93	0.80	1.06	0.94	0.72	0.67	1.00	0.77
12-month delay								
Imitate	0.85	0.76	0.78	0.65	0.83	0.86	0.94	0.80
Watch	0.70	0.88	0.78	0.94	0.44	0.51	0.89	1.08
16-month-olds								
1-month delay								
Imitate	0.73	0.65	0.65	0.59	0.89	0.68	0.67	0.69
Watch	0.56	0.69	0.72	0.83	0.56	0.70	0.39	0.50
3-month delay								
Imitate	0.91	0.85	0.89	0.96	0.89	0.83	0.94	0.80
Watch	0.59	0.63	0.72	0.75	0.50	0.51	0.56	0.62
6-month delay								
Imitate	0.63	0.81	0.78	1.00	0.61	0.70	0.50	0.71
Watch	0.63	0.81	0.83	0.92	0.61	0.85	0.44	0.62
9-month delay								
Imitate	0.49	0.60	0.44	0.51	0.35	0.48	0.67	0.77
Watch	0.65	0.68	0.83	0.86	0.78	0.55	0.33	0.49
12-month delay								
Imitate	0.70	0.77	0.56	0.62	0.78	0.81	0.78	0.88
Watch	0.67	0.75	0.56	0.78	0.89	0.76	0.56	0.70
Number of pairs of actions in the target order (max. = 3.0)								
20-month-olds								
1-month delay								
Imitate	0.18	0.42	0.24	0.42	0.18	0.38	0.12	0.47
Watch	0.18	0.38	0.00	—	0.35	0.48	0.18	0.38

(*continued*)

TABLE 1 (*continued*)

Age group/ Delay condition/ Experience	Sequence type							
	Overall		Enabling		Mixed		Arbitrary	
	Mean	SD	Mean	SD	Mean	SD	Mean	SD
3-month delay								
Imitate	0.23	0.42	0.24	0.42	0.22	0.43	0.22	0.43
Watch	0.16	0.41	0.24	0.55	0.24	0.42	0.00	—
6-month delay								
Imitate	0.15	0.41	0.17	0.51	0.12	0.32	0.17	0.38
Watch	0.15	0.41	0.22	0.55	0.22	0.43	0.00	—
9-month delay								
Imitate	0.17	0.42	0.22	0.55	0.22	0.43	0.06	0.24
Watch	0.07	0.26	0.11	0.32	0.06	0.24	0.06	0.24
12-month delay								
Imitate	0.15	0.36	0.06	0.24	0.17	0.38	0.22	0.43
Watch	0.13	0.48	0.17	0.51	0.00	—	0.22	0.65
16-month-olds								
1-month delay								
Imitate	0.04	0.19	0.06	0.24	0.06	0.24	0.00	—
Watch	0.06	0.23	0.11	0.32	0.06	0.24	0.00	—
3-month delay								
Imitate	0.19	0.44	0.28	0.57	0.11	0.32	0.17	0.38
Watch	0.04	0.19	0.11	0.32	0.00	—	0.00	—
6-month delay								
Imitate	0.15	0.41	0.22	0.55	0.11	0.32	0.11	0.32
Watch	0.09	0.35	0.11	0.47	0.11	0.32	0.06	0.24
9-month delay								
Imitate	0.04	0.19	0.00	—	0.00	—	0.11	0.32
Watch	0.04	0.19	0.11	0.32	0.00	—	0.00	—
12-month delay								
Imitate	0.09	0.29	0.00	—	0.11	0.32	0.17	0.38
Watch	0.06	0.23	0.00	—	0.11	0.32	0.06	0.24

$F(4,170) = 4.00$, $p < .004$, $MSE = 0.51$; main effects of group, $Fs(1,34) = 4.36$, 8.35, and 4.50, $ps < .05$, $MSEs = 0.65$, 0.34, and 0.75, for the 1-, 3-, and 6-month delay conditions, respectively]. In the 9-month delay condition, the performance of the 16- and the 20-month-olds on mixed event sequences that they would only watch did not differ. In the 12-month delay condition, the 16-month-olds produced a larger number of individual target actions of the mixed event sequences that they would only watch, relative to the 20-month-olds: $F(1,34) = 4.25$, $p < .05$, $MSE = 0.42$ (see Table 2 for relevant cell means). For the mixed event sequences that the children subsequently would be permitted to imitate, baseline levels of production of individual target actions by the 16-month-olds and the

TABLE 2

MEANS AND STANDARD DEVIATIONS FOR THE NUMBER OF INDIVIDUAL TARGET
ACTIONS AND PAIRS OF ACTIONS PRODUCED IN THE TARGET ORDER
AT IMMEDIATE RECALL BY CHILDREN TESTED ON FOUR-STEP EVENT SEQUENCES

Age group/ Delay condition	Sequence Type							
	Overall		Enabling		Mixed		Arbitrary	
	Mean	SD	Mean	SD	Mean	SD	Mean	SD
Number of individual target actions produced (max. = 4.0)								
20-month-olds								
1-month delay	3.93	0.26	3.94	0.24	3.89	0.32	3.94	0.24
3-month delay	3.78	0.54	3.72	0.67	3.83	0.51	3.78	0.43
6-month delay	3.93	0.26	4.00	—	3.89	0.32	3.89	0.32
9-month delay	3.93	0.33	3.89	0.47	3.94	0.24	3.94	0.24
12-month delay	3.85	0.41	3.89	0.32	3.78	0.55	3.89	0.32
16-month-olds								
1-month delay	3.28	0.90	3.33	1.03	3.06	1.00	3.44	0.62
3-month delay	3.24	0.99	3.22	1.17	3.22	1.00	3.28	0.83
6-month delay	3.54	0.86	3.56	0.86	3.39	1.09	3.67	0.59
9-month delay	3.48	0.75	3.67	0.59	3.22	0.94	3.56	0.62
12-month delay	3.41	0.74	3.39	0.78	3.28	0.89	3.56	0.51
Number of pairs of actions in the target order (max. = 3.0)								
20-month-olds								
1-month delay	2.20	0.68	2.44	0.78	2.17	0.51	2.00	0.69
3-month delay	2.09	0.83	2.28	0.83	2.22	0.81	1.78	0.81
6-month delay	2.26	0.68	2.56	0.62	2.44	0.51	1.78	0.65
9-month delay	2.07	0.70	2.28	0.75	2.33	0.49	1.61	0.61
12-month delay	2.00	0.82	2.39	0.78	2.00	0.84	1.61	0.70
16-month-olds								
1-month delay	1.54	0.82	1.67	0.91	1.56	0.86	1.39	0.70
3-month delay	1.46	0.77	1.61	0.92	1.56	0.78	1.22	0.55
6-month delay	1.61	0.90	1.78	0.88	1.72	0.96	1.33	0.84
9-month delay	1.65	0.89	2.06	0.80	1.56	1.04	1.33	0.69
12-month delay	1.56	0.88	1.78	0.88	1.50	0.99	1.39	0.78

20-month-olds did not differ significantly. Finally, on arbitrarily ordered event sequences there was a main effect of experience: $F(1,170) = 6.28$, $p < .02$, $MSE = 0.58$. Prior to modeling, the children produced a larger number of individual target actions of the arbitrarily ordered events that they subsequently would be permitted to imitate, relative to the events that they would only watch [$Ms = 0.84$ and 0.64 ($SDs = 0.80$ and 0.75), respectively]. There were no other reliable effects.

In terms of children's levels of production of pairs of actions in the target order, although analysis of variance revealed reliable effects of age and experience condition, analysis of covariance with the number of individual target actions produced as the covariate revealed no reliable effects. Thus, once the variance associated with differential levels of production of the individual target actions of the event sequences in some cells of the design was controlled, there were no significant differences in pre-modeling levels of production of pairs of actions in the target order.

In summary, children's performance during the baseline assessment period, prior to exposure to the events, was relatively low. That is, the children produced relatively few of the individual target actions that soon would be demonstrated for them, and even fewer of them in the target order. With some exceptions, the children's performance did not differ reliably across cells of the design. Children's production of the individual target actions of the sequences differed as a function of age, with the 20-month-olds generally producing more individual target actions, relative to the 16-month-olds. On one sequence type, namely, arbitrarily ordered events, children produced a greater number of the individual target actions of sequences that they subsequently would be permitted to imitate, relative to those that they would only watch. Because the mode of experience manipulation had not as yet been introduced, this effect can only be attributed to chance variation. Moreover, once the variance associated with differential baseline levels of production of the individual target actions of the events was controlled, children's production of pairs of actions in the target order did not differ across the cells of the design. Finally, the performance of the children in the different delay conditions did not differ reliably.

IMMEDIATE RECALL PERFORMANCE

Descriptive statistics on children's immediate recall performance are provided in Table 2. To determine whether the children learned the event sequences as a result of exposure to them, we compared their imitative performance (see Table 2) with their baseline performance (see Table 1) in 2 (modeling condition: pre-modeling, post-modeling) × 5 (delay) × 2 (age) × 3 (sequence type) mixed analyses of variance for each dependent measure. Mode of experience was not a variable in the analyses because it was only on sequences in the imitate condition that immediate recall performance measures were available (i.e., prior to imposition of the delay, children were not permitted to imitate event sequences in the watch condition).

Main effects of modeling condition revealed that, as a result of exposure to the modeled events, children learned both the individual target actions of the sequences, $F(1,170) = 3490.02$, $p < .0001$, $MSE = 0.61$, and the temporal order of the actions, $F(1,170) = 1504.32$, $p < .0001$, $MSE = 0.52$. That is, for both measures, there were reliable increases in performance after modeling [Ms = 3.64 and 1.84 (SDs = 0.70 and 0.85), for individual actions and pairs of actions, respectively], compared with before modeling [Ms = 0.83 and 0.14 (SDs = 0.80 and 0.37), for individual target actions and pairs of actions, respectively]. Main effects of age revealed higher levels of production of the individual target actions and of pairs of actions in the target order by the 20-month-olds compared with the 16-month-olds: $Fs(1,170)$ = 46.93 and 54.25, $ps < .0001$, $MSEs$ = 0.85 and 0.50, for individual target actions and pairs of actions in the target order, respectively [Ms for individual target actions produced = 2.42 and 2.04 (SDs = 1.59 and 1.57); Ms for pairs in target order = 1.15 and 0.83 (SDs = 1.15 and 0.97), for the 20- and the 16-month-olds, respectively]. Analyses of reliable Modeling condition × Age interactions on both dependent measures [$Fs(1,170)$ = 5.28 and 30.91, $ps < .03$, $MSEs$ = 0.61 and 0.52, for individual target actions and pairs of actions in target order, respectively] indicated that the sizes of the age effects were greater after modeling than they had been before modeling (M age differences after modeling of 0.49 and 0.57, for target actions and pairs of actions, respectively; M age differences prior to modeling of 0.28 and 0.07, for individual target actions and pairs of actions in target order, respectively). Across delay conditions, children's levels of acquisition of the target material did not differ: Neither the main effects of delay nor interactions involving it were significant, for either dependent measure. Thus, children in the different delay conditions exhibited equivalent levels of acquisition of the individual target actions of the event sequences. In terms of the number of individual target actions produced, there were no other reliable effects. Moreover, the patterns were not affected by controlling baseline levels of production of the individual target actions via analysis of covariance.

In terms of the number of pairs of actions produced in the target order, the main effect of sequence type was qualified by the interaction with modeling condition: $F(2,340) = 20.35$, $p < .0001$, $MSE = 0.32$. Separate analyses at each level of modeling condition revealed that prior to modeling, production of pairs of actions in the target order did not differ across sequence types [Ms = 0.15, 0.13, and 0.13 (SDs = 0.41, 0.33, and 0.36), for enabling, mixed, and arbitrarily ordered event sequences, respectively]. After modeling, the effect was reliable: $F(2,358) = 29.59$, $p < .0001$, $MSE = 0.46$. Children produced the largest number of pairs of actions in the target order on the enabling events ($M = 2.08$, $SD = 0.86$), followed by the mixed events ($M = 1.91$, $SD = 0.86$), followed by the arbitrarily ordered event sequences ($M = 1.54$, $SD = 0.73$); performance was reliably different for each sequence type. The pattern of differential immediate ordered recall across sequence types remained even after controlling for baseline levels of production of pairs of actions in the target order alone, $F(2,339) = 29.49$, $p < .0001$, $MSE = 0.46$, and after controlling for baseline levels in combination with post-modeling production of individual target actions, $F(2,338) = 47.53$, $p < .0001$, $MSE = 0.33$. There were no other reliable effects.

In summary, as measured by both dependent variables, children in the different delay conditions learned the to-be-remembered material. That is, as a result of exposure to the target event sequences, children's performance increased substantially and significantly, both in terms of production of the individual target actions of the event sequences and in terms of production of correctly ordered pairs of actions. At immediate testing, the children demonstrated levels of mastery of the event sequences that did not differ across delay conditions. The 20-month-olds demonstrated higher levels of production of individual target actions and ordered pairs of action, relative to the 16-month-olds. These effects were observed even with differential baseline levels of production controlled via analyses of covariance. The age-related differences in children's initial learning of the event sequences have implications for interpretation of patterns of delayed recall, described below.

Children's levels of production of the individual target actions of the events did not differ across sequence types. In contrast, the children evidenced superior ordered recall of event sequences that were wholly constrained by enabling relations, relative to those that were partially constrained; they evidenced superior ordered recall of event sequences partially constrained by enabling relations, relative to those that were wholly unconstrained. This pattern is consistent with that observed in previous related research (e.g., Bauer, Hertsgaard, et al., 1998).

DELAYED RECALL PERFORMANCE: EVENTS PREVIOUSLY EXPERIENCED COMPARED WITH NEW EVENTS

In previous research on children's recall over short to intermediate delays, we used comparisons of children's delayed recall performance with their baseline levels of performance to determine whether the children recalled the event sequences (e.g., Bauer & Hertsgaard, 1993; Bauer & Mandler, 1989). To the extent that delayed recall levels were reliably greater than baseline levels, we inferred memory. Over long retention intervals such as those used in the present research, such an approach is not adequate: as delay increased, so too did children's ages and thus, presumably, their abilities to detect the affordances of the materials presented to them, to make inferences about their properties and likely manner of combination, or both, whether or not they actually remembered them. In light of anticipated age-related increases in these abilities (hereafter referred to as "problem-solving abilities"), to determine whether they remembered the event sequences, we compared children's performance on the events to which they previously had been exposed to their performance on events that were new to the children at the time of delayed recall testing. Significant differences between performance on events previously imitated and events new to the children at Session 4 will be taken as evidence of recall.[3] Likewise, significant differences between performance on events previously only watched and on new events will be taken as evidence of recall.

To evaluate performance differences across the cells of the design, we conducted 5 (delay) × 2 (age) × 3 (sequence type) × 3 (experience: imitate, watch, new at Session 4) mixed analyses of variance on both the number of individual target actions produced and the number of pairs of actions produced in the target order. We conducted separate, parallel analyses evaluating children's performance before provision of the verbal labels for the event sequences and children's total recall performance. Because for both dependent measures, the effects were largely the same, to avoid redundancy, we report the results of the more conservative analyses of children's performance prior to provision of the verbal labels for the events and note exceptions when children's post-verbal-label performance was considered. In addition, only main effects of and interactions involving the variable experience are interpreted: Main effects and interactions not involving experience include the variance associated with performance on the event sequences new at Session 4 and as such, are not informative with respect to the influence of the other variables on children's long-term recall. Effects of each of the factors per se are evaluated in the next section. Descriptive statistics for all cells of the design are provided in Table 3.

Individual Target Actions Produced

The four-way mixed-factor analysis of variance revealed a main effect of experience: $F(2,340) = 98.29$, $p < .0001$, $MSE = 0.88$. Overall, the children produced larger numbers of individual target actions on events that they previously had imitated ($M = 1.71$, $SD = 1.21$) and on events that

---

[3]Strictly speaking, not all event sequences in the "imitate" experience condition were imitated by the children: Initial levels of performance on the event sequences were high but were not perfect. Nevertheless, for ease of exposition, we will refer to event sequences that the children had the opportunity to produce (i.e., those in the imitate experience condition) as the "imitate" events. The reader should keep in mind, however, that because a given event sequence was included in the imitate experience condition does not ensure that it necessarily was produced by the child, either in whole or even in part.

TABLE 3

MEANS AND STANDARD DEVIATIONS FOR THE NUMBER OF INDIVIDUAL TARGET
ACTIONS AND PAIRS OF ACTIONS PRODUCED IN THE TARGET ORDER
AT DELAYED TESTING BY CHILDREN TESTED ON FOUR-STEP EVENT SEQUENCES

Age group/ Delay condition/ Reminding/ Experience	Sequence Type							
	Overall		Enabling		Mixed		Arbitrary	
	Mean	SD	Mean	SD	Mean	SD	Mean	SD
Number of individual target actions produced (max. = 4.0)								
20-month-olds								
1-month delay								
Before reminder								
Imitate	2.83	1.21	2.72	1.32	2.50	1.20	3.28	1.02
Watch	3.02	1.11	2.67	1.24	2.83	1.20	3.56	0.62
New	0.89	0.92	0.78	0.88	0.72	0.75	1.17	1.10
Total production								
Imitate	3.28	0.98	3.11	1.13	3.06	1.06	3.67	0.59
Watch	3.39	0.96	3.33	1.03	3.06	1.16	3.78	0.43
New	1.22	1.06	1.00	0.84	1.39	1.24	1.28	1.07
3-month delay								
Before reminder								
Imitate	2.26	1.28	1.61	1.33	2.44	1.29	2.72	0.96
Watch	1.98	1.05	1.56	1.15	2.00	1.08	2.39	0.78
New	1.07	0.99	0.83	0.99	1.22	0.81	1.17	1.15
Total production								
Imitate	2.67	1.15	2.17	1.29	2.67	1.19	3.17	0.71
Watch	2.69	0.99	2.39	1.29	2.78	0.88	2.89	0.68
New	1.37	1.05	1.22	1.11	1.44	0.98	1.44	1.10
6-month delay								
Before reminder								
Imitate	1.63	1.23	1.67	1.50	1.22	1.11	2.00	0.97
Watch	1.56	1.09	1.33	1.33	1.56	1.10	1.78	0.81
New	1.02	0.81	1.22	0.81	1.06	0.80	0.78	0.81
Total production								
Imitate	2.11	1.24	2.39	1.50	1.56	0.98	2.39	1.04
Watch	2.00	1.20	1.78	1.31	1.89	1.18	2.33	1.08
New	1.53	0.92	1.67	1.08	1.71	0.89	1.22	0.73
9-month delay								
Before reminder								
Imitate	1.65	0.95	1.72	1.02	1.61	0.98	1.61	0.92
Watch	1.85	1.16	1.94	1.30	1.50	1.04	2.11	1.08
New	1.39	0.76	1.44	0.51	1.28	0.96	1.44	0.78
Total production								
Imitate	2.19	1.13	2.50	1.34	1.89	1.02	2.17	0.99
Watch	2.35	1.22	2.33	1.37	2.00	1.28	2.72	0.89
New	1.80	0.86	1.83	0.92	1.72	0.96	1.83	0.71

(*continued*)

TABLE 3 (*continued*)

Age group/ Delay condition/ Reminding/ Experience	Sequence Type							
	Overall		Enabling		Mixed		Arbitrary	
	Mean	SD	Mean	SD	Mean	SD	Mean	SD
12-month delay								
Before reminder								
Imitate	1.70	1.06	1.33	0.84	1.78	1.00	2.00	1.24
Watch	1.65	1.12	1.44	1.10	1.61	1.24	1.89	1.02
New	1.53	1.00	1.44	1.15	1.42	1.09	1.72	0.75
Total production								
Imitate	2.35	1.15	2.39	1.38	2.28	0.89	2.39	1.20
Watch	2.20	1.12	2.17	1.04	2.11	1.18	2.33	1.19
New	2.02	1.07	2.06	1.16	1.82	1.25	2.17	0.79
16-month-olds								
1-month delay								
Before reminder								
Imitate	2.37	1.26	1.94	1.43	2.44	1.10	2.72	1.18
Watch	2.17	1.22	2.22	1.40	2.06	1.06	2.22	1.26
New	0.85	0.81	0.56	0.51	1.00	0.84	1.00	0.97
Total production								
Imitate	2.84	1.12	2.53	1.24	2.72	1.13	3.28	0.89
Watch	2.74	1.18	2.67	1.46	2.56	0.86	3.00	1.19
New	1.15	0.98	1.12	0.96	1.06	0.87	1.28	1.13
3-month delay								
Before reminder								
Imitate	1.24	0.95	0.94	1.21	1.22	0.65	1.56	0.86
Watch	1.31	0.97	1.22	0.88	1.11	0.90	1.61	1.09
New	0.78	0.66	0.78	0.65	0.78	0.65	0.78	0.73
Total production								
Imitate	1.80	1.00	2.11	1.18	1.44	0.78	1.83	0.92
Watch	1.87	1.15	1.83	1.15	1.61	1.20	2.17	1.10
New	0.98	0.76	1.06	0.80	0.89	0.83	1.00	0.69
6-month delay								
Before reminder								
Imitate	1.26	0.83	1.39	0.70	0.83	0.62	1.56	0.98
Watch	1.13	0.97	0.89	0.76	0.83	0.92	1.67	1.03
New	0.96	0.80	0.78	0.65	0.94	0.73	1.17	0.99
Total production								
Imitate	1.63	0.96	1.61	0.85	1.22	0.65	2.06	1.16
Watch	1.81	1.08	1.83	1.38	1.44	0.78	2.17	0.92
New	1.19	0.84	1.11	0.76	1.17	0.86	1.28	0.96
9-month delay								
Before reminder								
Imitate	1.06	0.92	1.11	0.96	1.17	0.99	0.89	0.83
Watch	1.20	1.14	1.67	1.33	0.83	0.79	1.11	1.13
New	0.83	0.77	0.67	0.69	1.00	0.91	0.83	0.71

(*continued*)

TABLE 3 (*continued*)

Age group/ Delay condition/ Reminding/ Experience	Sequence Type							
	Overall		Enabling		Mixed		Arbitrary	
	Mean	*SD*	Mean	*SD*	Mean	*SD*	Mean	*SD*
Total production								
Imitate	1.50	1.00	1.44	0.92	1.72	1.23	1.33	0.84
Watch	1.52	1.09	1.94	1.30	1.11	0.83	1.50	0.99
New	1.19	0.89	0.94	0.94	1.28	1.02	1.33	0.69
12-month delay								
Before reminder								
Imitate	1.05	0.88	0.88	0.68	0.89	0.96	1.39	0.92
Watch	1.22	0.88	1.22	0.81	0.89	0.76	1.56	0.98
New	0.81	0.83	0.89	0.83	0.59	0.69	0.94	0.94
Total production								
Imitate	1.83	1.13	2.06	1.16	1.33	1.19	2.11	0.90
Watch	1.89	1.04	2.06	1.21	1.44	0.78	2.17	0.99
New	1.31	1.04	1.33	0.91	0.88	0.90	1.72	1.18
Number of pairs of actions in the target order (max. = 3.0)								
20-month-olds								
1-month delay								
Before reminder								
Imitate	1.37	1.09	1.44	1.34	1.33	1.08	1.33	0.84
Watch	1.28	1.02	1.28	1.32	1.33	1.03	1.22	0.65
New	0.11	0.32	0.11	0.32	0.11	0.32	0.11	0.32
Total production								
Imitate	1.59	0.98	1.67	1.24	1.61	0.92	1.50	0.79
Watch	1.50	0.93	1.72	1.07	1.39	0.98	1.39	0.70
New	0.26	0.59	0.11	0.32	0.50	0.86	0.17	0.38
3-month delay								
Before reminder								
Imitate	0.94	0.86	0.56	0.86	1.22	0.94	1.06	0.64
Watch	0.59	0.74	0.39	0.78	0.78	0.88	0.61	0.50
New	0.17	0.47	0.17	0.51	0.06	0.24	0.28	0.57
Total production								
Imitate	1.19	0.85	0.89	1.08	1.39	0.85	1.28	0.46
Watch	0.94	0.83	0.78	1.00	1.17	0.86	0.89	0.58
New	0.24	0.55	0.28	0.57	0.11	0.47	0.33	0.59
6-month delay								
Before reminder								
Imitate	0.57	0.84	0.72	1.02	0.39	0.78	0.61	0.70
Watch	0.43	0.74	0.50	0.92	0.39	0.78	0.39	0.50
New	0.17	0.42	0.22	0.43	0.18	0.51	0.11	0.32
Total production								
Imitate	0.81	0.93	1.22	1.17	0.50	0.79	0.72	0.67
Watch	0.70	0.84	0.67	0.97	0.61	0.85	0.83	0.71
New	0.36	0.55	0.44	0.62	0.41	0.60	0.22	0.43

(*continued*)

TABLE 3 (*continued*)

Age group/ Delay condition/ Reminding/ Experience	Sequence Type							
	Overall		Enabling		Mixed		Arbitrary	
	Mean	*SD*	Mean	*SD*	Mean	*SD*	Mean	*SD*
9-month delay								
Before reminder								
Imitate	0.44	0.66	0.50	0.62	0.39	0.70	0.44	0.70
Watch	0.59	0.84	0.67	0.97	0.33	0.49	0.78	0.94
New	0.26	0.48	0.28	0.46	0.28	0.57	0.22	0.43
Total production								
Imitate	0.67	0.80	0.83	0.86	0.50	0.71	0.67	0.84
Watch	0.83	0.84	0.83	0.92	0.67	0.69	1.00	0.91
New	0.44	0.63	0.44	0.78	0.50	0.62	0.39	0.50
12-month delay								
Before reminder								
Imitate	0.50	0.64	0.33	0.49	0.56	0.70	0.61	0.70
Watch	0.48	0.67	0.39	0.70	0.39	0.61	0.67	0.69
New	0.36	0.65	0.28	0.57	0.41	0.77	0.39	0.61
Total production								
Imitate	0.83	0.72	0.94	0.80	0.78	0.65	0.78	0.73
Watch	0.72	0.79	0.72	0.75	0.56	0.78	0.89	0.83
New	0.62	0.73	0.67	0.77	0.65	0.83	0.56	0.62
16-month-olds								
1-month delay								
Before reminder								
Imitate	0.94	0.90	0.82	1.10	1.17	0.86	0.83	0.71
Watch	0.83	0.88	0.78	1.00	0.94	0.94	0.78	0.73
New	0.09	0.29	0.00	—	0.11	0.32	0.17	0.38
Total production								
Imitate	1.13	0.85	1.12	1.02	1.22	0.88	1.06	0.64
Watch	1.07	0.91	1.06	1.11	1.17	0.86	1.00	0.77
New	0.23	0.46	0.29	0.57	0.11	0.32	0.28	0.46
3-month delay								
Before reminder								
Imitate	0.24	0.47	0.28	0.57	0.11	0.32	0.33	0.49
Watch	0.31	0.51	0.22	0.43	0.17	0.38	0.56	0.62
New	0.04	0.19	0.00	—	0.11	0.32	0.00	—
Total production								
Imitate	0.52	0.67	0.72	0.83	0.33	0.49	0.50	0.62
Watch	0.59	0.69	0.61	0.70	0.50	0.71	0.67	0.69
New	0.09	0.29	0.06	0.24	0.17	0.38	0.06	0.24
6-month delay								
Before reminder								
Imitate	0.26	0.44	0.22	0.43	0.11	0.32	0.44	0.51
Watch	0.19	0.39	0.06	0.24	0.17	0.38	0.33	0.49
New	0.13	0.34	0.00	—	0.17	0.39	0.22	0.43

(*continued*)

TABLE 3 (*continued*)

Age group/ Delay condition/ Reminding/ Experience	Sequence Type							
	Overall		Enabling		Mixed		Arbitrary	
	Mean	SD	Mean	SD	Mean	SD	Mean	SD
Total production								
Imitate	0.33	0.48	0.28	0.46	0.22	0.43	0.50	0.51
Watch	0.43	0.60	0.44	0.70	0.33	0.49	0.50	0.62
New	0.20	0.41	0.06	0.24	0.28	0.46	0.28	0.46
9-month delay								
Before reminder								
Imitate	0.17	0.42	0.22	0.43	0.17	0.51	0.11	0.32
Watch	0.26	0.56	0.44	0.78	0.11	0.32	0.22	0.43
New	0.11	0.32	0.06	0.24	0.22	0.43	0.06	0.43
Total production								
Imitate	0.35	0.59	0.39	0.61	0.44	0.70	0.22	0.43
Watch	0.37	0.59	0.61	0.78	0.17	0.38	0.33	0.49
New	0.26	0.52	0.11	0.32	0.39	0.61	0.28	0.57
12-month delay								
Before reminder								
Imitate	0.19	0.44	0.12	0.32	0.11	0.32	0.33	0.59
Watch	0.26	0.52	0.39	0.61	0.11	0.32	0.28	0.57
New	0.09	0.29	0.17	0.38	0.06	0.24	0.06	0.24
Total production								
Imitate	0.55	0.69	0.65	0.76	0.28	0.57	0.72	0.67
Watch	0.57	0.77	0.78	0.94	0.39	0.61	0.56	0.70
New	0.32	0.54	0.39	0.61	0.18	0.38	0.39	0.61

they previously had only watched ($M = 1.71$, $SD = 1.20$), relative to on events that were new to them at Session 4 ($M = 1.01$, $SD = 0.87$). This pattern is indicative of recall of the individual target actions of the event sequences. Although the main effect was qualified by the interaction with delay, $F(8, 340) = 15.69$, $p < .0001$, $MSE = 0.88$, separate one-way analyses of variance revealed evidence of recall of the individual target actions of the previously experienced event sequences in all delay conditions (see Figure 2, Panel A). That is, in all delay conditions, the main effects of experience were statistically significant: $Fs(2, 70) = 84.13, 22.68, 7.54, 5.69,$ and 3.14, $ps < .05$, $MSEs = 1.28, 0.96, 0.81, 0.83,$ and 0.69, for the 1-, 3-, 6-, 9-, and 12-month delay conditions, respectively. Moreover, Dunnett's tests revealed that in each delay condition, production of the individual target actions of the event sequences previously only watched was greater than production of the individual target actions of the new event sequences. In the 1-, 3-, 6-, and 9-month delay conditions, production of the individual target actions of the event sequences previously imitated

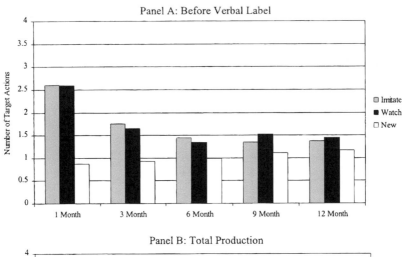

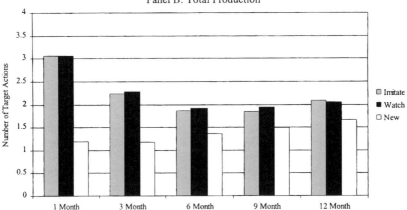

FIGURE 2.—Mean levels of production of the individual target actions of the four-step event sequences in the imitate, watch, and new experience conditions before provision of the verbal labels for the event sequences (Panel A) and the children's total production of individual target actions (Panel B), as a function of delay condition.

also was greater than production of the individual target actions of the new event sequences. In the 12-month delay condition, the effect fell just below the conventional level of statistical significance ($p < .06$; observed difference = .21; critical difference = .22).

When children's performance after provision of the verbal labels for the event sequences was considered, the children showed evidence of recall of the individual target actions both of event sequences previously only watched and of event sequences previously imitated, in all delay conditions (see Figure 2, Panel B). As reflected in Figure 2, the sizes of the differences between performance on previously experienced and on new event sequences were larger at the shorter, relative to the longer, delay intervals. In fact, at the longest delay interval, the average difference in performance on previously experienced and new event sequences was only 0.24 when the children were prompted by the event-related props alone (Figure 2, Panel A), and only 0.40 when the children were prompted by the props and by verbal labels for the event sequences (Figure 2, Panel B; see Chapter VIII: Implications of the Findings and Conclusions, for discussion of interpretation of these relative differences). Nevertheless, in all delay conditions, across age groups and sequence types, under conditions of maximum support for recall (i.e., when prompted by event-related props and verbal labels for the events), the children produced more of the individual target actions of the event sequences that they previously experienced, relative to the event sequences that were new to them.

The variable experience interacted with the variable of age: $F(2,340) =$ 3.97, $p < .02$, $MSE = 0.88$. To pursue the interaction, we conducted separate one-way analyses of variance for each age group. For both age groups, there were main effects of experience [$Fs(2,178) = 29.66$ and 43.31, $ps <$ .0001, $MSEs = 0.93$ and 1.44, for 16- and 20-month-olds, respectively]. Dunnett's tests revealed that, across delay conditions, for both age groups, performance on events previously imitated was greater than on events new to the children at Session 4; for both age groups, performance on events previously only watched was greater than on events new at Session 4 [16-month-olds: $Ms = 1.40$, 1.41, and 0.85 ($SDs = 1.09$, 1.11, and 0.77), for imitate, watch, and new, respectively; 20-month-olds: $Ms = 2.01$, 2.01, and 1.18 ($SDs = 1.24$, 1.22, and 0.93), for imitate, watch, and new, respectively]. Thus, both age groups showed evidence of recall of the individual target actions of the event sequences. The interaction reflected that the average size of the difference between performance on previously experienced event sequences and on new event sequences was greater for the 20-month-olds compared with the 16-month-olds (M differences $= 0.83$ and 0.55, respectively). When children's total production was evaluated, the Age × Experience interaction was not statistically significant. There were no other reliable effects either before or after provision of the verbal labels for the event sequences.

An important consideration in interpretation of the evidence of recall of the individual target actions of the event sequences is whether they are attributable to a general pattern of responding or to a small number of children within a cell. To address this question, we determined children's mean levels of performance across sequence types for events previously experienced (imitate and watch events) and event sequences new at Session 4. Use of the mean of the children's performances across sequence types and across the imitate and watch experience conditions was justified because with isolated exceptions, performance across the relevant cells of the design did not differ reliably. We then determined the number of children in each age group and each delay condition whose mean scores on events previously experienced were greater than their mean scores on new event sequences. Notice that this comparison depends on the direction of relative levels of performance on previously experienced and new event sequences, not their size; we merely note the number of children whose patterns of performance were indicative of memory for the events (i.e., higher performance on old event sequences than on new event sequences).

For the variable of individual target actions produced, the results of the comparison of children's performance in the old and new experience conditions, before and after the verbal reminders, are depicted in Figure 3 (Panels A and B for before verbal label and total production, respectively). As is evident from Figure 3, Panel A, when the children were prompted by the props alone, the smallest number of children for whom performance on old event sequences was nominally greater than performance on new event sequences was 10, or 56% of the sample. The number of 20-month-olds for whom pre-verbal-label performance on previously experienced events was greater than performance on new events was larger than would be expected by chance in all but the 12-month delay condition (sign tests for related samples maximum value $p < .02$; one-tailed; in this and subsequent analyses, tied cases were excluded). At the longest delay interval, the comparison against chance fell below the conventional level of statistical significance ($p < .10$). The number of 16-month-olds whose nominal levels of pre-verbal-label performance indicated recall of the individual target actions of the event sequences was greater than would be expected by chance in the 1-, 3-, 9-, and 12-month delay conditions (sign tests for related samples maximum value $p < .02$; one-tailed).

When post-verbal-label performance was evaluated (see Figure 3, Panel B), the smallest number of children who produced nominally greater numbers of individual target actions on the old event sequences relative to the new event sequences was 10, or 56% of the sample. The number of children for whom performance on previously experienced events was greater than performance on new events was larger than would be expected by chance for the 20-month-olds in all but the 12-month delay condition, and for the 16-month-olds in all but the 9-month delay condition (sign tests for related samples maximum value $p < .02$; one-tailed). These analyses provide support for the conclusion that the 20- and 16-month-olds remembered at least some of the individual target actions of the event sequences for periods of as many as 9 and 12 months.

Panel A: Individual Target Actions (before verbal label)

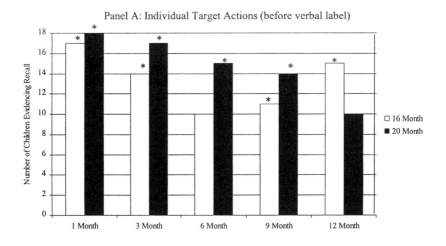

Panel B: Individual Target Actions (total production)

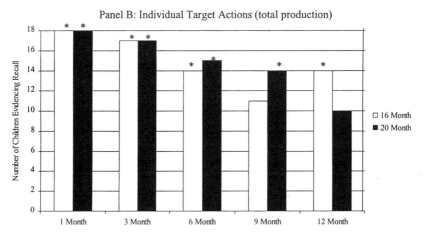

FIGURE 3.—The number of 20-month-old children and 16-month-old children tested on four-step event sequences who produced nominally higher numbers of the individual target actions of event sequences previously experienced than of new event sequences: before provision of the verbal labels for the event sequences (Panel A); children's total production (Panel B).

Pairs of Actions Produced in the Target Order

The four-way mixed-factor analysis of variance revealed a main effect of experience: $F(2, 340) = 71.53$, $p < .0001$, $MSE = 0.38$. When they were prompted by the event-related props alone, the children produced a larger number of pairs of actions in the target order on events previously imitated and previously only watched, relative to on events new at Session 4

[Ms = 0.56, 0.52, and 0.15 (SDs = 0.80, 0.77, and 0.40), for imitate, watch, and new, respectively]. This pattern is indicative of recall of the temporal order of the event sequences. The analysis also yielded interactions of Delay × Experience and Age × Experience.

To pursue the Delay × Experience interaction, $F(8,340)$ = 13.03, p < .0001, MSE = 0.38, we conducted separate analyses for each delay condition. As suggested by inspection of Figure 4, Panel A, in the 1-, 3-, and 6-month delay conditions, children produced larger numbers of pairs

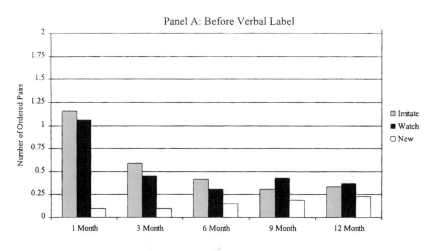

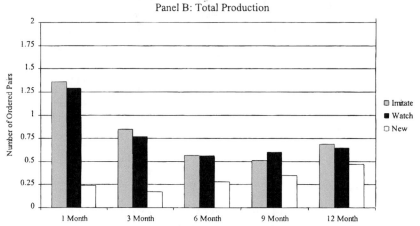

FIGURE 4.—Mean levels of production of pairs of actions in the target order of the four-step event sequences in the imitate, watch, and new experience conditions before provision of the verbal labels for the event sequences (Panel A) and the children's total production of pairs of actions in the target order (Panel B), as a function of delay condition.

of action in the target order on events previously imitated and previously only watched, relative to on events new at Session 4: $Fs(2,70)$ = 47.88, 20.77, and 6.29, ps < .004, $MSEs$ = 0.76, 0.33, and 0.31, for the 1-, 3-, and 6-month delay conditions, respectively. In the 9-month delay condition, analysis of the main effect, $F(2,70)$ = 4.79, p < .02, MSE = 0.33, indicated that children's levels of production of ordered pairs of actions on events previously only watched differed from those on events new at Session 4; children's levels of production of ordered pairs of actions on events previously imitated did not differ from that on events new at Session 4. In the 12-month delay condition, although the main effect was not statistically reliable (p < .11), Dunnett's test indicated that children's levels of production of ordered pairs of actions on events previously only watched differed from those on events new at Session 4; children's levels of production of ordered pairs of actions on events that they previously had been permitted to imitate and on events new to the children at Session 4 did not differ reliably. When total production was considered (Figure 4, Panel B), in the 12-month delay condition, children's levels of ordered recall of the events that they previously had imitated were significantly higher than on new event sequences. There were no other differences in the patterns of performance when pre-verbal-label compared with post-verbal-label performance was considered.

As was the case for children's production of the individual target actions of the event sequences, the sizes of the differences in performance on previously experienced and on new event sequences were larger at the shorter, relative to the longer, delay intervals. At the longest delay interval, the mean difference in performance on previously experienced and new event sequences was only 0.13 when the children were prompted by the event-related props alone, and only 0.20 when the children were prompted by the props and by the verbal labels for the event sequences. Although at the longer delay intervals, the differences were small in magnitude, the analyses nevertheless indicate recall by children in all delay conditions of temporal order information regarding the events that they previously had only watched, and by children in the 1-, 3-, 6-, and 12-month delay conditions of the order in which previously imitated events had occurred.

Analysis of the Age × Experience interaction, $F(2,340)$ = 7.41, p < .0007, MSE = 0.38, revealed that children in both age groups produced more ordered pairs of target actions of the event sequences that they had previously imitated and previously only watched, relative to of the event sequences new to them at Session 4: $Fs(2,178)$ = 20.15 and 36.38, ps < .0001, $MSEs$ = 0.33 and 0.65, for 16- and 20-month-olds, respectively [Ms = 0.36, 0.37, and 0.09 (SDs = 0.63, 0.64, and 0.29) and 0.77, 0.67, and 0.21 (SDs = 0.90, 0.86, and 0.48) for events imitated, watched, and new, for 16- and 20-month-olds, respectively]. Thus, both age groups showed evidence of

59

temporally ordered recall. The interaction resulted from the sizes of the differences between cell means. For the younger children, the average difference between performance on events previously experienced and events new at Session 4 was 0.28; for the older children, the average difference was 0.51. These patterns remained unchanged when children's total production was evaluated. There were no other reliable effects either before or after provision of the verbal labels for the event sequences.

For the variable of pairs of actions produced in the target order, the results of the nominal comparison of children's performance in the old and new experience conditions are depicted in Figure 5, for before (Panel A) and after (Panel B) the verbal labels for the event sequences were provided, respectively. For the 20-month-olds, whether evaluated when the children were prompted by the props alone or when they were prompted by the props and the verbal labels for the event sequences, the smallest number of children in any delay condition whose performance on previously experienced events was greater than on new events was 12, or fully 67% of the sample. The number of 20-month-olds whose pattern of performance was indicative of memory was greater than that which would be expected by chance in all delay conditions (sign tests for related samples maximum value $p < .05$; one-tailed). Thus, not only were the sizes of the differences between performance on old and new event sequences statistically reliable (above reported analyses of variance) but substantial and significant proportions of the 20-month-old children contributed to the effects. Prior to provision of the verbal labels for the events, the numbers of 16-month-olds contributing to the significant difference between performance on old and new event sequences were greater than would be expected by chance in the 1- and 3-month delay conditions only (sign tests for related samples maximum value $p < .001$; one-tailed); in the 12-month delay condition, the effect approached significance (sign tests for related samples maximum value $p < .10$; one-tailed). After the verbal labels were provided, the numbers of 16-month-olds contributing to the effect were greater than would be expected by chance in the 1-, 3-, and 6-month delay conditions (sign tests for related samples maximum value $p < .05$; one-tailed). At the longer delay intervals of 9 and 12 months, the number of 16-month-olds contributing to the effect fell below the level that would be expected by chance (sign tests for related samples minimum value $p > .10$). This result indicates that at the longer delay intervals, there is greater individual variability among the 16-month-olds than among the 20-month-olds.

Summary

The results of comparisons of children's performance on events previously experienced compared with events new to them at the time of

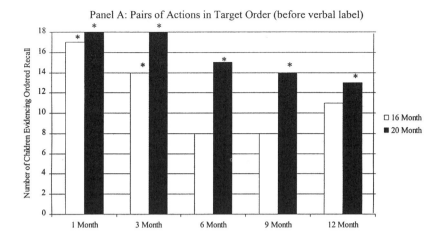

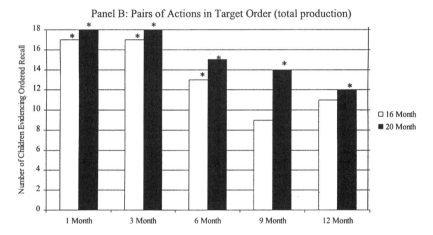

FIGURE 5.—The number of 20-month-old children and 16-month-old children tested on four-step event sequences who produced nominally higher numbers of pairs of actions in the target order of event sequences previously experienced than of new event sequences: before provision of the verbal labels for the event sequences (Panel A); children's total production (Panel B).

delayed recall testing indicate that they recalled information both about the individual target actions of the event sequences and about their temporal order. In all delay conditions, when prompted by the props alone, when prompted by the props and verbal labels for the event sequences, or both, children provided evidence of recall of some of the individual target actions of the event sequences that they previously had imitated as well as those that they had only watched. Whether tested before or after provision of the verbal labels for the events, the number of 20-month-old children who showed nominally higher levels of performance on old event sequences than on new event sequences was greater than would be expected by chance at all but the longest delay interval. With the exception of pre-verbal-label performance in the 6-month delay condition and post-verbal-label performance in the 9-month delay condition, the pattern of reliable performance was evident in the 16-month-olds as well.

In the 1-, 3-, 6-, and 12-month delay conditions, when prompted by the props alone, when prompted by the props and verbal labels for the event sequences, or both, the 16-month-olds and the 20-month-olds showed evidence of recall of information about the temporal order in which the events unfolded; the size of the effect was greater for the 20-month-olds compared with the 16-month-olds. In the 9-month delay condition, the children evidenced recall of order information regarding events that they previously had only watched, but not of events that they previously had been provided the opportunity to imitate. The number of 20-month-olds who showed nominally higher levels of production of pairs of actions in the target order on old event sequences than on new event sequences was greater than would be expected by chance at all delay intervals, both before and after provision of the verbal labels for the events. When they were prompted by the props alone, the number of 16-month-olds who showed nominally higher levels of production of pairs of actions in the target order on old event sequences than on new event sequences was greater than would be expected by chance in the 1- and 3-month delay conditions; when prompted by the props and verbal labels for the event sequences, the number of 16-month-olds whose patterns of performance were indicative of ordered recall was greater than would be expected by chance in the 1-, 3-, and 6-month delay conditions, but not in the 9- and 12-month delay conditions.

FACTORS AFFECTING DELAYED RECALL: EFFECTS OF DELAY, AGE, SEQUENCE TYPE, MODE OF EXPERIENCE, AND VERBAL REMINDING

Because the above analyses included the variance associated with performance on event sequences new to the children at the time delayed recall was tested, they could not be used to evaluate the direct and interactive effects on delayed recall of the factors of interest in this research, namely, length of the delay interval, age at the time of experience of the events, sequence type, mode of experience of the event sequences, and the availability of verbal reminders of the event sequences. To evaluate the effects of these factors on children's long-term recall, we conducted 5 (delay) × 2 (age) × 3 (sequence type) × 2 (experience: imitate, watch) mixed analyses of variance, for both dependent measures. We conducted separate, parallel analyses evaluating children's performance before provision of the verbal reminders and children's total recall performance. In addition, to determine whether conclusions regarding the factors affecting children's ordered recall performance were influenced by differences in their production of individual target actions, we conducted analyses of covariance with the number of pairs of actions produced in the target order at delayed recall as the dependent measure and the number of individual target actions produced at delayed recall as the covariate. With one exception (as noted below), introduction of the covariate did not modify the patterns obtained. For this reason, we focus on the results of the analyses of variance. We evaluated the effects of provision of verbal reminders by conducting t tests to determine whether the difference in performance prior to and after provision of the verbal reminders differed from zero. The results of the analyses are outlined below, for each potential effect on children's long-term recall in turn. Descriptive statistics for each cell of the design are provided in Table 3.

Length of the Delay Interval

For both dependent measures, both prior to and after provision of the verbal reminders, there were main effects of delay: $F(4,170) = 28.11$, 27.21, 28.61, and 24.75, ps $< .0001$, MSEs $= 2.02$, 1.89, 0.79, and 0.88, for the number of individual target actions produced before and after the verbal reminders and the number of pairs of actions produced in the target order before and after the verbal reminders, respectively. As reflected in Figure 6, for both dependent measures, whether evaluated before or after provision of the verbal reminders, performance in the 1-month delay condition was greater than in all other delay conditions. Performance prior to provision of the verbal reminder did not differ in the 3-, 6-, 9-, and 12-month delay conditions, for either dependent measure. Although on the measure of children's production of the individual target actions of the event sequences, the variable delay interacted with sequence type, the interaction did not qualify the main effect (see effects of *Sequence Type* for description of the interaction). When prompted by the props and verbal reminders, children's production of the individual target actions of the event sequences was greater in the 3-month delay condition, relative to the 6- and 9-month delay conditions, but not relative to the 12-month delay condition; performance in the 6-, 9-, and 12-month delay conditions did not differ. A similar yet more specific effect was observed on children's production of pairs of actions in the target order: when prompted by the props and verbal reminders, children's ordered recall of the event sequences was greater in the 3-month delay

63

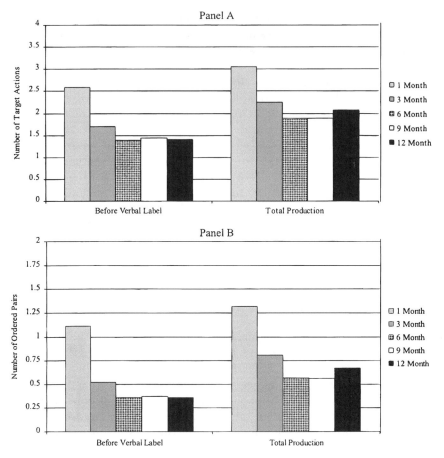

FIGURE 6.—Effects of delay on production of individual target actions (Panel A) and pairs of actions in the target order (Panel B) by 20-month-olds and 16-month-olds tested on four-step event sequences.

condition relative to the 9-month delay conditions, but not relative to the 6- and 12-month delay conditions; performance in the 6-, 9-, and 12-month delay conditions did not differ. Thus, whether evaluated with or without the support of verbal reminders, as measured by both dependent measures, children evidenced an initial decrement in performance between 1 and 3 months. Without the aid of verbal reminders, the children thereafter maintained stable levels of production both of the individual target actions of the event sequences and of pairs of actions in the target order. When performance was aided by verbal reminders, the children evidenced a somewhat more gradual decrement in performance, with decreases between 1 and 3 months (individual target actions and pairs of actions in target order), between 3 and 6 months (individual target actions), and 3 and 9 months (individual target actions and pairs of actions in target order).

Age at the Time of Exposure to the Event Sequences

For both dependent measures, both prior to and after provision of the verbal reminders, there were main effects of age: $F(1, 170) = 49.95$, 47.81, 43.49, and 45.95, $ps < .0001$, $MSEs = 2.02$, 1.89, 0.79, and 0.88, for the number of individual target actions produced before and after the verbal reminders and the number of pairs of actions produced in the target order before and after the verbal reminders, respectively. The 20-month-olds produced a larger number of individual target actions relative to the 16-month-olds [before verbal reminder: $Ms = 2.01$ and 1.40 ($SDs = 1.23$ and 1.10), respectively; after verbal reminder: $Ms = 2.52$ and 1.94 ($SDs = 1.20$ and 1.16), respectively]. The 20-month-olds also produced a larger number of pairs of actions in the target order relative to the 16-month-olds [before verbal reminder: $Ms = 0.72$ and 0.36 ($SDs = 0.88$ and .63), respectively; after verbal reminder: $Ms = 0.98$ and 0.59 ($SDs = 0.90$ and 0.74), respectively]. There were no interactions with age. Thus, overall, the older children performed at higher levels than the younger children, as assessed by both dependent measures, both before and after provision of the verbal reminders.

Sequence Type

In terms of the number of individual target actions produced, there were main effects of sequence type both prior to and after provision of the verbal reminders: $Fs(2, 340) = 23.60$ and 21.46, $ps < .0001$, $MSEs = 0.85$ and 0.96, respectively. The effects are illustrated in Figure 7, Panel A. Prior to the verbal reminders, the children produced a larger number of individual target actions of the arbitrarily ordered event sequences, relative to the enabling and mixed event sequences; performance on enabling and mixed event sequences did not differ reliably. Analysis of the Delay × Sequence type condition interaction, $F(8, 340) = 3.17$, $p < .002$, $MSE = 0.85$, revealed this pattern in all but the 9-month delay condition in which children's levels of production of the individual target actions of the event sequences did not differ reliably. After provision of the verbal reminders, across delay conditions, children exhibited relatively higher levels of performance on arbitrarily ordered event sequences relative to enabling and mixed event sequences. In addition, with provision of the

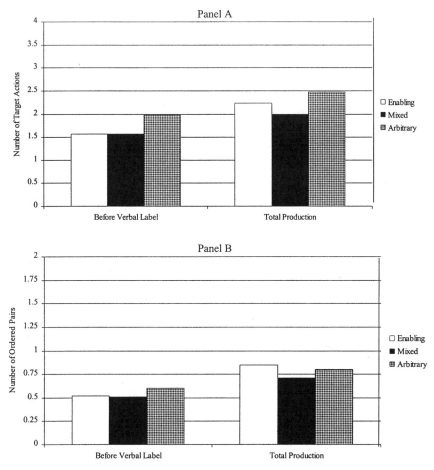

FIGURE 7.—Effects of sequence type on production of individual target actions (Panel A) and pairs of actions in the target order (Panel B) by 20-month-olds and 16-month-olds tested on four-step event sequences.

verbal reminders, there was a significant difference between children's levels of production of the individual target actions of the enabling event sequences relative to the mixed event sequences. These effects were not qualified by interactions.

In contrast to the relatively robust effects of sequence type on children's production of the individual target actions of the event sequences, children's production of pairs of actions in the target order was largely unaffected by the nature of the event sequences on which they were tested (see Figure 7, Panel B). When the children were prompted by the props alone, neither the main effect of sequence type nor interactions with sequence type were observed. That is, the number of pairs of actions that the children produced in the target order on the enabling, mixed, and arbitrarily ordered event sequences did not differ significantly. Introduction of the verbal reminders produced a reliable sequence type effect: $F(2,340) = 3.13$, $p < .05$, $MSE = 0.55$. The children produced a larger number of ordered pairs of actions on the enabling event sequences relative to the mixed event sequences; performance on the arbitrarily ordered event sequences was intermediate and did not differ from that on the other two sequence types. The patterns were unchanged when, in analyses of covariance, we controlled for the number of individual target actions produced.

It is notable that the sequence type effects obtained are precisely the opposite of those observed at immediate recall in the present research, and in previous related research when children's recall was tested after brief delays (e.g., Bauer & Dow, 1994; Bauer & Hertsgaard, 1993). That is, at immediate recall and over short delays, effects of sequence type were observed on children's ordered recall but not on their production of the individual target actions of the event sequences. In contrast, in the present research, after the delays, sequence type effects were more readily apparent on production of individual target actions than on production of pairs of actions in the target order. The pattern after the delay is, however, consistent with that observed in Bauer et al. (1994): After a delay interval of 8 months, we found that children's ordered recall of two-step event sequences was not affected by sequence type.

Mode of Experience

Whether evaluated before or after provision of the verbal reminders, children's levels of production of the individual target actions of the event sequences were not affected by whether they had been provided the opportunity to imitate the events prior to imposition of the delays (ps > .65). Likewise, whether they were prompted by the props alone or by both the props and the verbal reminders, the children's production of pairs of actions in the target order was not affected by experience condition (ps > .30). Thus, children's performance was not affected by whether they previously had been given the opportunity to imitate the events or whether they previously had only watched them being modeled. This finding is consistent with Meltzoff (1995). It suggests that, whereas the opportunity to imitate an event or event sequence prior to imposition of a short delay may, at least in some cases (e.g., Bauer et al., 1995), have a facilitating effect on recall, the effect at short delays is not ubiquitous, and over longer delays, it may have no apparent effect on children's performance.

Availability of Verbal Reminders

The analyses presented thus far have provided numerous suggestions of facilitating effects of verbal reminders on children's production of the individual target actions of the event sequences and of ordered pairs of actions of the sequences. To evaluate the effect formally, we conducted t tests (one-tailed) to determine whether the difference between children's performance after provision of the verbal reminders (i.e., total production) and before provision of the verbal reminders (i.e., before reminding) was greater than zero. We conducted separate tests for each delay condition, age group, and sequence type, for each dependent measure. Because in the above-reported analyses there were neither main effects of nor interactions involving mode of experience condition, in order to place some constraints on what in any case was to be a large number of statistical tests, we conducted the analyses across experience conditions.

For both age groups, the analyses revealed significant facilitating effects of verbal reminding on children's production of the individual target actions and pairs of actions in the target order of both the enabling and the arbitrarily ordered event sequences, at all delay intervals: $ts(17) > 2.20$, $ps < .05$. In addition, for both age groups, there were significant facilitating effects of verbal reminding on children's production of the individual target actions of the mixed event sequences, at all delay intervals: $ts(17) > 2.70$, $ps < .02$. In terms of ordered recall of the mixed event sequences, for the 20-month-olds, the effects were statistically reliable in the 1-, 3-, 6-, and 9-month delay conditions, indicating facilitating effects of reminding on children's ordered recall of the mixed events: $ts(17) > 2.90$, $ps < .01$. In the 12-month delay condition, the effect fell just below the conventional level of statistical significance: $t(17) = 1.94$, $p < .07$. For the 16-month-olds, the difference in children's ordered recall of the mixed event sequences when they were prompted by the props alone and when they were prompted by the props and verbal reminders was significantly greater than zero in the 3-, 9-, and 12-month delay conditions: $ts(17) > 2.05$, ps .05. In the 1- and 6-month delay conditions, the effect fell just below the conventional level of statistical significance: $ts(17) = 2.06$, $ps < .06$, for both delay conditions.

Summary

Both in terms of the number of individual target actions produced and the number of pairs of actions produced in the target order, children's performance declined significantly between the 1- and 3-month delay intervals. Without verbal reminders, children's performance leveled off thereafter. With verbal reminders, there was a somewhat more gradual decline in performance across the delay conditions. This pattern is similar to the initial steep decline in performance, followed by a substantially more gradual degradation in performance, observed in older children's recall (Schneider & Pressley, 1997).

Overall, the 20-month-old children in this research produced both a larger number of individual target actions and a larger number of pairs of actions in the target order, relative to the 16-month-olds. This suggests that, although both age groups showed evidence of memory for the event sequences (as indexed by differences in performance on events previously experienced as compared to events new to them at the time delayed recall was tested), the older children's memories were more robust.

Differentially robust memory was suggested for the individual target actions of the events wholly unconstrained by enabling relations, relative to events partially or totally constrained by them. Whether evaluated before or after provision of the verbal reminders, children's production of the individual target actions of the arbitrarily ordered event sequences was superior to that of the enabling and mixed event sequences. The only exception to this pattern was in the 9-month delay condition, before reminding, in which there were no effects of sequence type. Children's relative levels of production of the individual target actions of the events wholly and partially constrained by enabling relations differed as a function of the availability of verbal reminders: When prompted by the props alone, children's production of the individual target actions of the enabling and mixed event sequences did not differ; after provision of the verbal reminders, children produced more of the individual target actions of the enabling relative to the mixed event sequences. Evaluation of children's ordered recall revealed diminished sequence type effects. Indeed, prior to provision of the verbal reminders, levels of ordered recall did not differ across sequence types. When prompted by the props and verbal labels for the event sequences, children produced a larger number of ordered pairs of actions of the events wholly constrained by enabling relations, relative to the events that contained a mixture of enabling and arbitrary temporal relations. Children's ordered recall of arbitrarily ordered event sequences was intermediate and did not differ from that of either other sequence type. Possible explanations for these unusual and, therefore, unexpected sequence type effects are provided in Chapter VII (Summary and Interpretation of Major Findings).

Children's delayed recall performance was not affected by whether they had been given the opportunity to imitate the to-be-remembered event sequences prior to imposition of the delays. That is, levels of performance on events in the imitate and watch only conditions did not differ reliably. Neither did mode of experience interact with any of the other variables. There was no evidence then that the opportunity to imitate prior to imposition of the delay affected children's memory for the event sequences; the effects of age and of manipulation of delay interval and sequence type operated similarly on events imitated and events only watched.

Finally, the effects of provision of verbal reminders were robust and virtually uniform. The difference between children's production of the individual target actions of the event sequences when they were prompted by the props alone and when they were prompted by the props and by verbal labels for the events was significantly greater than zero for both age groups, for all three sequence types, at all delay conditions. The effects of reminding on children's ordered recall of the temporal order of the enabling and arbitrarily ordered event sequences were similarly robust. Verbal reminders were less effective in supporting children's ordered recall of the mixed event sequences. With this exception aside, it is reasonable to conclude that children 16 and 20 months of age benefit from verbal reminders, even after long delays; verbal reminders facilitate recall both of the individual actions of event sequences and of their temporal order.

SOURCES OF AGE AND SEQUENCE TYPE EFFECTS

The observed effects of age and sequence type seem to indicate more robust memory on the part of 20-month-olds compared with 16-month-olds, and for the individual target actions of events without enabling relations relative to with enabling relations. The differences need not necessarily be attributed to more robust memory, however. First, both age and sequence type effects were apparent in children's immediate recall. This raises the possibility that what appear to be age differences in levels of long-term recall could be an artifact of differential initial learning. Second, at the time of delayed testing, the children who had been 20 months of age at the time of enrollment in the study were, on average, older than the children who had been 16 months of age at the time of enrollment. Thus, age differences in children's problem-solving abilities might have contributed to the observed age effects whether or not the older children actually had better memory for the event sequences. In addition, some sequence types may more readily lend themselves to generation through trial-and-error, relative to others (see Bauer, Schwade, Wewerka, & Delaney, 1999, for discussion), thereby contributing to sequence type effects.

To determine whether differences in children's initial learning of the event sequences, as indexed by their immediate recall performance, might account for the observed age effects, the observed sequence type effects, or both, we conducted analyses of covariance on children's delayed recall performance on events previously imitated with their immediate recall performance as a covariate. Specifically, in one set of analyses of covariance, we examined children's delayed recall of individual target actions with the numbers of individual target actions produced at immediate recall as the covariates; we conducted separate analyses before and after provision of the verbal reminders. In another set of analyses, we examined children's delayed recall of pairs of actions in the target order with the number of pairs of actions produced in the target order at immediate recall as the covariates; pre-reminding and post-reminding performances were examined in separate analyses. We note that these analyses could be conducted only for event sequences in the imitate condition: No measures of immediate recall performance are available for the event sequences that the children only watched.

Evaluation of the possibility that apparent differences in children's memory for the event sequences could be due to age-related or sequence-type-related differences in problem-solving at the time of delayed testing required two steps. First, to determine whether there were observable differences in the target abilities at the time of delayed recall testing, we evaluated children's performance on the sequences that were new to them at Session 4. We conducted 5 (delay) × 2 (age) × 3 (sequence type) mixed analyses of variance for both dependent measures; separate analyses were conducted for children's performance before and after provision of the verbal labels that would, in the case of event sequences new to the children, function as "suggestions" of plausible activities. Second, to determine whether differential age or sequence type effects might account for the apparent differences in memory at the time of delayed testing, we conducted analyses of covariance on children's delayed recall performance with their performance on new event sequences as a covariate. In total, we conducted eight analyses of covariance; we conducted parallel sets of four analyses of covariance on children's performance prior to and after provision of the verbal suggestion: (a) children's delayed recall of individual target actions of events previously imitated with the number of individual target actions produced on new events as the covariate, (b) children's delayed recall of individual target actions of events previously only watched with the number of individual target actions produced on new events as the covariate, (c) children's delayed recall production of pairs of action in the target order on events previously imitated with the number of pairs of actions produced in the target order on new events as the covariate, and (d) children's delayed recall production of pairs of action in the target order on events previously only watched with the number of pairs of actions produced in the target order on new events as the covariate.

71

In a final address of the question of the source or sources of age and sequence type effects on children's long-term recall, for events in the imitate experience condition, we conducted analyses of covariance controlling for levels of initial learning and levels of problem-solving ability simultaneously. Specifically, in two analyses of covariance, we examined children's delayed recall of the individual target actions of the event sequences with the number of individual target actions produced at immediate recall and the number of individual target actions produced on sequences new at Session 4 as covariates; we conducted separate analyses before and after provision of the verbal labels for the event sequences. In another pair of analyses, we examined children's delayed recall of pairs of actions produced in the target order with the number of pairs of actions produced in the target order at immediate recall and the number of pairs of actions in the target order on new event sequences as covariates. Again, we conducted separate analyses before and after provision of the verbal labels for the event sequences. Because no measures of immediate recall performance are available for the event sequences that the children only watched, the simultaneous-control analyses could be conducted only for event sequences in the imitate condition. The results of each of the analyses of potential sources of age and sequence type effects are presented in turn below.

Age Effects

Differential Initial Learning

The analyses of covariance revealed some qualifications of the main effects of age in the above-reported analyses of variance. With the variance associated with differential initial learning (as indexed by immediate recall performance) controlled, main effects of age remained on both dependent variables, both prior to and after provision of the verbal reminders: $Fs(1,170)$ = 24.52, 22.10, 29.39, and 30.79, $ps < .0001$, $MSEs$ = 1.61, 1.40, 0.70, and 0.75, for the number of individual target actions produced before and after the verbal reminders and the number of pairs of actions produced in the target order before and after verbal reminders, respectively. For the number of individual target actions produced before the verbal reminders, there was no qualification to this effect. For children's performance after introduction of the verbal reminders, the interaction of Delay × Age × Sequence type was reliable: $F(8,339) = 2.14$, $p < .04$, $MSE = 1.00$. We pursued the interaction with separate analyses for each delay condition. With the variance associated with differential initial learning of the event sequences controlled, age differences no longer were apparent in the 1- and 6-month delay conditions. Additionally, in the 3-month delay condition, analysis of the Age × Sequence type interaction, $F(2,67) = 4.22$, $p < .02$, $MSE = 1.05$, revealed significant age effects on mixed and arbitrarily ordered event sequences only: $Fs(1,33) = 9.30$ and 18.54, $ps < .005$, $MSEs = 1.02$ and 0.69, for mixed and arbitrary, respectively; the age groups did not differ in their post-reminder production of the individual target actions of enabling event sequences. In both the 9- and 12-month delay conditions, effects of age were reliable, even after the variance associated with differential initial learning of the event sequences was controlled: $Fs(1,34) = 5.71$ and 4.39, $ps < .05$, $MSEs = 1.47$ and 1.00, respectively. The net result was that, even with the variance associated with differential initial learning controlled, when the children were prompted by the event-related props alone, age differences were apparent. Once the verbal reminders were introduced, age effects were largely confined to the longer delay conditions (i.e., the 9- and 12-month delay conditions).

With respect to the number of pairs of actions produced in the target order, prior to introduction of the verbal reminders, there was no qualification of the main effect of age. The main effect apparent in children's post-reminder performance was qualified by the interaction of Delay × Age × Sequence type: $F(8,339) = 2.04$, $p < .04$, $MSE = 0.51$. We pursued the interaction with separate analyses for each delay condition. As had been the case in analysis of the number of individual target actions that the children produced, with the variance associated with differential initial learning of the event sequences controlled, age differences in children's ordered recall no longer were apparent in the 1-month delay condition. In the 3-month delay condition, analysis of the Age × Sequence type interaction, $F(2,67) = 4.10$, $p < .02$, $MSE = 0.45$, revealed a pattern that again was identical to that observed in analysis of children's production of the individual target actions of the event sequences, namely, significant age effects on mixed and arbitrarily ordered event sequences only: $Fs(1,33) = 14.57$ and 20.31, $ps < .0006$, $MSEs = 0.48$ and 0.29, for mixed and arbitrary, respectively; the age groups did not differ in their post-reminder production of ordered pairs of actions of enabling event sequences. In the 6-month delay condition, analysis of the Age × Sequence type interaction, $F(2,67) = 4.06$, $p < .03$, $MSE = 0.38$, revealed that age effects were confined to the enabling event sequences: $F(1,33) = 6.62$, $p < .02$, $MSE = 0.80$. In both the 9- and 12-month delay conditions, effects of age were reliable, even after the variance associated with differential initial learning of the event sequences was controlled: $Fs(1,34) = 5.50$ and 5.01, $ps < .04$, $MSEs = 0.46$ and 0.40, respectively. In summary, as for children's production of the individual target actions of the event sequences, even with the variance associated with differential initial learning controlled, when the children were prompted by the event-related props alone, age differences in ordered recall were apparent. Once the verbal reminders were introduced, it was primarily at the longer delay intervals of 9 and 12 months that age effects were observed.

Differential Problem-Solving Abilities

The (delay) × 2 (age) × 3 (sequence type) mixed analyses of variance yielded significant main effects of age, indicating that both prior to and after provision of the verbal labels for the event sequences new to them at Session 4, the 20-month-olds "figured out" a larger number of individual target actions and a larger number of pairs of actions in the target order, relative to the 16-month-olds: $Fs(1,170)$ = 19.98, 23.51, 10.89, and 11.48, $ps < .002$, $MSEs$ = 0.75, 1.03, 0.18, and 0.32, for productions of the individual target actions of the event sequences prior to and after provision of the verbal suggestions and for production of pairs of actions of the event sequences in target order prior to and after provision of the verbal suggestions, respectively [Ms for individual target actions before verbal suggestion = 0.85 and 1.18 (SDs = 0.77 and 0.93), for 16- and 20-month-olds, respectively; Ms for individual target actions after verbal suggestion = 1.16 and 1.59 (SDs = 0.91 and 1.03), for 16- and 20-month-olds, respectively; Ms for pairs of actions in target order before verbal suggestion = 0.09 and 0.21 (SDs = 0.29 and 0.48), for 16- and 20-month-olds, respectively; Ms for pairs of actions in target order after verbal suggestion = 0.22 and 0.39 (SDs = 0.46 and 0.62), for 16- and 20-month-olds, respectively]. For the variable of production of pairs of actions in the target order, there were no other reliable effects. In terms of production of the individual target actions of the events, prior to provision of the verbal suggestions, the main effect of age was qualified by the interaction with delay condition: $F(4,170)$ = 3.28, $p < .02$, $MSE = 0.75$. Separate analyses revealed age effects in the 3-, 9-, and 12-month delay conditions [$Fs(1,34)$ = 4.55, 13.49, and 12.24, $ps < .04$, $MSEs$ = 0.52, 0.62, and 1.14, respectively]. In the 1- and 6-month delay conditions, age effects were not observed.

For the event sequences that the children previously had been given the opportunity to imitate, the results of the analyses of covariance controlling for differential age-related problem-solving abilities were identical to those when the variance associated with differential initial learning was controlled. Specifically, in terms of the number of individual target actions produced, when the variance associated with age-related differences in the children's performance when they were prompted only by the props for the new event sequences was controlled, the main effect of age was significant: $F(1,170) = 28.16$, $p < .0001$, $MSE = 1.59$. The effect was not qualified by interaction. When the variance associated with the children's performance when they were prompted by the new props and by verbal suggestions of how they might be combined was controlled, there again was a main effect of age: $F(1,170) = 32.37$, $p < .0001$, $MSE = 1.41$. The effect was, however, qualified by the interaction of Delay × Age × Sequence type: $F(8,339) = 2.11$, $p < .04$, $MSE = 1.00$. Analysis of the interaction revealed effects of age on children's recall of the individual target actions (a) of the mixed and arbitrarily ordered events sequences in the 3-month delay condition [Fs$(1,33) = 13.23$ and 29.12, ps $< .0009$, MSEs = 1.03 and 0.62, respectively; separate analyses by sequence type indicated by the interaction of Age × Sequence type, $F(2,67) = 4.61$, $p < .02$, $MSE = 1.05$], and (b) in the 9- and 12-month delay conditions [Fs$(1,34) = 8.86$ and 7.05, ps $< .02$, MSEs = 0.97 and 1.02, respectively]. In the 1- and 6-month delay conditions age effects were not apparent; in the 3-month delay condition, they were not apparent on enabling events. Thus, as was the case when the variance associated with children's immediate recall performance was controlled, for events previously imitated, effects of age on children's memories for the individual target actions of the events were more readily apparent when fewer prompts were provided (i.e., when performance was prompted by props alone) and at longer retention intervals (i.e., 9 and 12 months).

In terms of children's production of pairs of actions in the target order, when the variance associated with age-related differences in the children's performance on the new event sequences prior to provision of the verbal suggestions was controlled, the main effect of age was reliable: $F(1,170) = 32.36$, $p < .0001$, $MSE = 0.70$. The effect was not qualified by interaction. When the variance associated with the children's performance when they were prompted by the props and by verbal suggestions of how they might be combined was controlled, there again was a main effect of age: $F(1,170) = 34.65$, $p < .0001$, $MSE = 0.75$. The effect was qualified, however, by the interaction of Delay × Age × Sequence type: $F(8,339) = 2.06$, $p < .04$, $MSE = 0.51$. Analysis of the interaction revealed effects of age on children's recall of ordered pairs of actions (a) of the mixed and arbitrarily ordered events sequences in the 3-month delay condition [Fs$(1,33) = 20.33$ and 16.44, ps $< .0003$, MSEs = 0.49 and 0.31, respectively; separate analyses by sequence type indicated by the interaction of Age × Sequence type, $F(2,67) = 3.82$, $p < .03$, $MSE = 0.46$], (b) of the enabling event sequences in the 6-month delay condition [$F(1,33) = 4.56$, $p < .04$, $MSE = 0.66$; separate analyses by sequence type indicated by the interaction of Age × Sequence type, $F(2,67) = 3.42$, $p < .04$,

$MSE = 0.38$], and (c) in the 9- and 12-month delay conditions [$Fs(1,34) =$ 7.40 and 3.98, $ps < .05$, $MSEs = 0.46$ and 0.40, respectively]. In the 1-month delay condition age effects were not apparent; in the 3-month delay condition, they were not apparent on enabling event sequences; in the 6-month delay condition, they were not apparent on mixed and arbitrarily ordered event sequences.

For the event sequences that the children had only been permitted to watch, the analyses of covariance provided no qualifications of the main effects of age. That is, when the variance associated with age-related differences in the children's performance when they were prompted only by the props for the new event sequences was controlled, main effects of age were observed on children's production of the individual target actions of the event sequences and on their production of pairs of actions in the correct temporal order: $Fs(1,170) = 36.10$ and 22.69, $ps < .0001$, $MSEs = 1.25$ and 0.52, respectively. The effects were not qualified by interactions. Likewise, the main effects obtained when the variance associated with children's performance when they were prompted by the props and by verbal suggestions of how they might be combined was controlled: $Fs(1,170) = 25.34$ and 18.52, $ps < .0001$, $MSEs = 1.45$ and 0.72, for target actions and pairs of actions, respectively. The effects were not qualified by interactions. Thus, for events only watched, even after provision of verbal cues, effects of age were observed at the shorter as well as the longer retention intervals, for both dependent measures.

Differential Initial Learning and Problem-Solving Abilities

The results of the analyses of covariance that simultaneously controlled for the variance associated with children's initial learning and their problem-solving abilities did not differ from those when either source of variance was controlled separately. The patterns were the same for both dependent measures, and for performance both prior to and after provision of the verbal labels for the event sequences. Because the analyses shed no new light on children's performance, they are not reported here (details are available from PJB).

Summary of Sources of Age Effects

For performance prior to introduction of the verbal reminders, the analyses of covariance provided no qualifications to the effects of age observed in the analyses of variance. That is, when they were prompted by the event-related props alone, the older children produced both more individual target actions and more pairs of actions in the target order, relative to the younger children. Because age-related differences in the children's performance prior to introduction of the verbal reminders was not accounted for either by age-related differences in initial mastery of the to-be-remembered material or by differential problem-solving ability, it is reasonable to attribute them to age-related differences in the strength of the memory trace. Likewise, because the age effects for events that the children previously had only watched remained even after provision of the verbal labels for the event sequences, they too should be attributed to differences in the mnemonic performance of the older and younger children. For the events that the children had the opportunity to imitate, after provision of the verbal reminders, true age-related differences in mnemonic performance were confined to the longer retention intervals. That is, at the shorter retention intervals, when either differential levels of immediate recall performance or differential levels of problem solving were controlled, age effects were not observed (1-month delay condition) or were apparent on some sequence types but not others (3- and 6-month delay conditions). It was only at the longer retention intervals of 9 and 12 months that age differences not attributable to other sources of variance were observed. As a whole, this pattern is reminiscent of that observed in the literature on older children's verbal recall: age effects are larger in free recall and diminish as more prompts and probes are provided (e.g., Hamond & Fivush, 1991; Price & Goodman, 1990). Said another way, older children seem to require less support for recall, relative to younger children.

Sequence Type Effects

Differential Initial Learning

In terms of the number of individual target actions produced, the analyses of covariance controlling for differential initial learning yielded diminished sequence type effects, relative to those observed in the analyses of variance. Specifically, prior to introduction of the verbal reminders, the analysis of variance revealed lower and equivalent levels of production of the individual target actions of the enabling and mixed event sequences, relative to the arbitrarily ordered event sequences, in all but the 9-month delay condition. In the analysis of covariance controlling for immediate recall performance, analysis of the Delay × Sequence type interaction, $F(8,339) = 3.01$, $p < .003$, $MSE = 0.84$, revealed this pattern in the 1-month delay condition only [$F(2,69) = 5.30$, $p < .008$, $MSE = 0.80$].

Whereas there were main effects of sequence type in the 3-, 6-, and 12-month delay conditions [$Fs(2,69)$ = 6.38, 6.39, and 4.10, $ps < .02$, $MSEs$ = 1.07, 0.86, and 0.77, respectively], it was only in the 3- and 12-month delay conditions that performance on arbitrarily ordered event sequences was greater than that on sequences constrained by enabling relations; it was only in the 6-month delay condition that performance on arbitrarily ordered event sequences was greater than that on mixed event sequences. There were no sequence type effects in the 9-month delay condition; in no condition was performance on enabling and mixed event sequences reliably different.

In the analysis of variance, after provision of the verbal reminders, the children produced a larger number of individual target actions of the arbitrarily ordered event sequences, relative to the enabling event sequences, and a larger number of individual target actions of the enabling event sequences than of the mixed event sequences. With the variance associated with differential immediate recall performance controlled via analysis of covariance, the main effect was reliable, $F(2,339)$ = 8.14, $p < .004$, MSE = 1.00, but only arbitrary and mixed event sequences differed reliably. Moreover, even this effect was qualified by the interaction of Age × Delay × Sequence type mentioned above. Analysis of the interaction revealed that the difference in production of the individual target actions of the arbitrarily ordered and mixed event sequences was apparent in the 1- and 6-month delay conditions only: $Fs(2,67)$ = 5.75 and 7.64, $ps < .005$, $MSEs$ = 0.75 and 0.83, respectively. Differences between levels of performance on the arbitrarily ordered and enabling event sequences were apparent in the 1-month delay condition, and for the 20-month-olds in the 3-month delay condition [$F(2,33)$ = 4.28, $p < .03$, MSE = 1.10; separate analyses by age indicated an Age × Sequence type interaction: $F(2,67)$ = 4.22, $p < .02$, MSE = 1.05]. There were no sequence type effects in the 9- and 12-month delay conditions.

In terms of the number of pairs of actions produced in the target order, examination of children's performance when they were prompted by the props alone revealed that the results of the analysis of covariance and those of the analysis of variance were identical: There were no differences across sequence types in the number of pairs of actions produced in the target order. Whereas introduction of the verbal reminders produced a reliable sequence type effect in the analysis of variance, in the analysis of covariance, the main effect was not reliable. Instead, analysis of the Delay × Age × Sequence type interaction mentioned above revealed an isolated effect of sequence type in the 6-month delay condition. Specifically, analysis of the Age × Sequence type interaction (details above) revealed a main effect of sequence type for the 20-month-olds only: $F(2,33)$ = 4.58, $p < .02$, MSE = 0.58. The older children produced a greater number of pairs of actions in the target order on the enabling relative to the mixed event sequences; performance on arbitrarily ordered event sequences was intermediate and did not differ from that on the other two sequence types. This pattern is the same as the main effect in the analysis of variance. There were no other effects involving sequence type.

Differential Problem-Solving Abilities

Whereas the analyses of variance examining children's performance on event sequences new to them at Session 4 revealed reliable age effects, in no case did they reveal significant effects of sequence type. That is, neither main effects of sequence type nor interactions involving sequence type indicated that children were differentially successful at "figuring out" either the individual target actions of or the temporal order of the different sequence types, either before or after provision of the verbal labels for the events. For this reason, we do not present results of analyses controlling for sequence-type-related differential effects of problem solving. The absence of sequence type effects in children's problem solving also renders unnecessary analyses simultaneously controlling for differential initial learning and differential problem solving.

Summary of Sources of Sequence Type Effects

The analyses of covariance produced fewer sequence type effects, relative to the analyses of variance. In no instance were children's levels of production of the individual target actions of the enabling and mixed events found to differ. When sequence type effects were observed, they indicated higher levels of performance of the individual target actions of the arbitrarily ordered event sequences relative to the enabling event sequences (pre-verbal-reminders, in the 3- and 12-month delay conditions; post-verbal-reminders, in the 3-month delay condition, for the 20-month-olds only), the mixed event sequences (in the 6-month delay condition, both pre- and post-verbal-reminders), or both (1-month delay condition, both pre- and post-verbal-reminders). Just as in the analysis of variance, prior to provision of the verbal reminders, there was no effect of sequence type on children's ordered recall. After provision of the verbal reminders, the analysis of covariance indicated greater ordered recall performance on the enabling relative to the mixed event sequences by the 20-month-olds in the 6-month delay condition. There were no other effects of sequence type on children's ordered recall. Because children's performance on the event sequences that were new to them at Session 4 was

79

not affected by sequence type, on either dependent measure, either before or after provision of the verbal labels for the event sequences, we did not conduct analyses to control for that potential source of variance.

PATTERNS OF FORGETTING

To say that the children remembered both the individual target actions and the temporal order of actions over delay intervals of as many as 12 months is not to say that they did not also forget some of what they had learned about the events. To evaluate the amount of information forgotten over the various delay intervals we conducted 2 (recall condition: immediate, after verbal reminder) × 5 (delay) × 3 (sequence type) mixed analyses of variance, for both dependent measures (see Tables 2 and 3 for relevant means). Because of differential levels of initial learning by the 20-month-olds and the 16-month-olds, we conducted separate analyses for each age group. Moreover, note that these analyses involved the imitate condition only: immediate recall measures are not available on event sequences only watched prior to imposition of the delay. In addition, we note that we used children's performance when prompted by both the props and the verbal labels because it represents their best performance after the delay: If forgetting was apparent after exposure to the verbal reminders, it also would have been apparent before the verbal reminder. Because the focus of the analyses was on whether or not the children showed evidence of forgetting over the delays, only main effects of and interactions involving recall condition are discussed.

For the 20-month-old children, although for both dependent variables there were Recall condition × Delay interactions [$Fs(4,85)$ = 7.84 and 5.03, $ps < .002$, $MSEs$ = 0.81 and 0.66, for individual target actions and pairs of actions in target order, respectively], separate analyses at each delay condition revealed evidence of forgetting at all delays, for both dependent measures (i.e., in all delay conditions, immediate recall performance was greater than performance after the delay): $Fs(1,17)$ = 20.32, 47.22, 66.48, 80.93, and 139.25, $ps < .003$, MSE = 0.19, 0.24, 0.45, 0.34, and 0.15, for individual target actions in the 1-, 3-, 6-, 9-, and 12-month delay conditions, respectively; $Fs(1,17)$ = 21.21, 32.58, 63.84, 83.78, and 58.12, $ps < .0003$, $MSEs$ = 0.16, 0.23, 0.29, 0.21, and 0.21, for pairs of actions in target order in the 1-, 3-, 6-, 9-, and 12-month delay conditions, respectively. For both dependent measures, there also were interactions of Recall condition × Sequence type: $Fs(2,170)$ = 3.74 and 6.33, $ps < .03$, $MSEs$ = 0.60 and 0.62, for individual target actions and pairs of actions, respectively. Separate analyses for each sequence type revealed significant forgetting of both the individual target actions and pairs of actions in the target order for each sequence type (i.e., for all sequence types, immediate recall performance was greater than performance after the delay): $Fs(1,89)$ = 88.84, 163.50, and 91.53, ps < .0001, $MSEs$ = 0.96, 0.69, and 0.63, for individual target actions of enabling, mixed, and arbitrarily ordered event sequences, respectively; $Fs(1,89)$ = 103.75, 110.78, and 40.55, ps < .0001, $MSEs$ = 0.71, 0.66, and 0.65, for pairs of actions in target order of enabling, mixed, and arbitrarily ordered event sequences, respectively. There were no other reliable effects.

For the 16-month-old children, for both dependent measures, main effects of delay and recall condition were qualified by their interaction: $Fs(4,85)$ = 9.48 and 4.68, ps < .002, $MSEs$ = 1.09 and 0.75, for individual target actions and pairs of actions in target order, respectively. Separate analyses at each delay condition revealed that, with one exception, for both dependent measures, forgetting was apparent at all delays: $Fs(1,17)$ = 33.80, 107.03, 140.53, and 76.17, ps < .0001, $MSEs$ = 0.56, 0.31, 0.25, and 0.29, for individual target actions in the 3-, 6-, 9-, and 12-month delay conditions, respectively; $Fs(1,17)$ = 5.20, 22.64, 96.70, 66.32, and 39.06, ps < .04, $MSEs$ = 0.28, 0.35, 0.15, 0.23, and 0.23, for pairs of actions in target order in the 1-, 3-, 6-, 9-, and 12-month delay conditions, respectively. The exception was that for production of individual target actions, at the 1-month delay, the effect fell below the conventional level of statistical significance, $F(1,17)$ = 4.08, p < .06, MSE = 0.42, thereby indicating that children's immediate recall performance (M = 3.28, SD = 0.60) and delayed recall performance (M = 2.84, SD = 0.78) did not differ reliably. In terms of the number of individual target actions produced, there were no other reliable effects involving recall condition. In terms of the number of pairs of actions produced in the target order, the main effect of sequence type was qualified by the interaction with recall condition: $F(2,170)$ = 5.55, p < .005, MSE = 0.40. Separate analyses for each sequence type revealed significant forgetting of the order of all three sequence types (i.e., for all sequence types, immediate recall performance was greater than performance after the delay): $Fs(1,89)$ = 88.23, 89.08, and 58.53, ps < .0001, $MSEs$ = 0.67, 0.59, and 0.41, for enabling, mixed, and arbitrarily ordered event sequences, respectively.

These analyses make clear that, although the children remembered some of the individual target actions of the events, as well as the temporal order of the actions, over retention intervals of as many as 12 months, they nevertheless evidenced forgetting. For the 20-month-olds, forgetting was apparent after as little as 1 month. For the 16-month-olds, by 1 month, the children evidenced forgetting of the order of the event sequences; forgetting of the individual target actions of the event sequences was apparent by 3 months (i.e., the effect fell below the level of statistical significance in the 1-month delay condition).

SAVINGS IN RELEARNING

As the immediately preceding section made clear, although the children remembered the event sequences to which they had been exposed, they also evidenced forgetting. The presence of forgetting presents the opportunity to examine possible savings in relearning. At Session 4, after they had been tested for delayed recall, the children in the present research were once again exposed to the modeled events. They then had an opportunity to imitate them. We compared post-modeling performance on events in the imitate and watch experience conditions with that on events that were new at Session 4, in order to determine whether there was any evidence of savings in relearning of the sequences. Savings in relearning would be suggested by superior performance on the events to which the children were exposed prior to imposition of the delays, relative to on new event sequences.

To determine whether there was evidence of savings in relearning, we conducted 5 (delay) × 2 (age) × 3 (sequence type) × 3 (experience: imitate, watch, new at Session 4) mixed analyses of variance, for both dependent measures. Because the question of interest requires comparison of the different experience conditions, only effects involving experience are described.

In terms of the number of individual target actions produced, the interaction of Age × Experience condition was reliable: $F(2,340) = 3.75$, $p < .03$, $MSE = 0.41$. Separate analyses for each age group revealed evidence of savings in relearning by 16-month-olds of the event sequences that they previously had been permitted to watch but not to imitate: $F(2,178) = 4.32$, $p < .02$, $MSE = 0.57$ [$Ms = 3.66$ and 3.50 ($SDs = 0.74$ and 0.88), for watch and new event sequences, respectively]; performance on event sequences imitated prior to the delay ($M = 3.50$, $SD = 0.95$) did not differ from that on new event sequences. The performance of the 20-month-olds did not differ across experience conditions [$Ms = 3.77$, 3.79, and 3.79 ($SDs = 0.62$, 0.56, and 0.61), for watch, imitate, and new, respectively]. We note that one possible reason for the absence of a savings-in-relearning effect for the older children is their virtually ceiling level of production of the individual target actions of the event sequences across all cells of the design. Finally, there was no evidence of savings in relearning of the order of actions of the event sequences. The children's levels of production of ordered pairs of actions after modeling of the events at Session 4 did not differ across experience conditions [$Ms = 2.15$, 2.19, and 2.12 ($SDs = 0.85$, 0.84, and 0.86), for imitate, watch, and new at Session 4, respectively]. (Details on mean levels of performance in each cell of the design are available from PJB.)

IV. CHILDREN TESTED ON THREE-STEP EVENT SEQUENCES

The analytic strategy employed to examine the performance of the children tested on three-step event sequences is identical to that for the children tested on four-step event sequences.

BASELINE LEVELS OF PERFORMANCE

Descriptive statistics on the baseline performance of the 13-month-olds and the 16-month-old children tested on three-step event sequences are provided in Table 4. As had been the case for the children tested on four-step event sequences, although there were some differences in levels of performance across the cells of the design, they had no consequences for children's initial mastery of the to-be-remembered event sequences (see Immediate Recall Performance), and they contributed virtually no variance in children's long-term recall (see Chapter VI: Predictions of Long-Term Mnemonic Performance). We compared the values in 5 (delay: 1 month, 3 month, 6 month, 9 month, 12 month) × 2 (age: 13 month, 16 month) × 3 (sequence type: enabling, mixed, arbitrary) × 2 (experience: imitate, watch) mixed analyses of variance for each dependent measure.

In terms of the number of individual target actions produced, there was a main effect of age: $F(1,170) = 6.59$, $p < .02$, $MSE = 0.79$. The 13-month-olds' baseline levels of performance were lower than those of the 16-month-olds [$Ms = 0.62$ and 0.76 ($SDs = 0.74$ and 0.80), respectively]. The main effect was, however, qualified by Age × Experience condition and Delay × Age × Sequence type interactions. To pursue the Age × Experience condition interaction, $F(1,170) = 6.92$, $p < .01$, $MSE = 0.56$, we conducted separate analyses for each experience condition. The age groups differed reliably on the events that they would be permitted to imitate prior to the delay [$Ms = 0.55$ and 0.81 ($SDs = 0.70$ and 0.82), for 13- and 16-month-olds, respectively: $F(1,178) = 12.95$, $p < .0004$, $MSE = 0.70$], but not on the

TABLE 4

Means and Standard Deviations for the Baseline Number of Individual
Target Actions and Pairs of Actions Produced in the Target Order
by Children Tested on Three-Step Event Sequences

Age group/ Delay condition/ Experience	Sequence Type							
	Overall		Enabling		Mixed		Arbitrary	
	Mean	SD	Mean	SD	Mean	SD	Mean	SD
Number of individual target actions produced (max. = 3.0)								
16-month-olds								
1-month delay								
Imitate	0.83	0.88	0.89	0.90	0.61	1.04	1.00	0.69
Watch	0.81	0.75	0.78	0.65	0.89	0.90	0.78	0.73
3-month delay								
Imitate	0.96	0.85	1.06	0.94	1.00	0.84	0.83	0.79
Watch	0.76	0.75	0.67	0.77	0.89	0.83	0.72	0.67
6-month delay								
Imitate	0.80	0.79	1.06	0.80	0.78	0.88	0.56	0.62
Watch	0.83	0.88	1.33	1.03	0.56	0.70	0.61	0.70
9-month delay								
Imitate	0.76	0.82	1.06	0.64	0.67	0.97	0.56	0.78
Watch	0.61	0.68	0.67	0.69	0.61	0.70	0.56	0.70
12-month delay								
Imitate	0.70	0.77	1.00	0.77	0.44	0.70	0.67	0.77
Watch	0.56	0.74	0.89	0.76	0.56	0.78	0.22	0.55
13-month-olds								
1-month delay								
Imitate	0.63	0.81	1.06	0.94	0.56	0.78	0.28	0.46
Watch	0.87	0.89	1.00	0.97	0.78	0.88	0.83	0.86
3-month delay								
Imitate	0.63	0.71	0.78	0.65	0.56	0.78	0.56	0.70
Watch	0.78	0.82	0.83	0.99	0.67	0.69	0.83	0.79
6-month delay								
Imitate	0.59	0.77	0.61	0.70	0.22	0.55	0.94	0.87
Watch	0.63	0.65	0.83	0.71	0.56	0.70	0.50	0.51
9-month delay								
Imitate	0.56	0.63	0.83	0.79	0.33	0.49	0.50	0.51
Watch	0.54	0.75	0.39	0.61	0.56	0.62	0.67	0.97
12-month delay								
Imitate	0.36	0.55	0.56	0.51	0.24	0.64	0.28	0.46
Watch	0.67	0.73	0.56	0.62	0.56	0.70	0.89	0.83
Number of pairs of actions in the target order (max. = 2.0)								
16-month-olds								
1-month delay								
Imitate	0.13	0.34	0.22	0.43	0.17	0.38	0.00	—
Watch	0.13	0.34	0.11	0.32	0.17	0.38	0.11	0.32

(*continued*)

TABLE 4 (*continued*)

Age group/ Delay condition/ Experience	Sequence Type							
	Overall		Enabling		Mixed		Arbitrary	
	Mean	SD	Mean	SD	Mean	SD	Mean	SD
3-month delay								
Imitate	0.15	0.41	0.17	0.51	0.22	0.43	0.06	0.24
Watch	0.09	0.35	0.11	0.32	0.11	0.47	0.06	0.24
6-month delay								
Imitate	0.15	0.41	0.28	0.57	0.17	0.38	0.00	—
Watch	0.17	0.50	0.39	0.78	0.11	0.32	0.00	—
9-month delay								
Imitate	0.13	0.34	0.11	0.32	0.17	0.38	0.11	0.32
Watch	0.07	0.26	0.06	0.24	0.11	0.32	0.06	0.24
12-month delay								
Imitate	0.07	0.33	0.17	0.51	0.06	0.24	0.00	—
Watch	0.09	0.29	0.22	0.43	0.06	0.24	0.00	—
13-month-olds								
1-month delay								
Imitate	0.07	0.33	0.11	0.32	0.11	0.47	0.00	—
Watch	0.19	0.39	0.33	0.49	0.22	0.43	0.00	—
3-month delay								
Imitate	0.07	0.26	0.06	0.24	0.11	0.32	0.06	0.24
Watch	0.11	0.32	0.28	0.46	0.06	0.24	0.00	—
6-month delay								
Imitate	0.06	0.30	0.06	0.24	0.00	—	0.11	0.47
Watch	0.07	0.26	0.11	0.32	0.11	0.32	0.00	—
9-month delay								
Imitate	0.04	0.19	0.11	0.32	0.00	—	0.00	—
Watch	0.07	0.26	0.06	0.24	0.06	0.24	0.11	0.32
12-month delay								
Imitate	0.02	0.14	0.00	—	0.06	0.24	0.00	—
Watch	0.02	0.14	0.00	—	0.06	0.24	0.00	—

event sequences that they would only watch [Ms = 0.70 and 0.71 (SDs = 0.77 and 0.77), for 13- and 16-month-olds, respectively].

To pursue the Delay × Age × Sequence type interaction, $F(8,340)$ = 1.96, p = .05, MSE = 0.53, we conducted separate analyses for each delay condition. In the 1-, 3-, and 9-month delay conditions, there were no reliable effects. In the 6-month delay condition, the main effect of sequence type, $F(2,68)$ = 7.26, $p < .002$, MSE = 0.49, indicated greater production of the individual target actions of enabling event sequences ($M = 0.96$, $SD = 0.85$), relative to mixed events ($M = 0.53$, $SD = 0.73$) and arbitrarily ordered event sequences ($M = 0.65$, $SD = 0.70$); levels of performance on the mixed and arbitrarily ordered event sequences did not differ. In addition, analysis of the Age × Sequence type interaction, $F(2,68) = 3.61$, $p < .04$, $MSE = 0.49$, revealed an age effect on enabling event sequences, $F(1,34) = 4.99$, $p < .04$, $MSE = 0.80$, indicating lower levels of production of individual target actions by the 13-month-olds relative to the 16-month-olds [$Ms = 0.72$ and 1.19 ($SDs = 0.70$ and 0.92), respectively]. In the 12-month delay condition, the main effect of sequence type, $F(2,68) = 3.80$, $p < .03$, $MSE = 0.48$, indicated greater production of individual target actions of enabling event sequences ($M = 0.75$, $SD = 0.69$) relative to mixed event sequences ($M = 0.45$, $SD = 0.71$); performance on arbitrarily ordered event sequences ($M = 0.51$, $SD = 0.71$) was intermediate and did not differ from the other two sequence types.

In terms of children's baseline levels of production of ordered pairs of actions, although analysis of variance revealed reliable effects of both age and sequence type, analysis of covariance with the number of individual target actions produced as the covariate revealed only an effect of sequence type: $F(2,340) = 9.88$, $p < .0001$, $MSE = 0.07$. The effect indicated higher and equivalent levels of production of pairs of actions in the target order on enabling event sequences ($M = 0.15$, $SD = 0.40$) and on mixed event sequences ($M = 0.11$, $SD = 0.33$), relative to arbitrarily ordered event sequences ($M = 0.03$, $SD = 0.19$). Given the virtually floor levels of spontaneous production of pairs of actions in the target order, this effect is suspect.

In summary, prior to exposure to the event sequences, the performance of the age groups differed such that (a) on event sequences that the children subsequently would be permitted to imitate; and (b) for children in the 6-month delay condition, on enabling event sequences, the younger children produced a smaller number of individual target actions, relative to the older children. With the variance associated with differential production of the individual target actions controlled, the age groups did not differ in their spontaneous production of pairs of actions in the target order.

Prior to modeling, some effects of sequence type were observed. In the 6-month delay condition, the difference was between production of the individual target actions of enabling relative to arbitrarily ordered event sequences; in the 12-month delay condition, the difference was between production of the individual target actions of enabling relative to mixed event sequences. With the variance associated with differential levels of spontaneous production of the individual target actions of the event sequences controlled, children were found to have lower levels of production of ordered pairs of actions on arbitrarily ordered event sequences relative to enabling or mixed event sequences. Whereas the order of magnitude of the observed differences was small, their consistency suggests that both the individual target actions and the structure of the three-step event sequences with enabling relations were more transparent, relative to those of the three-step mixed and arbitrarily ordered event sequences. This apparent fact does not, however, compromise the integrity of the conclusions that can be drawn from this research: As discussed in Chapter VI (Predictions of Long-Term Mnemonic Performance), in regression analyses, baseline levels of performance contribute little variance in predicting children's long-term recall.

IMMEDIATE RECALL PERFORMANCE

Descriptive statistics on children' levels of immediate recall are provided in Table 5. To determine whether the children learned the event sequences as a result of exposure to them, we compared their imitative performance (see Table 5) with their baseline levels of performance (see Table 4 for relevant means) in 2 (modeling condition: pre-modeling, post-modeling) × 5 (delay) × 2 (age) × 3 (sequence type) mixed analyses of variance for both dependent measures. Main effects of modeling condition revealed that, as a result of exposure to the test events, there were reliable increases in production of both the individual target actions, $F(1,170) = 1700.21$, $p < .0001$, $MSE = 0.56$ [$Ms = 0.68$ and 2.57 ($SDs = 0.77$ and 0.74), for before and after modeling, respectively], and pairs of actions in the target order, $F(1,170) = 924.22$, $p < .0001$, $MSE = 0.29$ [$Ms = 0.09$ and 1.08 ($SDs = 0.32$ and 0.73), for before and after modeling, respectively]. Thus, the children learned both the individual target actions of the events and their temporal order.

Main effects of age revealed higher levels of production of individual target actions and pairs of actions in the target order by the 16-month-olds compared with the 13-month-olds: $Fs(1,170) = 44.75$ and 35.88, $ps < .0001$, $MSEs = 0.83$ and 0.35, for individual target actions and pairs of actions in the target order, respectively [Ms for individual target action = 1.81 and 1.44 ($SDs = 1.20$ and 1.19); Ms for pairs in target order = 0.69 and 0.48 ($SDs = 0.79$ and 0.69), for 16- and 13-month-olds, respectively]. Reliable Modeling condition × Age interactions on both dependent measures [$Fs(1,170) = 6.03$ and 19.16, $ps < .02$, $MSEs = 0.56$ and 0.29, for individual target actions and pairs of actions in target order, respectively] indicated that the sizes of the age effects were greater after modeling than they had been before modeling (M age differences after modeling of 0.48 and 0.36, for target actions and pairs of actions, respectively; M age differences prior to modeling of 0.26 and 0.08, for individual target actions and pairs of actions in target order, respectively). Across delay conditions, children's levels of acquisition of the target material did not differ: Neither the main effects of delay nor any interactions with delay

TABLE 5

Means and Standard Deviations for the Number of Individual Target
Actions and Pairs of Actions Produced in the Target Order
on Three-Step Event Sequences at Immediate Recall by Children Tested
on Three-Step Event Sequences

Age group/	Sequence Type							
Delay condition	Overall		Enabling		Mixed		Arbitrary	
	Mean	SD	Mean	SD	Mean	SD	Mean	SD
Number of individual target actions produced (max. = 3.0)								
16-month-olds								
1-month delay	2.81	0.52	2.89	0.47	2.72	0.67	2.83	0.38
3-month delay	2.89	0.32	2.94	0.24	2.94	0.24	2.78	0.43
6-month delay	2.85	0.41	2.89	0.32	2.89	0.47	2.78	0.43
9-month delay	2.74	0.56	2.78	0.55	2.67	0.69	2.78	0.43
12-month delay	2.75	0.55	2.89	0.47	2.59	0.69	2.78	0.43
13-month-olds								
1-month delay	2.13	0.99	2.44	0.92	1.94	1.00	2.00	1.03
3-month delay	2.44	0.72	2.61	0.61	2.39	0.92	2.33	0.59
6-month delay	2.37	0.94	2.22	1.00	2.39	0.98	2.50	0.86
9-month delay	2.30	0.77	2.56	0.62	2.06	1.00	2.28	0.57
12-month delay	2.39	0.92	2.56	0.62	2.18	1.20	2.44	0.86
Number of pairs of actions in the target order (max. = 2.0)								
16-month-olds								
1-month delay	1.22	0.69	1.61	0.61	1.28	0.67	0.78	0.55
3-month delay	1.43	0.66	1.94	0.24	1.44	0.62	0.89	0.58
6-month delay	1.37	0.65	1.83	0.51	1.28	0.57	1.00	0.59
9-month delay	1.17	0.75	1.67	0.59	1.11	0.76	0.72	0.57
12-month delay	1.13	0.65	1.44	0.62	1.12	0.68	0.83	0.51
13-month-olds								
1-month delay	0.85	0.79	1.33	0.77	0.67	0.69	0.56	0.70
3-month delay	0.91	0.71	1.22	0.81	0.83	0.62	0.67	0.59
6-month delay	0.93	0.70	1.00	0.84	0.94	0.64	0.83	0.62
9-month delay	0.83	0.80	1.33	0.84	0.61	0.70	0.56	0.62
12-month delay	1.00	0.67	1.33	0.59	0.88	0.68	0.78	0.65

were reliable, for either dependent variable. For the number of individual target actions produced, the effect of sequence type was reliable: $F(2,340) = 15.18$, $p < .0001$, $MSE = 0.48$. Across modeling conditions, children produced a larger number of individual target actions on events constrained by enabling relations ($M = 1.78$, $SD = 1.15$) relative to events that lacked enabling relations ($M = 1.58$, $SD = 1.19$) or were partially constrained by enabling relations ($M = 1.51$, $SD = 1.28$); performance on the latter two event types did not differ reliably. For production of individual target actions, there was a three-way interaction among age, delay, and sequence type. We did not pursue the interaction because, once baseline levels of production of individual target actions were controlled via analysis of covariance, the interaction no longer was reliable.

For the variable of production of pairs of actions in the target order, the significant main effect of sequence type was qualified by interactions with age and with modeling condition. Separate analyses by age of the Age × Sequence type interaction, $F(2,340) = 5.23$, $p < .006$, $MSE = 0.23$, revealed sequence type effects for both age groups: $Fs(2,267) = 15.96$ and 43.87, $ps < .0001$, $MSEs = 0.28$ and 0.26, for 13-month-olds and 16-month-olds, respectively. Among the 13-month-olds, production of pairs of actions in the target order was greater on enabling event sequences ($M = 0.66$, $SD = 0.82$), relative to on mixed events ($M = 0.42$, $SD = 0.62$) and arbitrarily ordered events ($M = 0.36$, $SD = 0.58$); performance on mixed and arbitrarily ordered event sequences did not differ reliably. Among the 16-month-olds, production of pairs of actions in the target order was greatest on event sequences wholly constrained by enabling relations ($M = 0.94$, $SD = 0.91$), followed by sequences partially constrained by enabling relations ($M = 0.70$, $SD = 0.76$), followed by sequences wholly unconstrained by enabling relations ($M = 0.44$, $SD = 0.58$); levels of production of ordered pairs of actions of each sequence type differed reliably.

Analysis of the Modeling condition × Sequence type interaction, $F(2,340) = 41.50$, $p < .0001$, $MSE = 0.22$, revealed that the pattern observed among the 16-month-olds was apparent after exposure to the modeled event sequences: $F(2,537) = 52.13$, $p < .0001$, $MSE = 0.45$ [$Ms = 1.47$, 1.02, and 0.76 ($SDs = 0.70$, 0.70, and 0.60), for enabling, mixed, and arbitrarily ordered event sequences, respectively]. Prior to modeling, whereas performance on enabling and arbitrarily ordered event sequences differed reliably, production of ordered pairs of actions of the mixed sequences was intermediate and did not differ from that on the other two sequence types: $F(2,537) = 4.47$, $p < .02$, $MSE = 0.10$ [$Ms = 0.13$, 0.11, and 0.03 ($SDs = 0.38$, 0.33, and 0.21), for enabling, mixed, and arbitrarily ordered event sequences, respectively]. The patterns of performance at immediate recall were not affected by analysis of covariance controlling for baseline levels of production of pairs of actions in the target order alone. Control both of baseline levels of production of pairs of actions in the target order and of post-modeling production of individual target actions eliminated the age effect, such that levels of immediate ordered recall by the 13-month-olds and 16-month-olds no longer differed reliably.

In summary, as had the children tested on four-step sequences, the children tested on three-step sequences learned both the individual target actions and the temporal order of actions of the events to which they were exposed. The children in the different delay conditions demonstrated equivalent levels of mastery of the to-be-remembered material. Children produced a larger number of the individual target actions of the event sequences that were wholly constrained by enabling relations, relative to sequences that were partially constrained or unconstrained by them. The same pattern was observed in 13-month-olds' production of pairs of actions in the target order. In contrast, the 16-month-olds demonstrated a pattern of ordered recall that was similar to their counterparts tested on four-step sequences, namely, superior ordered recall of events that were wholly constrained by enabling relations, relative to events that were partially constrained, and superior ordered recall of events partially constrained by enabling relations, relative to events that were wholly unconstrained. Finally, the older children in the sample demonstrated higher levels of production of the individual target actions of the event sequences, relative to the younger children. As noted for the children tested on four-step event sequences, the age-related differences have implications for interpretation of patterns of delayed recall, outlined below. With the variance associated with both differential pre-modeling levels of production of ordered pairs of actions and of post-modeling production of individual target actions controlled, the age groups did not differ in their levels of mastery of the temporal order of the event sequences.

DELAYED RECALL PERFORMANCE: EVENTS PREVIOUSLY EXPERIENCED COMPARED WITH NEW EVENTS

Descriptive statistics on children's levels of production of individual target actions and pairs of actions in the target order on events that the children had the opportunity to imitate prior to imposition of the delays, events only watched prior to imposition of the delays, and events new to the children at the time of delayed recall testing are provided in Table 6. To evaluate performance differences, we conducted 5 (delay) × 2 (age) × 3 (sequence type) × 3 (experience: imitate, watch, new at Session 4) mixed analyses of variance on both dependent measures. We conducted separate, parallel analyses evaluating children's performance before and after provision of the verbal labels for the event sequences. To avoid redundancy, we report the results of the more conservative analyses of children's performance prior to provision of the verbal labels and note exceptions to the patterns when children's total production was considered. Following the logic outlined in discussion of the results of analyses of the performance of the children tested on four-step event sequences, only main effects of and interactions involving the variable experience will be interpreted.

TABLE 6

Age group/ Delay condition/ Reminding/ Experience	Sequence Type							
	Overall		Enabling		Mixed		Arbitrary	
	Mean	SD	Mean	SD	Mean	SD	Mean	SD
Number of individual target actions produced (max. = 3.0)								
16-month-olds								
1-month delay								
Before reminder								
Imitate	2.41	0.90	2.44	0.86	2.00	1.14	2.78	0.43
Watch	2.15	0.96	2.33	0.97	1.89	1.08	2.22	0.81
New	0.98	0.79	1.22	0.94	0.67	0.69	1.06	0.64
Total production								
Imitate	2.63	0.71	2.72	0.46	2.33	1.03	2.83	0.38
Watch	2.44	0.74	2.61	0.70	2.22	0.81	2.50	0.71
New	1.37	0.81	1.44	0.78	1.22	0.94	1.44	0.70
3-month delay								
Before reminder								
Imitate	1.74	1.12	1.94	1.16	1.50	1.20	1.78	1.00
Watch	1.72	1.00	1.61	0.92	1.72	1.27	1.83	0.79
New	1.04	0.82	1.06	0.73	0.83	0.92	1.24	0.81
Total production								
Imitate	1.94	1.04	2.06	1.00	1.67	1.14	2.11	0.96
Watch	2.04	0.95	1.89	0.83	2.06	1.11	2.17	0.92
New	1.23	0.86	1.17	0.79	1.00	1.03	1.53	0.70
6-month delay								
Before reminder								
Imitate	1.31	0.95	1.83	0.79	1.06	0.80	1.06	1.06
Watch	1.24	1.01	1.28	0.89	1.28	1.18	1.17	0.99
New	0.79	0.76	1.06	0.64	0.56	0.62	0.67	0.59
Total production								
Imitate	1.56	0.95	2.06	0.73	1.44	0.92	1.17	0.99
Watch	1.76	0.93	2.06	0.73	1.72	1.13	1.50	0.86
New	1.13	0.80	1.28	0.75	1.06	1.06	0.83	0.62
9-month delay								
Before reminder								
Imitate	1.26	0.96	1.33	0.91	1.22	1.00	1.22	1.00
Watch	1.19	0.91	1.11	0.90	1.17	0.92	1.28	0.96
New	1.24	0.89	1.11	0.83	1.00	0.91	0.89	0.76
Total production								
Imitate	1.72	0.92	1.72	0.83	1.61	1.14	1.83	0.79
Watch	1.54	0.91	1.56	0.92	1.44	0.92	1.61	0.92
New	1.61	0.96	1.33	0.84	1.67	1.08	1.33	0.84

(*continued*)

TABLE 6 (*continued*)

Age group/ Delay condition/ Reminding/ Experience	Overall		Enabling		Mixed		Arbitrary	
	Mean	SD	Mean	SD	Mean	SD	Mean	SD
12-month delay								
Before reminder								
Imitate	1.32	1.02	1.61	1.04	1.24	0.94	1.11	1.08
Watch	1.43	0.98	1.67	1.03	1.44	0.92	1.17	0.99
New	1.22	0.98	1.33	0.69	1.11	1.08	1.28	0.89
Total production								
Imitate	1.79	1.00	2.00	1.08	1.65	0.84	1.72	1.07
Watch	1.96	0.97	2.17	0.86	2.00	1.08	1.72	0.96
New	1.63	1.07	1.56	0.92	1.61	1.14	1.67	0.84
13-month-olds								
1-month delay								
Before reminder								
Imitate	1.61	1.09	2.06	0.94	0.94	1.11	1.83	0.92
Watch	1.35	1.07	1.33	1.19	1.06	1.11	1.67	0.84
New	0.76	0.87	0.61	0.70	0.83	1.10	0.83	0.79
Total production								
Imitate	1.98	1.02	2.39	0.78	1.44	1.15	2.11	0.90
Watch	1.83	0.95	1.83	0.99	1.56	1.04	2.11	0.76
New	0.98	0.84	0.89	0.68	0.94	1.11	1.11	0.68
3-month delay								
Before reminder								
Imitate	1.07	0.89	1.50	0.62	0.61	0.85	1.11	0.96
Watch	1.15	0.98	1.24	0.88	0.71	0.82	1.50	1.10
New	0.72	0.68	0.67	0.59	0.78	0.81	0.72	0.67
Total production								
Imitate	1.39	0.96	1.78	0.73	1.06	0.94	1.33	1.08
Watch	1.68	0.96	1.65	0.90	1.29	1.02	2.11	0.83
New	1.19	0.93	1.22	0.81	1.28	1.13	1.06	0.87
6-month delay								
Before reminder								
Imitate	1.16	0.84	1.06	0.73	0.83	0.71	1.59	0.91
Watch	0.89	0.79	0.89	0.90	0.72	0.75	1.06	0.73
New	0.76	0.64	1.06	0.64	0.56	0.62	0.67	0.59
Total production								
Imitate	1.38	0.83	1.39	0.78	1.06	0.80	1.71	0.82
Watch	1.15	0.88	1.00	0.84	0.89	0.83	1.56	0.86
New	1.06	0.83	1.28	0.75	1.06	1.06	0.83	0.62
9-month delay								
Before reminder								
Imitate	1.02	0.98	0.89	0.83	0.94	1.16	1.22	0.94
Watch	1.06	1.02	1.00	1.14	1.11	0.96	1.06	1.00
New	1.00	0.82	1.11	0.83	1.00	0.91	0.89	0.76

(*continued*)

TABLE 6 (*continued*)

Age group/ Delay condition/ Reminding/ Experience	Sequence Type							
	Overall		Enabling		Mixed		Arbitrary	
	Mean	SD	Mean	SD	Mean	SD	Mean	SD
Total production								
Imitate	1.37	0.94	1.33	0.84	1.22	1.06	1.56	0.92
Watch	1.44	1.02	1.44	1.04	1.61	0.98	1.28	1.07
New	1.44	0.92	1.33	0.84	1.67	1.08	1.33	0.84
12-month delay								
Before reminder								
Imitate	1.38	0.99	1.50	0.86	1.18	1.04	1.47	1.09
Watch	1.19	0.95	0.94	0.87	1.33	1.03	0.29	0.96
New	1.33	0.91	1.44	0.62	1.39	1.24	1.17	0.79
Total production								
Imitate	1.77	0.96	1.72	0.89	1.88	1.02	1.71	1.02
Watch	1.57	0.94	1.33	1.08	1.72	0.83	1.65	0.90
New	1.72	0.94	1.89	0.68	1.72	1.07	1.56	1.04
Number of pairs of actions in the target order (max. = 2.0)								
16-month-olds								
1-month delay								
Before reminder								
Imitate	1.00	0.73	1.33	0.77	0.78	0.65	0.89	0.68
Watch	0.81	0.73	1.17	0.92	0.67	0.59	0.61	0.50
New	0.19	0.44	0.44	0.62	0.06	0.24	0.06	0.24
Total production								
Imitate	1.17	0.64	1.56	0.51	1.00	0.59	0.94	0.64
Watch	0.96	0.73	1.33	0.84	0.72	0.57	0.83	0.62
New	0.31	0.51	0.50	0.62	0.28	0.46	0.17	0.38
3-month delay								
Before reminder								
Imitate	0.65	0.76	0.89	0.83	0.61	0.70	0.44	0.70
Watch	0.48	0.64	0.61	0.78	0.50	0.62	0.33	0.49
New	0.19	0.39	0.17	0.38	0.17	0.38	0.24	0.42
Total production								
Imitate	0.74	0.78	0.89	0.83	0.67	0.77	0.67	0.77
Watch	0.63	0.68	0.72	0.83	0.67	0.59	0.50	0.62
New	0.25	0.43	0.28	0.46	0.24	0.42	0.24	0.42
6-month delay								
Before reminder								
Imitate	0.28	0.53	0.44	0.70	0.22	0.43	0.17	0.38
Watch	0.30	0.50	0.39	0.61	0.33	0.49	0.17	0.38
New	0.13	0.34	0.06	0.24	0.12	0.32	0.22	0.43
Total production								
Imitate	0.41	0.60	0.67	0.77	0.39	0.50	0.17	0.38
Watch	0.52	0.67	0.78	0.81	0.56	0.62	0.22	0.43
New	0.28	0.45	0.17	0.38	0.29	0.46	0.39	0.50

(*continued*)

TABLE 6 (*continued*)

Age group/ Delay condition/ Reminding/ Experience	Sequence Type							
	Overall		Enabling		Mixed		Arbitrary	
	Mean	SD	Mean	SD	Mean	SD	Mean	SD
9-month delay								
Before reminder								
Imitate	0.35	0.59	0.44	0.70	0.39	0.61	0.22	0.43
Watch	0.22	0.46	0.22	0.55	0.28	0.46	0.17	0.38
New	0.24	0.47	0.22	0.43	0.33	0.59	0.17	0.38
Total production								
Imitate	0.52	0.69	0.61	0.78	0.56	0.78	0.39	0.50
Watch	0.35	0.55	0.39	0.70	0.33	0.49	0.33	0.49
New	0.39	0.60	0.39	0.61	0.50	0.71	0.28	0.46
12-month delay								
Before reminder								
Imitate	0.36	0.62	0.56	0.78	0.29	0.57	0.22	0.43
Watch	0.44	0.60	0.61	0.78	0.44	0.51	0.28	0.46
New	0.28	0.45	0.22	0.43	0.39	0.50	0.22	0.43
Total production								
Imitate	0.62	0.71	0.78	0.81	0.47	0.61	0.61	0.70
Watch	0.67	0.70	0.78	0.73	0.72	0.67	0.50	0.71
New	0.44	0.60	0.61	0.78	0.50	0.51	0.22	0.43
13-month-olds								
1-month delay								
Before reminder								
Imitate	0.56	0.74	1.06	0.87	0.28	0.57	0.33	0.49
Watch	0.41	0.60	0.56	0.70	0.28	0.46	0.39	0.61
New	0.15	0.36	0.11	0.32	0.22	0.43	0.11	0.32
Total production								
Imitate	0.76	0.75	1.17	0.86	0.61	0.70	0.50	0.51
Watch	0.61	0.68	0.78	0.73	0.50	0.51	0.56	0.78
New	0.19	0.39	0.17	0.38	0.28	0.46	0.11	0.38
3-month delay								
Before reminder								
Imitate	0.22	0.46	0.44	0.62	0.11	0.32	0.11	0.32
Watch	0.27	0.48	0.29	0.57	0.12	0.32	0.39	0.50
New	0.07	0.26	0.06	0.24	0.06	0.24	0.11	0.32
Total production								
Imitate	0.39	0.60	0.72	0.75	0.22	0.43	0.22	0.43
Watch	0.48	0.63	0.47	0.70	0.35	0.59	0.61	0.61
New	0.28	0.53	0.33	0.59	0.39	0.61	0.11	0.59
6-month delay								
Before reminder								
Imitate	0.17	0.38	0.17	0.38	0.06	0.24	0.29	0.46
Watch	0.11	0.32	0.11	0.32	0.17	0.38	0.06	0.24
New	0.07	0.26	0.17	0.38	0.06	0.24	0.00	—

(*continued*)

TABLE 6 (*continued*)

Age group/ Delay condition/ Reminding/ Experience	Sequence Type							
	Overall		Enabling		Mixed		Arbitrary	
	Mean	SD	Mean	SD	Mean	SD	Mean	SD
Total production								
Imitate	0.25	0.43	0.22	0.43	0.17	0.38	0.35	0.48
Watch	0.19	0.44	0.11	0.32	0.28	0.46	0.17	0.51
New	0.20	0.45	0.28	0.57	0.28	0.46	0.06	0.24
9-month delay								
Before reminder								
Imitate	0.26	0.52	0.22	0.55	0.33	0.59	0.22	0.43
Watch	0.26	0.48	0.33	0.49	0.22	0.43	0.22	0.55
New	0.20	0.45	0.28	0.57	0.22	0.43	0.11	0.32
Total production								
Imitate	0.39	0.60	0.44	0.70	0.39	0.61	0.33	0.49
Watch	0.39	0.60	0.50	0.62	0.33	0.49	0.33	0.69
New	0.41	0.57	0.38	0.61	0.50	0.51	0.33	0.59
12-month delay								
Before reminder								
Imitate	0.44	0.60	0.44	0.70	0.41	0.49	0.47	0.61
Watch	0.28	0.49	0.28	0.57	0.33	0.49	0.24	0.42
New	0.33	0.55	0.39	0.50	0.44	0.70	0.17	0.38
Total production								
Imitate	0.61	0.65	0.67	0.77	0.65	0.59	0.53	0.61
Watch	0.39	0.53	0.39	0.61	0.50	0.51	0.29	0.46
New	0.52	0.67	0.72	0.67	0.44	0.70	0.39	0.61

Individual Target Actions Produced

The four-way mixed-factor analysis of variance revealed a main effect of experience: $F(2, 340) = 34.29$, $p < .0001$, $MSE = 0.86$. Overall, the children produced a larger number of individual target actions on events that they previously had been given the opportunity to imitate ($M = 1.43$, $SD = 1.04$) and on events that they previously had only watched ($M = 1.34$, $SD = 1.02$), relative to on events that were new to them at Session 4 ($M = 0.99$, $SD = 0.84$). This pattern is indicative of recall of the individual target actions of the event sequences. The effect was, however, qualified by lower-order interactions of Delay × Experience, Age × Experience, and Sequence type × Experience. To pursue the interaction of Delay × Experience, $F(8, 340) = 7.40$, $p < .0001$, $MSE = 0.86$, we conducted separate one-way analyses of variance at each level of delay. The analyses revealed that, as suggested by inspection of Figure 8, Panel A, children could be said to recall the material in the 1-, 3-, and 6-month delay conditions only: Fs $(2, 70) = 43.82$, 11.59, and 8.89, ps $< .0004$, MSEs $= 0.88$, 0.90, and

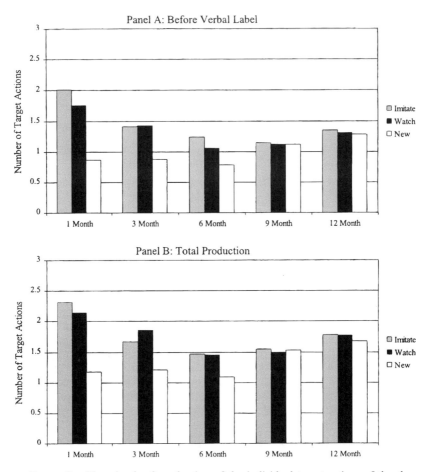

FIGURE 8.—Mean levels of production of the individual target actions of the three-step event sequences in the imitate, watch, and new experience conditions before provision of the verbal labels for the event sequences (Panel A) and the children's total production of individual target actions (Panel B), as a function of delay condition.

0.66, for the 1-, 3-, and 6-month delay conditions, respectively; in the 9- and 12-month delay conditions, the effects of experience were not reliable. In the delay conditions in which the children showed evidence of recall of the individual target actions of the event sequences, they recalled the actions of the events that they had only watched, as well as the events that they had imitated. These patterns remained unchanged when children's total production was evaluated (Figure 8, Panel B).

To pursue the interaction of Age × Experience, $F(2,340) = 3.34$, $p <$ .04, $MSE = 0.86$, we conducted separate one-way analyses of variance for each age group. For both age groups, there were main effects of experience [$Fs(2,178)$ = 8.92 and 22.51, $ps < .0002$, $MSEs$ = 0.87 and 1.10, for 13- and 16-month-olds, respectively]. Dunnett's tests revealed that, across delay conditions, for both age groups, performance on events previously imitated was greater than on events new to the children at Session 4; for both age groups, performance on events previously only watched was greater than on events new at Session 4 [13-month-olds: Ms = 1.25, 1.13, and 0.91 (SDs = 0.98, 0.97, and 0.82); 16-month-olds: Ms = 1.61, 1.54, and 1.06 (SDs = 1.08, 1.03, and 0.86), for imitate, watch, and new, respectively]. Thus, both age groups showed evidence of recall of the individual target actions of the event sequences. The average size of the difference between performance on previously experienced event sequences and on new event sequences was almost twice as large for the 16-month-olds compared with the 13-month-olds (M differences = 0.52 and 0.28, respectively). These patterns remained unchanged when children's total production was evaluated.

To pursue the interaction of Sequence type × Experience, $F(4,680)$ = 2.77, $p < .03$, MSE = 0.86, we conducted separate analyses for each sequence type. The analyses revealed no exceptions to the conclusion that the children recalled the individual target actions of the event sequences. That is, for each sequence type, children produced greater numbers of individual target actions of the events that they previously had experienced relative to event sequences new to them at Session 4: $Fs(2,358)$ = 18.13, 4.50, and 16.51, $ps < .02$, $MSEs$ = 0.85, 0.98, and 0.88, for enabling, mixed, and arbitrarily ordered event sequences, respectively [enabling event sequences: Ms = 1.62, 1.34, and 1.04 (SDs = 0.97, 1.04, and 0.78); mixed event sequences: Ms = 1.15, 1.24, and 0.94 (SDs = 1.05, 1.06, and 0.96); arbitrary event sequences: Ms = 1.52, 1.42, and 0.98 (SDs = 1.06, 0.97, and 0.78), for imitate, watch, and new, respectively]. When children's post-reminder performance was considered, the Sequence type × Experience interaction was not statistically reliable. There were no other reliable effects before or after provision of the verbal labels for the event sequences.

As noted in discussion of the patterns of performance for the children tested on four-step event sequences, an important consideration in interpretation of the observed effects is whether they are attributable to a general pattern of responding or to a small number of children within a cell. To address this question, we determined the number of children in each age group and each delay condition whose mean scores on previously experienced events were nominally greater than their mean scores on new event sequences. For the variable of individual target actions produced, the results of the comparison are depicted in Figure 9 (Panels A and B, for children's performance prior to and after provision of the

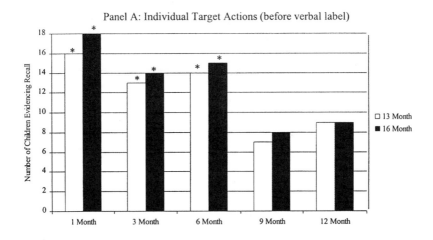

Panel A: Individual Target Actions (before verbal label)

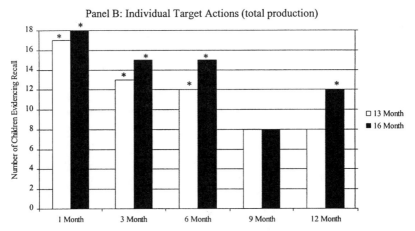

Panel B: Individual Target Actions (total production)

FIGURE 9.—The number of 13-month-old children and 16-month-old children tested on three-step event sequences who produced nominally higher numbers of the individual target actions of event sequences previously experienced than of new event sequences: before provision of the verbal labels for the event sequences (Panel A); children's total production (Panel B).

verbal labels for the event sequences, respectively). Consistent with the analysis of variance which indicated that the children remembered the individual target actions of the event sequences for 1, 3, and 6 months, but not for longer, the number of children for whom performance on previously experienced events was greater than performance on new events was larger than would be expected by chance in the 1-, 3-, and 6-month delay conditions, for both age groups, both prior to and after provision of the

98

verbal labels for the events (sign tests for related samples maximum value $p < .05$; one-tailed). In addition, for the 16-month-olds, after provision of the verbal labels, performance on previously experienced event sequences was greater than on new event sequences in the 12-month delay condition (sign test for related samples, $p < .05$; one-tailed). For the 13-month-olds, at the longer delay intervals of 9 and 12 months, whether evaluated when the children were prompted by the props alone or by the props and the verbal labels for the event sequences, the number of children for whom performance on previously experienced events was greater than performance on new events fell below the level that would be expected by chance (sign tests for related samples minimum value $p > .10$).

Pairs of Actions Produced in the Target Order

Analyses of children's levels of production of pairs of actions in the target order largely paralleled those for the variable of production of individual target actions. The four-way mixed-factor analysis of variance revealed a main effect of experience: $F(2,340) = 30.25$, $p < .0001$, $MSE = 0.28$. Overall, the children produced a larger number of pairs of actions in the target order on events that they previously had been given the opportunity to imitate ($M = 0.43$, $SD = 0.64$) and on events that they previously had only watched ($M = 0.36$, $SD = 0.57$), relative to on events that were new to them at Session 4 ($M = .19$, $SD = .41$). This pattern is indicative of temporally ordered recall of the event sequences. The effect was, however, qualified by lower-order interactions of Delay × Experience, Age × Experience, and Sequence type × Experience. Analysis of the Delay × Experience interaction, $F(8,340) = 5.41$, $p < .0001$, $MSE = 0.28$, revealed that, as suggested by inspection of Figure 10 (Panel A), the children could be said to recall the material in the 1- and 3-month delay conditions only: $Fs(2,70) = 32.96$ and 7.85, $ps < .0008$, $MSEs = 0.33$ and 0.35, for the 1- and 3-month delay conditions, respectively; in the 6-, 9-, and 12-month delay conditions, the effects of experience were not reliable. In the two delay conditions in which they showed evidence of recall of pairs of actions in the target order, the children recalled the order of the events that they had only watched, as well as of the events that they had imitated. These patterns remained unchanged when children's total production was evaluated (Figure 10, Panel B).

To pursue the Age × Experience interaction, $F(2,340) = 3.80$, $p < .03$, $MSE = 0.28$, we conducted separate one-way analyses of variance for each age group. For both age groups, there were main effects of experience [$Fs(2,178) = 7.29$ and 20.81, $ps < .0009$, $MSEs = 0.25$ and 0.37, for 13- and 16-month-olds, respectively]. Dunnett's tests revealed that, across delay conditions, for both age groups, performance on events that the children

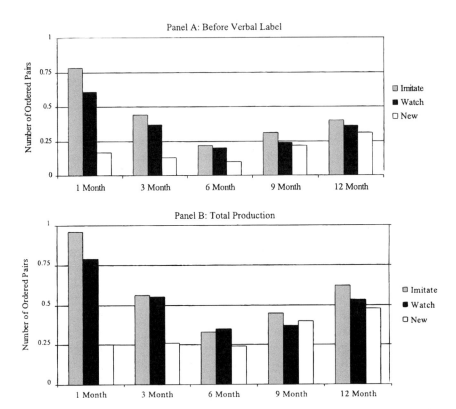

FIGURE 10.—Mean levels of production of pairs of actions in the target order of the three-step event sequences in the imitate, watch, and new experience conditions before provision of the verbal labels for the event sequences (Panel A) and the children's total production of pairs of actions in the target order (Panel B), as a function of delay condition.

had been provided the opportunity to imitate was greater than on events new to the children at Session 4; for both age groups, performance on events previously only watched was greater than on events new at Session 4 [13-month-olds: $Ms = 0.33, 0.27$, and 0.17 ($SDs = 0.57, 0.49$, and 0.40); 16-month-olds: $Ms = 0.53, 0.45$, and 0.21 ($SDs = 0.70, 0.62$, and 0.42), for imitate, watch, and new, respectively]. Thus, both age groups showed evidence of ordered recall of the event sequences. The average size of the difference between performance on previously experienced event sequences and on new event sequences was twice as large for the 16-month-olds compared with the 13-month-olds (M differences $= 0.28$ and 0.13, respectively). For the children who had been 16 months at the time of exposure to the event sequences, these patterns remained unchanged when children's total production was evaluated. For the children who had been

13 months at the time of exposure to the event sequences, after provision of the verbal labels for the events, the difference between levels of production of pairs of actions in the target order on events previously only watched ($M = 0.41$, $SD = 0.59$) and on events new at Session 4 ($M = 0.32$, $SD = 0.54$) fell below the level of statistical significance ($p < .06$; observed difference $= .09$; critical difference $= .10$). The difference between performance on events that the children previously had been permitted to imitate ($M = 0.48$, $SD = 0.64$) and on new events was reliable.

To pursue the interaction of Sequence type × Experience, $F(4,680) = 2.99$, $p < .02$, $MSE = 0.26$, we conducted separate analyses for each sequence type. The analyses revealed no exceptions to the conclusion that the children recalled information about the temporal order of the event sequences. That is, for each sequence type, children produced greater numbers of pairs of actions in the target order of the events that they previously had experienced relative to event sequences new to them at Session 4: $Fs(2,358) = 18.59$, 4.01, and 9.98, $ps < .02$, $MSEs = 0.37$, 0.25, and 0.20, for enabling, mixed, and arbitrarily ordered event sequences, respectively [enabling event sequences: $Ms = 0.60$, 0.46, and 0.21 ($SDs = 0.77$, 0.70, and 0.44); mixed event sequences: $Ms = 0.35$, 0.33, and 0.21 ($SDs = 0.56$, 0.50, and 0.45); arbitrary event sequences: $Ms = 0.34$, 0.28, and 0.13 ($SDs = 0.54$, 0.48, and 0.34), for imitate, watch, and new, respectively]. When children's post-verbal-label performance was considered, the Experience × Sequence type interaction was not statistically reliable.

The number of children whose relative levels of performance in the old and new experience conditions are indicative of memory is reflected in Figure 11 (Panels A and B, for before and after provision of the verbal labels for the event sequences, respectively). For the 16-month-olds, prior to provision of the verbal labels for the event sequences, the number of children for whom performance on previously experienced events was superior to performance on new events was reliably greater than chance only in the 1- and 3-month delay conditions (sign tests for related samples maximum value $p < .02$; one-tailed); in the 6-month delay condition, the effect approached significance ($p < .10$). When performance was evaluated after provision of the verbal labels for the event sequences, the number of children showing evidence of temporally ordered recall was reliably greater than chance in the 1-, 3-, and 6-month delay conditions (sign tests for related samples maximum value $p < .02$; one-tailed). Thus, although in the 6-month delay condition, the size of the difference between performance in the old and new experience conditions was not sufficient to produce a statistically reliable effect in the analysis of variance, after provision of verbal labels for the event sequences, a substantial and significant number of the 16-month-old children evidenced a

Panel A: Pairs of Actions in Target Order (before verbal label)

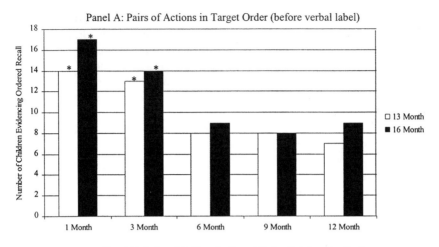

Panel B: Pairs of Actions in Target Order (total production)

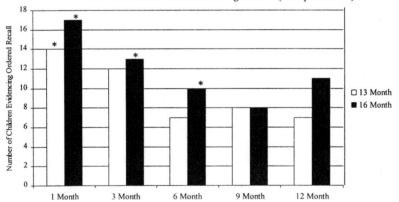

FIGURE 11.—The number of 13-month-old children and 16-month-old children tested on three-step event sequences who produced nominally higher numbers of pairs of actions in the target order of event sequences previously experienced than of new event sequences: before provision of the verbal labels for the event sequences (Panel A); children's total production (Panel B).

pattern consistent with the conclusion that they remembered the temporal order of the event sequences over delays as long as 6 months.

When the 13-month-olds were prompted by the event-related props alone, the number of children for whom performance on previously experienced events was greater than performance on new events exceeded the level that would be expected by chance in the 1- and 3-month delay conditions (sign tests for related samples, $p < .02$; one-tailed). When they were prompted by the event-related props and by the verbal labels for the event sequences, the number of children evincing the pattern indicative of recall of the order of the event sequences was larger than would be expected by chance in the 1-month delay condition only (sign test for related samples, $p < .001$); in the 3-month delay condition, the effect approached significance ($p < .10$). The result indicates greater individual variability among the 13-month-olds compared with the 16-month-olds, even at the relatively shorter delay intervals, and even with the aid of verbal reminders.

Summary

The results of analysis of variance comparing children's performance on events previously experienced with events new to them at Session 4 indicate that the children recalled the individual target actions of the event sequences over delay intervals of 1, 3, and 6 months, but not for 9 and 12 months. The pattern was apparent on events that the children previously had been permitted to imitate as well as on events previously only watched; the pattern was apparent across sequence types. The results of analyses of the number of children who showed nominally higher levels of performance on old event sequences than on new event sequences were consistent with the results of the analysis of variance.

The 13-month-olds and 16-month-olds tested on three-step event sequences showed evidence of recall of pairs of actions of the event sequences in the correct temporal order over delay intervals of 1 and 3 months, but not over intervals of 6, 9, and 12 months. Consistent with this finding, when they were prompted by the event-related props alone, the number of 16-month-old children who showed nominally higher levels of performance on previously experienced events than on new events was greater than the number that would be expected by chance in the 1- and 3-month delay conditions only; the number of children exhibiting the pattern approached significance in the 6-month delay condition. When they were prompted both by the event-related props and by verbal labels for the event sequences, a substantial and significant number of 16-month-old children showed nominally higher levels of production of pairs of actions in the target order on previously experienced events than on new events in the 1-, 3-, and 6-month delay conditions. This effect parallels that among the 16-month-olds tested on four-step event sequences. In contrast, for the 13-month-olds, before exposure to the verbal labels for the event sequences, the pattern of performance indicative of recall of the temporal order of the event sequences was apparent in the 1- and 3-month delay conditions; after exposure to the verbal labels, the pattern was apparent only in the 1-month delay condition.

FACTORS AFFECTING DELAYED RECALL: EFFECTS OF DELAY, AGE, SEQUENCE TYPE, MODE OF EXPERIENCE, AND VERBAL REMINDING

To evaluate the direct and interactive effects on delayed recall of the factors of delay, age, sequence type, and mode of experience, we conducted Delay × Age × Sequence type × Experience condition mixed analyses of variance for both dependent measures. Because the children tested on three-step event sequences showed evidence of recall of the individual target actions of the events for 1, 3, and 6 months, but not for 9 and 12 months, we included in the analysis only the 1-, 3-, and 6-month delay conditions. Likewise, because the children showed evidence of recall of the temporal order of the events for only 1 and 3 months, we included in the analysis only the first two levels of delay. We conducted separate, parallel analyses evaluating children's performance before provision of the verbal reminders and children's total recall performance. We evaluated the effects of provision of verbal reminders by conducting t tests to determine whether the difference in performance prior to and after provision of the verbal reminders differed from zero. Descriptive statistics for each cell of the design are provided in Table 6. The results for each potential effect on children's long-term recall are outlined in turn below.

Length of the Delay Interval

For both dependent measures, both prior to and after provision of the verbal reminders, there were main effects of delay: $Fs(2,102) = 21.92$, 26.89, 16.06, and 14.48, $ps < .0002$, $MSEs = 1.34$, 1.18, 0.56, and 0.74, for the number of individual target actions produced before and after the verbal reminders and the number of pairs of actions produced in the target order before and after verbal reminders, respectively. As reflected in Figure 12, for both dependent measures, whether evaluated before or after provision of the verbal reminders, children's performance was greater after 1 month than after 3 months. In addition, whether prompted by the props alone or by the props and verbal labels for the event sequences, children produced a smaller number of individual target actions after 6 months than after 3 months (Figure 12, Panel A). For the variable of pairs of actions in the target order, there were no other effects involving delay (Figure 12, Panel B). The effect of delay was observed even with the number of individual target actions produced at delayed recall controlled via analysis of covariance.

For the variable of number of individual target actions produced, prior to provision of the verbal reminders, delay interacted with age; after provision of the verbal reminders, delay interacted with age as well as sequence type. To pursue the interaction of Delay × Age (prior to verbal

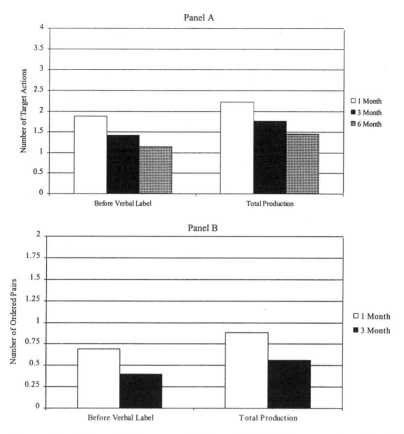

FIGURE 12.—Effects of delay on production of individual target actions (Panel A) and pairs of actions in the target order (Panel B) by 13-month-olds and 16-month-olds tested on three-step event sequences.

reminders), $F(2,102) = 3.09$, $p < .05$, $MSE = 1.34$, we conducted separate analyses for each age group. For the 16-month-olds, the pattern indicated by the main effect obtained: The children showed significant decrements in performance in the 3-month delay condition ($M = 1.73$, $SD = 1.06$) relative to the 1-month delay condition ($M = 2.28$, $SD = 0.94$), and in the 6-month delay condition ($M = 1.28$, $SD = 0.97$) relative to the 3-month delay condition [$F(2,51) = 19.17$, $p < .0001$, $MSE = 1.41$]. For the younger children, the decline in performance was less gradual: The 13-month-olds showed lower and equivalent levels of performance in the 3-month delay condition ($M = 1.11$, $SD = 0.93$) and in the 6-month delay condition ($M = 1.02$, $SD = 0.82$), relative to the 1-month delay condition ($M = 1.48$, $SD = 1.08$) [$F(2,51) = 5.05$, $p < .01$, $MSE = 1.26$].

After provision of the verbal reminders, delay and age interacted with one another and also with sequence type: $F(4,204) = 3.62$, $p < .008$, $MSE = 0.65$. To pursue the interaction, we conducted separate analyses for each age group. The younger children's levels of production of the individual target actions of the event sequences was lower in the 6-month delay condition ($M = 1.27$, $SD = 0.86$) relative to the 1-month delay condition ($M = 1.91$, $SD = 0.98$); performance in the 3-month delay condition ($M = 1.54$, $SD = 0.97$) was intermediate and did not differ from that in the other two delay conditions [$F(2,51) = 8.16$, $p < .0008$, $MSE = 1.37$]. Among the 16-month-olds, analysis of the Delay × Sequence type interaction, $F(4,102) = 3.52$, $p < .01$, $MSE = 0.64$, revealed significant effects of delay for all sequence types: $Fs(2,51) = 7.68$, 4.29, and 28.74, $ps < .02$, $MSEs = 0.67$, 1.02, and 0.56, for enabling, mixed, and arbitrary, respectively. For all sequence types, performance in the 1-month delay condition [$Ms = 2.67$, 2.27, and 2.67 ($SDs = 0.59$, 0.91, and 0.59), for enabling, mixed, and arbitrary, respectively] was greater than that in the 6-month delay condition [$Ms = 2.06$, 1.58, and 1.33 ($SDs = 0.71$, 1.02, and 0.93), for enabling, mixed, and arbitrary, respectively]. On enabling event sequences, performance in the 3-month delay condition ($M = 1.97$, $SD = 0.91$) was less than that in the 1-month condition and did not differ from that in the 6-month condition. On mixed event sequences, performance in the 3-month delay condition ($M = 1.86$, $SD = 1.13$) was intermediate and did not differ from that in either the 1- or 6-month delay condition. Finally, on arbitrarily ordered event sequences, performance in the 3-month delay condition ($M = 2.14$, $SD = 0.93$) was intermediate and differed from that in the 1-month as well as the 6-month delay condition.

Age at the Time of Exposure to the Event Sequences

In terms of the number of individual target actions produced, both prior to and after provision of the verbal reminders, there were main effects of age, indicating higher levels of production by the 16-month-olds relative to the 13-month-olds: $Fs(1,102) = 37.57$ and 33.26, $ps < .0001$, $MSEs = 1.34$ and 1.18, for before and after reminders, respectively [before verbal reminder: $Ms = 1.76$ and 1.21 ($SDs = 1.07$ and 0.97), for 16- and 13-month-olds, respectively; after verbal reminder: $Ms = 2.06$ and 1.57 ($SDs = 0.96$ and 0.97), for 16- and 13-month-olds, respectively]. Although as noted above in the discussion of the effects of delay, age participated in interactions with delay (before verbal reminders) and with delay and sequence type (after verbal reminders), in all cases, the analyses indicated superior performance by the 16-month-olds relative to the 13-month-olds.

Analyses of variance indicated that children's levels of recall of the temporal order of the event sequences were affected by age, both before and after provision of the verbal reminders. However, analyses of covariance with the number of individual target actions produced at delayed recall controlled indicated that the effects were not reliable.

Sequence Type

In terms of production of individual target actions, there were main effects of sequence type both prior to and after provision of the verbal reminders: $Fs(2,204) = 17.36$ and 16.14, $ps < .0001$, $MSEs = 0.79$ and 0.65, respectively. The effects are illustrated in Figure 13, Panel A. Both prior to and after provision of the verbal reminders, the children produced larger and equivalent numbers of individual target actions of the enabling and arbitrarily ordered event sequences, relative to the mixed event sequences. The main effect was qualified by interactions with age [before verbal reminder: $F(2,204) = 2.96$, $p = .05$, $MSE = 0.79$] and both age and delay [after verbal reminder: $F(4,204) = 3.62$, $p < .008$, $MSE = 0.65$]. In both cases, we pursued the interactions with separate analyses for each age group.

For the 13-month-olds, the analyses revealed the same pattern as in the overall main effect. That is, the pattern of higher and equivalent levels of production of the individual actions of the enabling and arbitrarily ordered event sequences, relative to the mixed event sequences, obtained for the younger children in the sample both when they were prompted by the props alone and when they were prompted by the props and verbal labels for the event sequences [Ms before verbal reminders = 1.34, 1.46, and 0.81 (SDs = 0.95, 0.94, and 0.90); Ms after verbal reminders = 1.67, 1.82, and 1.22 (SDs = 0.93, 0.92, and 0.98), for enabling, arbitrary, and mixed event sequences, respectively]: before verbal reminder, $F(2,106) = 16.53$, $p < .0001$, $MSE = 0.78$; after verbal reminder, $F(2,102) = 16.29$, $p < .0001$, $MSE = 0.66$.

For the 16-month-olds, prior to provision of the verbal reminders (Figure 14, Panel A), production of individual target actions of the enabling event sequences was greater than of the mixed event sequences; production of the individual target actions of the arbitrarily ordered event sequences was intermediate and did not differ from the other two sequence types: $F(2,106) = 3.85$, $p < .03$, $MSE = 0.82$. When the children were prompted by the props and by verbal labels for the event sequences (Figure 14, Panel B), analysis of the interaction of Sequence type × Delay (values provided above) revealed no sequence type effect in either the 1- or the 3-month delay condition. In the 6-month delay condition, children produced a larger number of individual target actions of the enabling event sequences relative to the arbitrarily ordered event sequences; production of the individual target actions of the mixed event sequences was

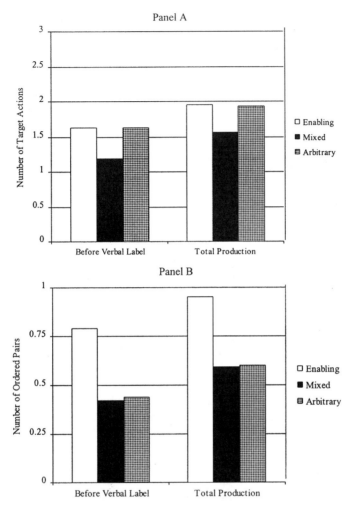

FIGURE 13.—Main effects of sequence type on production of individual target actions (Panel A) and pairs of actions in the target order (Panel B) by 13-month-olds and 16-month-olds tested on three-step event sequences.

intermediate and did not differ from that of the other two sequence types: $F(2,34) = 6.26$, $p < .005$, $MSE = 0.77$.

Children's ordered recall performance also was affected by sequence type: $Fs(2,136) = 17.33$ and 17.24, $ps < .0001$, $MSEs = 0.37$ and 0.35, before and after reminders, respectively. As suggested by inspection of Figure 13, Panel B, whether they were prompted by the props alone or

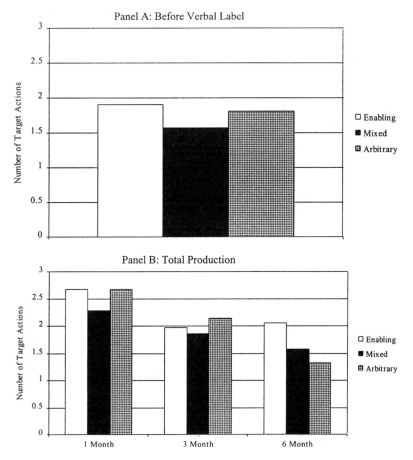

FIGURE 14.—Effects of sequence type on production of the individual target actions of the three-step event sequences by 16-month-olds before provision of the verbal labels for the event sequences (Panel A) and children's total production, as a function of delay condition (Panel B).

by the props and verbal labels for the event sequences, the children produced larger numbers of pairs of actions in the target order on enabling event sequences than on either mixed or arbitrarily ordered event sequences. Consistent with the pattern observed among the 13-month-olds at immediate recall, children's levels of ordered reproduction of events partially constrained and totally unconstrained by enabling relations did not differ reliably, either before or after verbal reminding. The pattern of differences among sequence types was observed even with the

109

number of individual target actions produced at delayed recall controlled via analyses of covariance. The effects of sequence type were not qualified by interactions with any of the other variables.

Mode of Experience

As had been the case in analysis of the performance of the children tested on four-step event sequences, the mnemonic performance of the children tested on three-step event sequences was largely unaffected by whether or not they had been given the opportunity to imitate the events prior to imposition of the delays. In terms of the number of individual target actions produced, analysis of children's performance when they were prompted by the event-related props alone revealed an interaction of Sequence type × Experience: $F(2,204) = 3.22$, $p < .05$, $MSE = 0.78$. Prior to provision of the verbal reminders, there was an effect of mode of experience condition on children's production of the individual target actions of event sequences wholly constrained by enabling relations: $F(1,107) = 9.85$, $p < .003$, $MSE = 0.71$. The children produced more of the individual target actions of the enabling event sequences that they had been permitted to imitate ($M = 1.81$, $SD = 0.95$), relative to the enabling event sequences that they had only watched ($M = 1.45$, $SD = 1.04$). For the mixed and arbitrarily ordered event sequences, there were no mode of experience effects. Once the verbal reminders were provided, the effect of mode of experience on children's performance on the enabling event sequences no longer obtained: Analysis of children's production of the individual target actions of the event sequences when they were prompted by the props and by verbal labels revealed neither a main effect nor any interactions involving mode of experience. The children's production of pairs of actions in the target order on events imitated and events only watched did not differ reliably, either before or after provision of the verbal reminders. The effects were not altered when, in analyses of covariance, we controlled for the number of individual target actions produced at delayed recall.

Availability of Verbal Reminders

To evaluate the efficacy of verbal reminders on the children's performance we calculated scores reflecting the difference in levels of performance when the children were prompted by the event-related props alone and when they were prompted by the props as well as the verbal labels for the event sequences. We then subjected the difference scores to t tests (one-tailed), to determine whether they were different from zero. We conducted separate analyses for each age group and sequence type. We tested the effects of verbal reminding on children's recall of the individual target actions of the event sequences in the 1-, 3-, and 6-month delay conditions; we tested the effects of verbal reminding on children's recall of pairs of actions in the target order in the 1- and 3-month delay conditions. With one exception, the tests indicated that the differences in children's pre- and post-verbal-reminder performance were reliably greater than zero: $ts(17) > 2.05$, $ps < .05$. The exception was among the 16-month-olds in the 3-month delay condition whose ordered recall of the enabling event sequences was not facilitated by the verbal reminders. In all other delay conditions, for both age groups, and on all three sequence types, verbal reminders facilitated children's recall of the individual target actions as well as of the temporal order of actions of the to-be-remembered events.

Summary

The effects of delay on the children tested on three-step events was similar to the effects on the children tested on four-step event sequences: Children's ordered recall performance declined significantly between the 1- and 3-month delay intervals. With one exception, children's production of the individual target actions of the event sequences also declined between 1 and 3 months and again between 3 and 6 months. The exception was among the 13-month-olds. Prior to introduction of the verbal labels for the event sequences, the younger children's performance declined more sharply than did the older children's performance (significant difference between 1 and 3 months with no difference in performance between 3 and 6 months). After exposure to the verbal labels for the events, the decline was more gradual, with significant differences appearing between the 1- and 6-month delay conditions only. Whereas both age groups showed evidence of recall of the individual target actions of the events for as many as 6 months, the 16-month-olds showed more robust recall, relative to the 13-month-olds. Once the variance associated with the differential levels of recall of the individual target actions by the age groups was controlled, the 13- and 16-month-olds did not differ in their levels of temporally ordered recall.

The children's performance was affected by sequence type. For the 13-month-olds, both prior to and after introduction of the verbal reminders of the event sequences, production of individual target actions was greater on events totally constrained by enabling relations and on events wholly unconstrained by enabling relations, relative to on mixed event sequences. When they were prompted by the event-related props alone, the 16-month-olds produced more of the individual target actions of the enabling relative to the mixed event sequences. When they were prompted by both the props and the verbal reminders of the event sequences, the 16-month-olds showed no effects of sequence type in their production of the individual target actions of the event sequences in either the 1- or the 3-month delay condition. In the 6-month delay condition, the 16-month-olds produced more of the individual target actions of the enabling event sequences relative to the arbitrarily ordered events; production of the individual target actions of the mixed event sequences was intermediate and did not differ from that of either enabling or arbitrarily ordered sequences. Children's ordered recall followed a somewhat different pattern, such that, whether evaluated before or after provision of the verbal labels for the event sequences, events totally constrained by enabling relations were better recalled, relative to those that were only partially constrained or wholly unconstrained by enabling relations.

As was the case for the children tested on four-step event sequences, the delayed recall performance of children tested on three-step event sequences was largely unaffected by whether or not they had been provided the opportunity to imitate the event sequences prior to imposition of the delays. Specifically, prior to introduction of the verbal reminders for the event sequences, the children showed superior levels of production of the individual target actions of enabling event sequences that they had been permitted the opportunity to imitate, relative to those that they had only watched. There was no effect of mode of experience on the other two sequence types. Moreover, after introduction of the verbal reminders for the event sequences, no effects of mode of experience were observed. Neither were levels of ordered recall performance affected by mode of experience, either before or after verbal reminding: Production of pairs of actions in the target order on events previously imitated and on events merely watched did not differ.

Finally, with the exception of one cell of the design, children's performance was facilitated by provision of verbal reminders. That is, they produced both more individual target actions and more pairs of actions in the target order when prompted by the props and verbal reminders than when prompted by the props alone. The exception was among the 16-month-olds in the 3-month delay condition whose ordered recall of enabling event sequences was not facilitated by verbal reminders.

SOURCES OF AGE AND SEQUENCE TYPE EFFECTS

The observed effects of age seem to indicate more robust memory for the individual target actions of the event sequences on the part of 16-month-olds compared with 13-month-olds. They also seem to indicate more robust memory for the individual target actions of events wholly constrained and wholly unconstrained by enabling relations, relative to events partially constrained by such relations, as well as more robust memory for the temporal order of actions of events totally constrained by enabling relations, relative to events only partially constrained or totally lacking enabling relations. However, as was the case for the children tested on four-step event sequences, alternative explanations are possible. First, both age and sequence type effects were apparent in children's immediate recall. Second, it is likely that children who were older at the time delayed recall was tested had more sophisticated problem-solving abilities, relative to the children who were younger. To evaluate these alternatives, following the same analytic strategy as followed for evaluation of performance by the children tested on four-step event sequences, for children tested on three-step event sequences, we examined the possible effects of differential initial learning of the event sequences and of differential problem-solving abilities.

Age Effects

Differential Initial Learning

To determine whether differences in children's initial learning of the event sequences might account for the observed age effects, we conducted analyses of covariance on children's delayed recall performance with their immediate recall performance as covariates. Because once the variance associated with children's production of the individual target actions of the event sequences was controlled, age effects were not apparent in children's ordered recall, we conducted the analyses only on children's production of the individual target actions of the event sequences. For the variable of production of individual target actions, both prior to and after introduction of the verbal reminders of the event sequences, overall main effects of age indicated patterns consistent with the analyses of variance (i.e., higher levels of production of individual target actions by 16- relative to 13-month-olds) [$Fs(1,102) = 11.11$ and 7.63, $ps < .007$, $MSEs = 1.03$ and 0.94, before and after verbal reminders, respectively]. However, analyses of the Delay × Age × Sequence type interactions [$Fs(4,203) = 2.72$ and 2.75, $ps < .03$, $MSEs = 0.70$ and 0.65, before and after verbal reminders, respectively] suggested different conclusions regarding the relative levels of performance of the younger and older children.

When the children were prompted by the event-related props alone, even with the variance associated with differential initial learning of the individual target actions of the event sequences controlled, there were

113

main effects of age in both the 1- and the 3-month delay conditions, indicating that the performance of the 13-month-olds was lower than that of the 16-month-olds: $Fs(1,34)$ = 9.64 and 5.42, $ps < .03$, $MSEs$ = 0.93 and 1.30, for the 1- and 3-month delay conditions, respectively. In the 6-month delay condition, analysis of the Age × Sequence type interaction, $F(2,67)$ = 5.67, $p < .006$, MSE = 0.58, indicated significant effects of age for production of the individual target actions of the enabling and arbitrarily ordered event sequences [$Fs(1, 33)$ = 5.61 and 5.14, $ps < .03$, $MSEs$ = 0.57 and 0.83, respectively], but not for the mixed event sequences. When the children were prompted by the props and by the verbal labels for the event sequences, control of the variance associated with differential initial learning of the target actions of the event sequences produced age effects in the 1-month delay condition only: $F(1,34)$ = 3.99, $p = .05$, MSE = 0.77. In the 3- and 6-month delay conditions, once the variance associated with children's differential initial levels of learning were controlled, age effects no longer were apparent.

Differential Problem-Solving Abilities

As we did in evaluation of whether differences in the problem-solving abilities of the children tested on four-step event sequences might account for the observed age effects, we first determined whether there were observable age-related differences in problem-solving abilities at the time of delayed recall testing. To do so, we evaluated children's performance on the sequences that were new to them at Session 4 by conducting 3 (delay: 1 month, 3 month, 6 month) × 2 (age) × 3 (sequence type) mixed analyses of variance on children's performance before and after the verbal suggestions were provided. Again, because age effects on children's ordered recall were not apparent, we conducted the analyses only on children's production of the individual target actions of the event sequences. Prior to introduction of the verbal suggestions for plausible activities to perform, the 13-month-olds produced fewer individual target actions, relative to the 16-month-olds: $F(1,102)$ = 5.09, $p < .03$, MSE = 0.58 [Ms = 0.75 and 0.94 (SDs = 0.73 and 0.69), respectively]. Once the verbal suggestions were provided, the performance of the age groups no longer differed reliably.

To determine whether control of age-related differences in children's pre-verbal-label problem-solving abilities affected the delayed recall patterns observed, we conducted 3 (delay) × 2 (age) × 3 (sequence type) analyses of covariance on children's delayed recall of the individual target actions of events that they had been permitted to imitate with the number of individual target actions produced on new events as the covariate, and on children's delayed recall of the individual target actions of events previously only watched with the number of individual target actions produced on new events as the covariate. Since age effects were apparent only when children's pre-suggestion performance was evaluated, we conducted the analyses of covariance only on children's performance when prompted by the event-related props alone. For events previously imitated, the main effect of age, $F(1,102) = 21.38$, $p < .0001$, $MSE = 1.11$, was qualified by the interaction of Delay × Age × Sequence type: $F(4,203) = 2.91$, $p < .03$, $MSE = 0.72$. Separate analyses for each delay condition indicated that even with the variance associated with differential problem solving controlled, age effects were apparent in the 1- and 3-month delay conditions: $Fs(1,34) = 15.12$ and 8.36, $ps < .007$, $MSEs = 1.07$ and 1.33, respectively. In the 6-month delay condition, analysis of the Age × Sequence type interaction, $F(2,67) = 5.20$, $p < .008$, $MSE = 0.56$, indicated age effects on the enabling event sequences only: $F(1,33) = 6.16$, $p < .02$, $MSE = 0.51$. On the mixed and arbitrarily ordered event sequences, once the variance associated with differential problem solving was controlled, age effects were not apparent. For events previously only watched, the main effect of age was significant even when the variance associated with differential problem solving was controlled: $F(1,102) = 25.19$, $p < .0001$, $MSE = 1.14$. The effect was not qualified by interactions.

Differential Initial Learning and Differential Problem-Solving Abilities

For the variable of pairs of individual target actions produced, we conducted an analysis of covariance on children's performance in the imitate condition, controlling for differential initial learning and for differential problem solving simultaneously. Because age effects in children's problem-solving ability were only apparent prior to provision of the verbal labels for the event sequences, we evaluated performance only prior to verbal reminding. The patterns of results of the analysis of covariance controlling for both differential initial learning and differential problem-solving abilities were identical to those obtained when only differential problem-solving abilities were controlled. Because the analysis sheds no new light on children's performance, it is not reported here (details are available from PJB).

Summary of Sources of Age Effects

Age effects were not observed in children's ordered recall. Accordingly, no analyses of covariance were conducted on that dependent measure. In terms of the individual target actions of the event sequences, the results of the analyses of variance indicated more robust memory on the part of 16-month-olds compared with 13-month-olds. Controlling the variance associated with differential learning of the event sequences yielded some qualifications to this conclusion. As had been the case for the children tested on four-step event sequences, when the children tested on three-step sequences were prompted by the event-related props alone, age effects were observed. The only exception was in the 6-month delay condition, on mixed event sequences. In contrast, when the children were prompted by the event-related props and by the verbal labels for the event sequences, age effects were observed in the 1-month, but not in the 3- and 6-month delay conditions. This pattern of post-reminder performance is the opposite of that observed among the children tested on four-step event sequences, for whom age-related differences were more apparent at the longer, rather than the shorter, retention intervals.

Differences in the 13-month-olds' and the 16-month-olds' problem-solving abilities were apparent prior to introduction of the verbal labels for the event sequences; they were not apparent after introduction of the verbal labels. To determine whether differential problem-solving abilities might explain the age-related differences in children's pre-reminder recall of the individual target actions of the event sequences, we conducted analyses of covariance controlling for that source of variance. For events previously imitated, the pattern of results was highly similar to that obtained when differential initial learning was controlled. Specifically, age effects were apparent in the 1- and 3-month delay conditions, and in the 6-month delay condition on enabling event sequences. For events previously only watched, age effects were apparent across delay conditions and sequence types. For events previously imitated, controlling both for the variance associated with differential problem-solving abilities and for differential initial learning produced a pattern identical to that obtained when only the variance associated with differential problem-solving abilities was controlled.

Sequence Type Effects

Differential Initial Learning

To determine whether differences in children's initial learning of the event sequences might account for the observed sequence type effects, we conducted analyses of covariance on children's delayed recall performance with their immediate recall performance as covariates. For the variable of production of the individual target actions of the event sequences, as noted above, both prior to and after provision of the verbal labels for the event sequences, there were interactions of Delay × Age × Sequence type (values provided above). For the 13-month-olds, there were no qualifications to the effects in the analyses of variance: Main effects revealed that both prior to and after introduction of the verbal reminders, the younger children's levels of production of the individual target actions of the enabling and arbitrarily ordered event sequences were equivalent and greater than levels of production of the individual target actions of the mixed event sequences [$Fs(2,101)$ = 14.20 and 9.63, $ps < .0001$, $MSEs$ = 0.67 and 0.65, for prior to and after verbal reminders, respectively].

For the 16-month-olds, when the children were prompted by the event-related props alone, controlling for levels of initial learning produced no qualification to the effect observed in the analysis of variance: The main effect revealed that children produced a larger number of individual target actions of the enabling relative to the mixed event sequences; the number of individual target actions of the arbitrarily ordered event sequences produced was intermediate and did not differ from the other two sequence types [$F(2,101)$ = 5.44, $p < .006$, MSE = 0.75]. With the variance associated with differential initial learning of the event sequences controlled, the same effect was apparent in children's post-reminder performance [$F(2,101)$ = 4.26, $p < .02$, MSE = 0.68].

In terms of the number of pairs of actions produced in the target order, the analyses of covariance provided no qualifications to the main effects observed in the analyses of variance. Specifically, both prior to and after provision of the verbal labels for the event sequences, the analyses of covariance revealed main effects of sequence type: $Fs(2,135)$ = 10.68 and 7.63, $ps < .0007$, $MSEs$ = 0.35 and 0.35, respectively. The children produced a larger number of pairs of actions in the target order on the event sequences that were wholly constrained by enabling relations, relative to the event sequences that were only partially constrained by enabling relations, or that were not characterized by enabling relations. Ordered recall performance on the mixed and arbitrarily ordered event sequences did not differ reliably.

Differential Problem-Solving Abilities

As had been the case for the children tested on four-step event sequences, the analyses of variance of children's performance on event sequences new to them at Session 4 revealed no effects of sequence type. That is, neither main effects of sequence type nor interactions involving sequence type indicated that children were differentially successful at "figuring out" either the individual target actions or the temporal order of actions of the different sequences types, either before or after provision of the verbal labels for the events. For this reason, we do not report results of analyses of covariance controlling for sequence-type-related differential effects of problem solving. The absence of sequence type effects in children's problem solving also renders unnecessary analyses simultaneously controlling for differential initial learning and differential problem solving.

Summary of Sources of Sequence Type Effects

The analyses of covariance suggest that, for both age groups, children's memories for the individual target actions of the enabling event sequences were more robust than their memories for the actions of the mixed event sequences. The indication was apparent both when children were prompted by the event-related props alone and when they were prompted by the props and the verbal labels for the event sequences. For the younger age group only, children's memories for the individual target actions of the arbitrarily ordered event sequences also were more robust than their memories for the actions of the mixed event sequences. Again, the effect was apparent both prior to and after provision of the verbal reminders of the events. For neither age group were there indications of differentially robust memories for the individual target actions of the enabling and arbitrarily ordered event sequences.

With regard to children's memories for the temporal order of the actions of the event sequences, the analyses of covariance controlling for differential initial learning produced no qualifications to the effects obtained in the analyses of variance. That is, there were indications of more robust memory for the temporal order of actions of event sequences constrained by enabling relations, relative to event sequences only partially or wholly unconstrained by enabling relations. It seems that we are on firm ground when we conclude that, for children tested on three-step event sequences, memory for the temporal order of events is more robust for event sequences wholly constrained by enabling relations, relative to event sequences that are partially or totally unconstrained by enabling relations.

PATTERNS OF FORGETTING

As for the children tested on four-step event sequences, to evaluate the amount of information that the 13-month-olds and 16-month-olds tested on three-step events forgot over the various delay intervals we conducted Recall condition (immediate, after verbal reminder) × Delay × Sequence type mixed analyses of variance for both dependent measures (see Tables 5 and 6 for relevant means). Because children showed evidence of recall of the individual target actions in the 1-, 3-, and 6-month delay conditions, the analysis of that variable included three levels of delay; because the children showed evidence of recall of the temporal order of the event sequences in the 1- and 3-month delay conditions only, the analysis of that variable included two levels of delay. Because of differential levels of initial learning by the 16-month-olds and 13-month-olds, we conducted separate analyses for each age group.

For the 16-month-old children, for both dependent measures, main effects of delay and recall condition were qualified by their interaction: $F(2,51)$ = 22.44, p < .0001, MSE = 0.39, for individual target actions; $F(2,34)$ = 12.78, p < .002, MSE = 0.42, for pairs of actions in target order. Separate analyses at each delay condition revealed that, for both dependent measures, forgetting was apparent at delays of longer than 1 month: $Fs(1,17)$ = 39.30 and 137.01, ps < .0001, $MSEs$ = 0.20 and 0.11, for individual target actions in the 3- and 6-month delay conditions, respectively; $F(1,17)$ = 27.54, p < .0001, MSE = 0.15, for pairs of actions in target order in the 3-month delay condition. In the 1-month delay condition, for the variable of production of individual target actions, the effect fell below the conventional level of statistical significance: $F(1,17)$ = 4.21, p < .06, MSE = 0.07. For the variable of production of pairs of action in the target order, the effect was not significant: $F(1,17)$ = 0.22, p > 0.60. Thus, there was a trend toward forgetting of the individual target actions over the delay [Ms = 2.81 and 2.63 (SDs = 0.31 and 0.48), for immediate and delayed recall, respectively]; there was no evidence of forgetting of the order of the actions over the 1-month delay [Ms = 1.22 and 1.17 (SDs = 0.36 and 0.45), for immediate and delayed recall, respectively].

For both dependent measures, there also were interactions of Recall condition × Sequence type: $F(2,102)$ = 3.42, p < .04, MSE = 0.34, for individual target actions; $F(2,68)$ = 4.94, p < .01, MSE = 0.32, for pairs of actions in target order. Separate analyses for each sequence type revealed evidence of 16-month-olds' forgetting of the individual target actions of all three sequence types: $Fs(1,106)$ = 27.43, 41.06, and 24.02, ps < .0001, $MSEs$ = 0.39, 0.71, and 0.65, for enabling, mixed, and arbitrarily ordered event sequences, respectively [Ms after provision of the verbal reminders = 2.28, 1.81, and 2.04 (SDs = 0.81, 1.08, and 1.06); Ms at immediate testing = 2.91, 2.85, and 2.80 (SDs = 0.35, 0.49, and 0.41), for enabling, mixed, and arbitrary, respectively]. There was evidence of forgetting of pairs of actions in the target order of the enabling and mixed event sequences: $Fs(1,70)$ = 12.67 and 11.21, p < .002, $MSEs$ = 0.41 and 0.45, for enabling and mixed, respectively; the effect of recall condition was not reliable for the arbitrarily ordered event sequences, indicating no significant forgetting of the temporal order of arbitrarily ordered event sequences over the delays [Ms after provision of the verbal reminders = 1.22, 0.83, and 0.81 (SDs = 0.76, 0.70, and 0.71); Ms at immediate testing = 1.78, 1.36, and 0.83 (SDs = 0.48, 0.64, and 0.56), for enabling, mixed, and arbitrary, respectively].

For the 13-month-old children, for both variables, main effects of recall were qualified by interactions with delay: $F(2,51)$ = 9.14, p < .0004, MSE = 0.75, for individual target actions; $F(1,34)$ = 5.94, p < .02, MSE = 0.41, for pairs of actions in target order. Separate analyses for each delay

119

condition revealed no evidence of forgetting over the 1-month delay. That is, 13-month-old children's levels of production of individual target actions and pairs of actions in the target order after provision of the verbal reminders [Ms = 1.98 and 0.76 (SDs = 0.67 and 0.48), respectively] were not significantly different from those in evidence at immediate recall testing [Ms = 2.13 and 0.85 (SDs = 0.76 and 0.49), for individual target actions and pairs of actions in target order, respectively]. In the 3- and 6-month delay conditions, there was evidence of forgetting of the individual target actions of the event sequences: $Fs(1,17)$ = 42.32 and 33.57, ps < .006, $MSEs$ = 0.24 and 0.26, for the 3- and 6-month delay conditions, respectively; in the 3-month delay condition, there was evidence of forgetting of the temporal order of the event sequences: $F(1,17)$ = 13.12, p < .006, MSE = 0.18.

For the variable of number of individual target actions produced, the interaction of Recall condition × Sequence type was reliable: $F(2,102)$ = 3.82, p < .03, MSE = 0.56. Separate analyses for each sequence type revealed evidence of 13-month-olds' forgetting of the individual target actions of all three sequence types: $Fs(1,106)$ = 12.09, 31.88, and 10.05, ps < .002, $MSEs$ = 0.74, 0.94, and 0.85, for enabling, mixed, and arbitrarily ordered, respectively [Ms after provision of the verbal reminders = 1.85, 1.19, and 1.72 (SDs = 0.86, 0.97, and 0.98); Ms at immediate testing = 2.43, 2.24, and 2.28 (SDs = 0.86, 0.97, and 0.86), for enabling, mixed, and arbitrary, respectively]. There were no other significant effects involving recall condition, for either dependent measure.

SAVINGS IN RELEARNING

To determine whether there was evidence of savings in relearning, we conducted 5 (delay) × 2 (age) × 3 (sequence type) × 3 (experience) mixed analyses of variance, for both dependent measures. In terms of the number of individual target actions produced, although the interaction of Age × Experience was statistically significant, $F(2,340)$ = 3.20, p < .05, MSE = 0.39, separate analyses for each group revealed that performance in the three experience conditions did not differ reliably. Thus, there was no evidence of savings in relearning of the individual target actions of the previously experienced events. On the variable of number of pairs of actions produced in the target order, there was neither a main effect of nor any interactions involving the factor experience. There was no evidence, then, of savings in relearning of either the individual target actions or the temporal order of the actions of the event sequences. (Details on mean levels of performance in each cell of the design are available from PJB.)

V. SIXTEEN-MONTH-OLDS TESTED ON FOUR-STEP EVENT SEQUENCES COMPARED WITH 16-MONTH-OLDS TESTED ON THREE-STEP EVENT SEQUENCES

The analyses just described indicate that, overall, the immediate and long-term recall performance of the 16-month-olds tested on four-step event sequences and of the 16-month-olds tested on three-step event sequences was affected in similar ways by the factors investigated in this research. For example, the recall of both groups of 16-month-olds was facilitated by provision of verbal reminders of the event sequences and neither group was profoundly affected by whether they had been provided the opportunity to imitate the event sequences prior to the delay. Nevertheless, one glaring difference between the two groups of same-age children emerged. Whereas the children tested on four-step event sequences showed evidence of recall of both the individual target actions and the temporal order of actions of the event sequences at all delay intervals, the children tested on three-step event sequences showed evidence of recall of the individual target actions of the event sequences for only 6 months, and recall of the temporal order of the actions of the event sequences for only 3 months. There are several possible reasons for this dramatic difference in the performance of the two groups of 16-month-olds, each of which is examined in turn below.

UNCONTROLLED DIFFERENCES BETWEEN COMPOSITION OR TREATMENT OF THE FOUR-STEP AND THREE-STEP GROUPS

One possible explanation for the differences in long-term recall performance by the 16-month-olds tested on four-step event sequences and their peers tested on three-step event sequences is uncontrolled differences in the composition of the groups at the time of enrollment. We deem this an unlikely explanation. First, as reported in Chapter II (Method and Analytic Strategy), the two groups of 16-month-olds did not differ in age at the time of enrollment in the study. Second, at the time of enrollment, using the MacArthur Productive Vocabulary Checklist for Infants, we collected from the parents of the majority of the sample information on the children's productive vocabulary. In total, we had completed inventories on 167 of our 180 16-month-olds. To determine whether random assignment to groups inadvertently resulted in differences between the three-step and the four-step groups, we conducted a 2 (group: 16-month-olds tested on three-step event sequences, 16-month-olds tested on four-step event sequences) × 5 (delay: 1 month, 3 month, 6 month, 9 month, 12 month) between-subjects analysis of variance on children's reported productive vocabulary. The analysis revealed that the groups were closely matched on reported productive vocabulary [Ms = 43.54 and 46.95 (SDs = 58.82 and 55.89), for three-step and four-step groups, respectively]. Moreover, the interaction of Group × Delay was not reliable, thus indicating that there was no systematic relation between step-length group and delay condition. Uncontrolled differences between the two groups of 16-month-olds does not then appear to be a likely explanation for the observed differences in performance.

Another possible explanation for the apparent differences in long-term retention is that the two groups of 16-month-olds were treated differently in terms of the lengths of delays between exposure sessions or the lengths of delays between the final exposure and the delayed recall test sessions. However, as reported in Chapter II (Method and Analytic Strategy), the two groups did not differ on these features. Thus, differential treatment is not a viable explanation for the apparent differences in the performance of the two groups of 16-month-olds.

DIFFERENTIAL INITIAL LEARNING OF THE EVENT SEQUENCES

Group differences in levels of mastery of the to-be-remembered material is another potential explanation for the apparent differences in length of long-term retention by the two groups of 16-month-olds. Specifically, it is possible that the children tested on three-step event sequences learned the to-be-remembered material less well, relative to their peers exposed to four-step event sequences. The previous sections made clear that levels of initial learning impacted long-term retention, making this possibility a source of potential concern.

To evaluate levels of initial learning, we conducted 2 (group) × 5 (delay) × 3 (sequence type: enabling, mixed, arbitrary) mixed analyses of variance on the proportion of individual target actions produced and the proportion of pairs of actions produced in the target order at immediate testing. It was necessary to use proportions, rather than raw scores, because the children were tested on sequences of different lengths. The analyses yielded group effects: Fs$(1,170)$ = 19.80 and 14.43, ps < .0002, MSEs = 0.05 and 0.11, for individual target actions and pairs of actions in the target order, respectively. In both cases, the 16-month-olds tested on three-step event sequences demonstrated proportionally higher levels of performance, relative to their peers tested on four-step event sequences [M proportions for individual target actions = 0.94 and 0.85 (SDs = 0.16 and 0.21); M proportions for pairs of actions in the target order = 0.63 and 0.52 (SDs = 0.34 and 0.28), for three-step and four-step, respectively]. There were no interactions involving the variable group. These analyses indicate that greater initial mastery of the to-be-remembered material by the 16-month-olds tested on four-step event sequences, relative to their peers tested on three-step event sequences, is an unlikely explanation for the observed differences in long-term recall performance.

DIFFERENTIAL LONG-TERM RETENTION OF THE EVENT SEQUENCES

As reviewed above, the conclusion that the 16-month-olds tested on three-step and four-step event sequences remembered the material for different amounts of time was based on differential relations between their performances on previously experienced and new event sequences. The source of the difference in conclusions drawn thus could reside either in children's performance on previously experienced event sequences or in their performance on the event sequences that were new to them. It is critical to determine the locus of the difference because different loci lead to different conclusions regarding the factors that affect long-term memory. If the two groups of 16-month-olds differed in terms of their levels of performance on previously experienced event sequences, that would suggest that it was "easier" to remember four-step event sequences relative to three-step event sequences. If, however, the two groups differed in terms of their levels of performance on the event sequences that were new to them at the time of delayed testing, that would suggest that it was more difficult to detect memory in the group of children tested on three-step event sequences, relative to the group tested on four-step event sequences: Higher levels of performance on new event sequences makes obtaining a reliable difference between performance on previously experienced and new event sequences less likely. To determine the locus or loci of differences between the two groups of 16-month-olds, in separate analyses, we evaluated their performance on previously experienced and on new event sequences.

To determine whether, at delayed recall, the 16-month-olds tested on three-step event sequences had lower levels of performance on events previously experienced, relative to the 16-month-olds tested on four-step event sequences, we conducted 2 (group) × 5 (delay) × 3 (sequence type) × 2 (experience condition: imitate, watch) mixed analyses of variance on the proportion of individual target actions produced and the proportion of pairs of actions produced in the target order. We conducted parallel analyses before and after provision of the verbal reminders of the event sequences. All four analyses revealed main effects of group as well as Group × Delay × Sequence type interactions: $Fs(8,340)$ = 2.69, 2.59, 2.31, and 2.14, $ps < .04$, $MSEs$ = 0.06, 0.07, 0.06, and 0.07, for individual target actions before and after verbal reminders and pairs of actions in the target order before and after verbal reminders, respectively. Separate analyses for each delay condition revealed that, without exception, the 16-month-olds tested on three-step event sequences performed at levels that were either greater than or did not differ from the levels of performance of the 16-month-olds tested on four-step event sequences. The patterns remained the same when, via analyses of covariance, we controlled levels of immediate recall performance. These findings make clear that on event sequences to which they previously had been exposed, the 16-month-olds tested on three-step event sequences were not performing at lower levels relative to their peers tested on four-step event sequences.

To determine whether the 16-month-olds tested on three-step events had higher levels of performance on event sequences new to them at the time delayed recall was tested, relative to the 16-month-olds tested on four-step event sequences, we conducted 2 (group) × 5 (delay) × 3 (sequence type) mixed analyses of variance on the proportion of individual target actions produced and the proportion of pairs of actions produced in the target order. We conducted parallel analyses before and after provision of the verbal suggestions of plausible event sequences. In terms of the number of individual target actions produced, the analyses revealed main effects of group: $Fs(1,170)$ = 44.52 and 58.88, $ps < .0001$, $MSEs$ = 0.06 and 0.07, for before and after verbal suggestions, respectively. Relative to their peers tested on four-step event sequences, the 16-month-olds tested on three-step event sequences had proportionally higher levels of production of the individual target actions of the new event sequences [M proportions before verbal suggestions = 0.35 and 0.21 (SDs = 0.29 and 0.19); M proportions after verbal suggestions = 0.46 and 0.29 (SDs = 0.31 and 0.23), for three-step and four-step, respectively]. Whereas for children's production of the individual target actions of the event sequences prior to provision of the verbal suggestions, group interacted with delay, $F(4,170)$ = 2.60, $p < .04$, MSE = 0.06, follow-up analyses revealed that in each delay condition, the performance of the 16-month-olds tested on three-step event sequences either was greater than performance of the 16-month-olds tested on four-step event sequences (1-, 3-, 9-, and 12-month delay conditions) or did not differ from performance of the 16-month-olds tested on four-step event sequences (6-month delay condition). Thus, the interaction produced no qualification of the main effect.

In terms of the number of pairs of actions produced in the target order, the analyses revealed main effects of group: $Fs(1,170) = 29.27$ and 32.94, $ps < .0001$, $MSEs = 0.02$ and 0.04, for before and after verbal suggestions, respectively. Relative to their peers tested on four-step event sequences, the 16-month-olds tested on three-step event sequences had proportionally higher levels of production of pairs of actions in the target order of the new event sequences [M proportions before verbal suggestions = 0.10 and 0.03 (SDs = 0.21 and 0.10); M proportions after verbal suggestions = 0.17 and 0.07 (SDs = 0.26 and 0.15), for three-step and four-step, respectively]. When the variance associated with children's production of the individual target actions of the event sequences was controlled, the main effects of group were no longer statistically reliable.

The finding of an advantage in deducing or inferring the individual target actions and likely order of actions of three-step relative to four-step event sequences, coupled with that of equivalent or higher levels of performance on previously experienced events by children tested on three-step compared with four-step event sequences, leads to an important conclusion regarding the mnemonic competence of the 16-month-olds in the two different step-length groups. The findings suggest that the long-term retention abilities of the two groups of 16-month-olds were roughly comparable, but that in the case of the children tested on three-step event sequences, mnemonic competence was more difficult to detect, due to proportionally higher levels of performance on event sequences new to the children at Session 4.

VI. PREDICTIONS OF LONG-TERM MNEMONIC PERFORMANCE

In this section we present the results of regression analyses examining the proportion of variance in long-term recall performance that is associated with each of a number of potential predictor variables. Because the regressions were exploratory, we elected to use step-wise procedures. To avoid an excessive number of analyses we conducted them on the means for events previously imitated and events previously only watched, after exposure to the verbal reminders, collapsed across sequence type. This approach was justified because whether or not the children had been permitted to imitate the event sequences prior to imposition of the delay periods had little effect on conclusions regarding whether or not they subsequently recalled the event sequences, and reminding had relatively uniform effects across all cells of the design. Moreover, although there were some effects associated with sequence type, with few exceptions, conclusions as to whether or not the children remembered the event sequences over the delays imposed were consistent across sequence types. These consistencies in performance permit elimination of the factors of experience condition, reminding condition, and sequence type from these exploratory analyses.

The predictor variables that we examined included (a) age at the time of exposure to the event sequences, (b) the number of steps in the to-be-remembered event sequences, (c) the child's gender, (d) the child's level of productive vocabulary at the time of exposure to the to-be-remembered event sequences,[4] (e) experimenter, (f) the delay interval imposed, (g) performance in baseline, (h) performance at immediate testing, and (i) performance on the event sequences new to the children at Session 4. Because the predictive utility of a given variable might differ

---

[4]Inclusion of children's productive vocabulary at the time of enrollment resulted in loss of degrees of freedom because the productive language estimate was not available for all participants. Because the number of missing values differed across delay conditions, available degrees of freedom also varied.

over different retention intervals, we conducted the regression analyses both across delay conditions and for each delay condition separately. In each analysis, the dependent measure was the proportion of individual target actions produced or the proportion of pairs of actions produced in the target order. Use of proportion scores was necessary, since half of the children were tested on four-step event sequences and half of the children were tested on three-step event sequences.

PROPORTION OF INDIVIDUAL TARGET ACTIONS PRODUCED

Across delay intervals, the variables that proved to be predictive of children's production of the individual target actions of the event sequences at delayed recall were (in order of entry into the regression equation) (i) the delay imposed ($R^2 = .13$), (ii) children's immediate recall performance (cumulative $R^2 = .20$), (iii) children's performance on the event sequences new at Session 4 (cumulative $R^2 = .25$), (iv) children's level of productive vocabulary (cumulative $R^2 = .27$), (v) the number of steps in the to-be-remembered event sequences (cumulative $R^2 = .28$), and (vi) children's age at the time of exposure to the to-be-remembered event sequences (cumulative $R^2 = .32$): $F(6,329) = 25.75$, $p < .0001$. Across delay conditions, the factors that facilitated recall of the individual target actions of the event sequences thus included higher levels of initial learning of the individual target actions of the event sequences, higher levels of problem-solving ability, and larger reported productive vocabulary, all of which are associated with the final positive predictor, namely, older age at the time of exposure to the event sequences. The factors that represented challenges to children's recall were long delays between exposure to and test for recall of the event sequences and being tested on longer four-step versus shorter three-step event sequences. With the exception of reported productive vocabulary at the time of exposure to the event sequences, each of the variables contributed unique variance even after the variance associated with all of the other predictor variables had been removed.

Separate analyses for each delay condition revealed that the factors that predicted retention of event-related information over time varied as a function of the length of the delay imposed. In the 1-month delay condition the only significant predictors of long-term recall were (i) level of initial learning of the individual target actions of the event sequences ($R^2 = .34$), and (ii) children's problem-solving abilities at the time delayed recall was tested (cumulative $R^2 = .38$): $F(2,64) = 19.88$, $p < .0001$. Once the variance associated with all of the other potential predictor variables had been removed, only level of initial learning contributed unique variance.

In the 3-month delay condition, the predictors of the number of individual target actions that the children produced at delayed recall were (i) baseline levels of performance (R^2 = .15), (ii) children's reported level of productive vocabulary (cumulative R^2 = .21), (iii) the number of steps in the to-be-remembered event sequences (cumulative R^2 = .28), and (iv) age at the time of exposure to the event sequences (cumulative R^2 = .37): $F(4,62)$ = 9.12, p < .0001. Spontaneous production of the target actions of the event sequences, step length, and age each contributed unique variance even after that associated with all of the other potential predictor variables had been accounted for.

In the 6-month delay condition, the predictors of retention were (i) level of initial learning of the individual target actions of the event sequences (R^2 = .15), (ii) children's problem-solving abilities at the time delayed recall was tested (cumulative R^2 = .20), and (iii) the number of steps in the to-be-remembered event sequences (cumulative R^2 = .28): $F(3,64)$ = 6.37, p < .0002. After the variance associated with all of the other potential predictor variables had been removed, only level of initial learning contributed unique variance.

In the 9-month delay condition, the predictors of retention were (i) children's problem-solving abilities at the time delayed recall was tested (R^2 = .21), and (ii) level of initial learning of the individual target actions of the event sequences (cumulative R^2 = .38): $F(2,65)$ = 20.03, p < .0001. Both variables contributed unique variance even after that associated with all of the other potential predictor variables had been removed.

In the 12-month delay condition, the predictors of retention were (i) the number of steps in the to-be-remembered event sequences (R^2 = .23), and (ii) children's age at the time of exposure to the event sequences (cumulative R^2 to .32): $F(2,61)$ = 14.53, p < .0001. However, when the variance associated with all of the other potential predictor variables had been removed, only step length remained as a unique predictor.

PROPORTION OF PAIRS OF ACTIONS PRODUCED IN THE TARGET ORDER

Across delay intervals, the predictors of the amount of temporal order information that children retained were (i) delay imposed (R^2 = .12), (ii) immediate recall performance (cumulative R^2 = .18), (iii) performance on the new event sequences (cumulative R^2 = .20), (iv) children's age at the time of exposure to the event sequences (cumulative R^2 to .22), and (v) the number of steps in the to-be-remembered event sequence (cumulative R^2 to .26): $F(5,330)$ = 23.66, p < .0001. Each of the variables contributed unique variance above and beyond that contributed by all of the other potential predictor variables.

As was the case for the variable of production of individual target actions, separate analyses for each delay condition revealed that the factors that predicted retention of temporal order information over time varied as a function of the length of the delay imposed. In the 1-month delay condition significant predictors of long-term ordered recall were (i) level of initial learning of the temporal order in which the event sequences occurred (R^2 = .32), (ii) children's problem-solving abilities at the time delayed recall was tested (cumulative R^2 = .36), and (iii) children's reported productive vocabulary at the time of exposure to the event sequences (cumulative R^2 = .41): $F(3,64)$ = 14.70, $p < .0001$. Once the variance associated with all of the other potential predictor variables had been accounted for, only level of initial learning and reported productive vocabulary contributed unique variance.

In the 3-month delay condition, the predictors of children's ordered recall were (i) reported productive vocabulary at the time of exposure to the event sequences (R^2 = .12), and (ii) baseline levels of production of pairs of actions in the target order (cumulative R^2 = .21): $F(2,64)$ = 8.61, $p < .0005$. Both variables predicted unique variance even after that associated with all of the other predictor variables had been removed.

In the 6-month delay condition, age (R^2 = .16) and the number of steps in the to-be-remembered event sequences (cumulative R^2 = .22) were the only variables to enter into the regression equation: $F(2,66)$ = 9.52, $p < .0002$. With the variance associated with all of the other potential predictor variables removed, age alone contributed unique variance. Similarly, in the 9-month delay condition, whereas (i) children's problem-solving abilities at the time delayed recall was tested (R^2 = .08), (ii) age at the time of exposure to the event sequences (cumulative R^2 = .14), and (iii) the number of steps in the event sequences (cumulative R^2 = .19) all entered into the equation [$F(3,64)$ = 5.03, $p < .004$], after the variance associated with all of the other potential predictor variables had been accounted for, age alone contributed unique variance. Finally, in the 12-month delay condition (i) the number of steps in the event sequences (R^2 = .08) and (ii) children's age at the time of exposure to the event sequences (cumulative R^2 = .17) both entered into the equation: $F(2,61)$ = 6.07, $p < .004$; both variables contributed unique variance even after that accounted for by all other potential predictor variables had been removed.

SUMMARY

The regression analyses revealed that, across delay conditions, the most significant predictors both of the proportion of individual target actions produced and the proportion of pairs of actions produced in the target order at delayed testing were (a) the amount of time over which event-related information had to be retained, (b) how well memory for the event sequences was instantiated before the delay, and (c) in this particular paradigm, children's problem-solving abilities at the time their long-term recall was tested. Also contributing unique variance were (d) the number of steps in the to-be-remembered event sequences, and (e) children's age at the time of exposure to the to-be-remembered event sequences. Separate analyses by delay condition revealed not only that the variables that proved to be significant in predicting children's performance varied across delays, but that they varied across dependent measures as well.

In terms of the number of individual target actions produced, children's levels of initial mastery of the to-be-remembered event sequences predicted unique variance in the 1-, 6-, and 9-month delay conditions. It was the only significant predictor in the 1- and 6-month delay conditions. In contrast, children's initial level of acquisition of the temporal order of the event sequences predicted unique variance only at the shortest retention interval (i.e., in the 1-month delay condition). Conversely, whereas children's age at the time of exposure to the event sequences predicted unique variance in their production of temporally ordered pairs of actions in the 6-, 9-, and 12-month delay conditions, and was the only unique predictor in the 6- and 9-month delay conditions, only in the 3-month delay condition did age account for unique variance in children's delayed recall of the individual target actions of the event sequences. These patterns indicate that age-related changes and developments play a larger role in maintenance and subsequent retrieval of temporally ordered event representations, relative to the role played in retention of information about individual target actions. The role of age-related changes and developments in supporting maintenance and subsequent retrieval is most apparent at the longer retention intervals. Even at longer delay intervals, what is most important for retention of the individual elements of the event sequences is a high level of initial mastery of them.

There are three final comments to be made regarding the results of the regression analyses predicting children's long-term recall performance. First, two of the variables that we included in the regression analyses, namely, the child's gender and the experimenter who conducted the testing sessions, failed to account for any significant variance in children's performance. Thus, although we observed some differences in performance as a function of children's gender and the experimenter by whom they were tested (see Appendix C: Potential Effects on Children's Performance of Child Language and Gender and Appendix B: Potential Effects on Children's Performance of Features of the Research Design, respectively), the differences apparently were of negligible consequence.

Second, the pattern of prediction of the performance of the children in the 3-month delay condition was different from that of all of the other delay conditions. This was true for both dependent measures. Because delay condition was a between-subjects variable, it is impossible to know whether the atypical pattern is a function of differences among the children in the 3-month delay condition, compared with the children in the other delay conditions, or whether it is a function of performance after a delay of 3 months, compared with performance after a shorter or longer delay.

Third, the variables that we entered into the regression equations combined to account for between 28% and 38% of the variance in children's long-term recall of the individual target actions of the event sequences. The cumulative proportion of variance accounted for was relatively constant across the different retention intervals (i.e., 38%, 37%, 28%, 38%, and 32%, for the 1-, 3-, 6-, 9-, and 12-month delay conditions, respectively). In contrast, the proportion of variance in children's delayed recall production of pairs of actions in the target order varied from as little as 17% to as much as 41%. The cumulative proportion of variance accounted for was largest at the shortest retention interval and decreased with increasingly delay (i.e., 41%, 21%, 22%, 19%, and 17%, for the 1-, 3-, 6-, 9-, and 12-month delay conditions, respectively). These differences likely are at least in part the result of the greater variability at the longer delays in children's production of individual target actions, relative to their variability in production of pairs of action in the target order (i.e., levels of production of ordered pairs of actions were more uniformly low as the length of the delay interval increased).

VII. SUMMARY AND INTERPRETATION OF MAJOR FINDINGS

In this research we tested the ability of children 13, 16, and 20 months of age at the time of exposure to specific target event sequences to remember the events over delay intervals of 1, 3, 6, 9, and 12 months. All of the 20-month-olds and half of the 16-month-olds were tested on event sequences four steps in length; half of the 16-month-olds and all of the 13-month-olds were tested on event sequences three steps in length. For each step-length group, equal numbers of event sequences were completely constrained by enabling relations among the individual elements ("enabling" events), partially constrained by enabling relations among the individual elements ("mixed" events), and totally unconstrained by enabling relations ("arbitrary" events). Children were exposed to each event sequence at three sessions, each of which was spaced 1 week apart. At the final exposure session, they were permitted to imitate one sequence of each type ("imitate" experience condition); the other sequence of each type they were only permitted to watch ("watch" experience condition).

When the children returned after their appointed delays of 1 to 12 months, they first experienced a response period during which their recall was prompted by the event-related props alone. The children then were provided with verbal reminders of the event sequences in the form of verbal labels for them. Finally, after the delayed recall periods, each event sequence was demonstrated and the children had the opportunity to imitate, thereby allowing for assessment of savings in relearning of the sequences to which the children previously had been exposed. Because the major questions in this report concern children's performance after imposition of the 1- to 12-month delays, we concentrate in this summary on the long-term recall patterns observed and on the factors that affected children's remembering and forgetting.

Children's performance after the delays was evaluated in two ways. First, for each step-length group, we determined the retention interval over which recall was apparent. By the time delayed recall was tested in this research, some of the children were as much as 1 year older than they had been at the time of their first experience of the event sequences. For this reason, as our means of establishing whether or not the children remembered the event sequences, we used comparisons of children's performance on the event sequences to which they previously had been exposed (three event sequences in the imitate experience condition and three event sequences in the watch experience condition; in each experience condition, one sequence of each type [enabling, mixed, arbitrary]) with their performance on three event sequences that were new to the children at the time delayed recall was tested (one sequence of each type; "new" experience condition). Evidence of recall was derived from higher levels of performance on events that the children previously had been permitted to imitate compared with new events, and from higher levels of performance on events previously only watched compared with new event sequences (see Tables 3 and 6 for relevant means for the children tested on four-step and three-step event sequences, respectively). Second, for the delay intervals at which retention of event-related information was apparent, we examined how the factors of interest in this research affected recall of the event sequences that the children had the opportunity to imitate prior to imposition of the delays and of the event sequences that they had only watched. We discuss the effects on children's long-term recall of the variables of delay, age at the time of exposure to the event sequences, sequence type, mode of experience, availability of verbal reminders, and the length of the to-be-remembered event sequences, in turn.

EFFECTS OF DELAY

Whether prompted by the event-related props alone or by the props and verbal labels for the to-be-remembered events, the children tested on four-step sequences provided evidence that they recalled at least some of the individual target actions of the events that they experienced 1 to 12 months previously. The children remembered the individual target actions of the event sequences that they previously had been permitted to imitate and that they had only watched. Moreover, both before and after provision of verbal labels for the event sequences, in all delay conditions, the children tested on four-step event sequences showed evidence of temporally ordered recall of the event sequences that they had only watched. When prompted by the props alone, temporally ordered recall of the events that the children previously had been permitted to imitate was apparent in the 1-, 3-, and 6-month delay conditions. After provision of the verbal labels for the events, temporally ordered recall of sequences in the imitate condition was apparent in the 1-, 3-, 6-, and 12-month delay conditions. Although prior to provision of the verbal labels for the event sequences, girls' recall was in some cases more temporally restricted than that of boys, after provision of the verbal reminders, there were no effects of gender on the length of time over which recall was apparent (see Appendix C). The patterns of performance on previously experienced compared with new event sequences could not be attributed to children spending greater amounts of time manipulating the props associated with the event sequences that they had seen before relative to the event sequences that were new to them at the time delayed recall was tested (see Appendix B). Nor was evidence of recall of the previously experienced event sequences confined to specific sequences (see Appendix B).

Whereas among the children tested on four-step event sequences, evidence of recall of the individual target actions and of the temporal order of actions of the event sequences was apparent at even the longest retention interval, the children nevertheless forgot significant amounts of event-related information over the delays. Specifically, among the children tested on four-step event sequences, with one exception, performance after even 1 month was lower than performance at immediate testing (the exception was for 16-month-olds, among whom forgetting of the individual target actions of the event sequences was not apparent until 3 months). When the children were prompted by the event-related props alone, performance after the 1-month delay was greater than performance after the 3-, 6-, 9-, and 12-month delays; performance in the 3-, 6-, 9-, and 12-month delays did not differ. This pattern of a steep initial decline in performance, followed by a more shallow forgetting function, is consistent with existing research on recall over long delay intervals (e.g., Klein & Meltzoff, 1999; Meltzoff, 1995). With provision of verbal reminders for the event sequences, the decline in performance was somewhat more gradual (i.e., decreases in performance between 3 and 6 months as well as between 1 and 3 months).

Among the children tested on three-step event sequences, whether evaluated before or after the verbal reminders, evidence of recall of some of the individual target actions of the to-be-remembered event sequences was apparent in the 1-, 3-, and 6-month delay conditions, but not in the 9- and 12-month delay conditions. The length of time over which the children tested on three-step event sequences showed temporally ordered recall was even more restricted: Even after provision of verbal labels for the event sequences, the children showed evidence of ordered recall in the 1- and 3-month delay conditions only. When recall was apparent it could not be attributed to children spending greater amounts of time manipulating the props associated with the previously experienced event sequences relative to the event sequences that were new to them at Session 4 (see

Appendix B). Nor was evidence of recall of the previously experienced event sequences confined to specific sequences (see Appendix B).

Although, compared with the children tested on four-step sequences, the children tested on three-step sequences evidenced recall over a shorter absolute length of time, their initial rate of decline in performance was not as steep as that observed among the children tested on four-step events. As indexed by both dependent measures, relative to immediate testing, the children who experienced three-step events evidenced no significant decline in performance after a delay of 1 month. Performance after 3 months not only was lower than that at immediate testing (i.e., forgetting was in evidence), but also generally was lower than after 1 month. In addition, production of individual target actions after 6 months was either no different from (13-month-olds) or lower than (16-month-olds) production of individual target actions after 3 months. The apparently more rapid loss of event-related information by the children tested on the four-step compared with the three-step event sequences likely should be attributed to greater initial mastery of the shorter event sequences (see Chapter V for evidence consistent with this suggestion).

EFFECTS OF AGE AT THE TIME OF EXPOSURE TO THE EVENT SEQUENCES

There are four different sources of evidence with which to evaluate potential effects of children's age at the time of exposure to the event sequences on their ability to remember over the delays: (a) age-related differences in the lengths of time over which performance on old event sequences was greater than on new event sequences, (b) age-related differences in the sizes of differences between performance on old event sequences and new event sequences, (c) age-related differences in the reliability with which children in each step-length group performed at nominally higher levels on old event sequences than on new event sequences, and (d) age-related differences in absolute levels of performance on old event sequences. In neither step-length group was there evidence of age-related differences in the lengths of time over which performance on old event sequences was greater than on new event sequences. In contrast, the other three sources of evidence of effects of age at the time of exposure to the event sequences were apparent in both step-length groups.

For the children tested on four-step sequences, evidence of effects of age at the time of exposure to the events was particularly apparent prior to introduction of the verbal labels for the events. When the children were prompted by the event-related props alone, for both dependent measures, the sizes of the differences in performance on old and new event

135

sequences were larger for the 20-month-olds than for the 16-month-olds. In addition, for the older age group, the number of children whose relative levels of production of ordered pairs of actions of previously experienced event sequences and of new event sequences was indicative of recall was reliably greater than chance in all delay conditions. For the 16-month-olds, it was only in the 1- and 3-month delay conditions that a substantial and significant number of children showed nominally higher levels of ordered production on previously experienced event sequences relative to on new event sequences. Moreover, prior to introduction of the verbal reminders of the events, there were reliable age differences in children's absolute levels of production of both the individual target actions and the temporal order of actions of the old event sequences. The age effects were observed even when differential levels of initial learning, differential levels of problem-solving ability, or both, were controlled.

Introduction of the verbal reminders of the event sequences produced somewhat diminished, yet nevertheless apparent, age-related differences in the children's performance. Once again, the sizes of the differences in children's performance on old and new event sequences were larger for the 20-month-olds than for the 16-month-olds. However, with the aid of verbal reminders, the effect was apparent only on children's ordered recall. Second, for the 20-month-olds, the numbers of children whose relative levels of performance on previously experienced event sequences and on new event sequences were indicative of recall of the individual target actions of the events were reliably greater than chance in all but the 12-month delay condition. For the 16-month-olds, the number of children whose performance was indicative of recall of the individual target actions of the event sequences was reliably greater than chance in all but the 9-month delay condition. Age-related differences were apparent in patterns of ordered recall. A substantial and significant number of 20-month-olds produced nominally higher numbers of ordered pairs of actions on previously experienced event sequences than on new event sequences at all delay intervals. For the 16-month-olds, it was only in the 1-, 3-, and 6-month delay conditions that the numbers of children whose relative levels of performance on previously experienced events and on new events were indicative of ordered recall were reliably greater than chance. Finally, after introduction of the verbal reminders of the events, there were reliable age differences in children's absolute levels of production of both the individual target actions and the temporal order of actions of the old event sequences. For events previously only watched, the age effects were observed even when differential levels of problem-solving ability were controlled. For events that the children previously had been permitted to imitate, with differential levels of initial learning, differential levels of problem-solving ability, or both, controlled, age effects no longer were observed at the shorter retention intervals but nevertheless were apparent at the longer retention intervals of 9 and 12 months.

Whereas for the children tested on four-step event sequences, age-related effects were most obvious prior to introduction of the verbal reminders, for the children tested on three-step event sequences, age effects were in evidence both prior to and after introduction of the verbal reminders. First, when they were prompted by the event-related props alone and when they were prompted by the props and the verbal labels for the event sequences, the sizes of the differences in children's performance on old and new event sequences were larger for the 16-month-olds than for the 13-month-olds. The differences in the older and younger children's levels of performance were observed on both dependent measures.

Second, in terms of the number of individual target actions produced, prior to introduction of the verbal labels for the event sequences, for both the 16-month-olds and the 13-month-olds, the numbers of children whose relative levels of performance on old and new event sequences were indicative of recall were reliably greater than chance in the 1-, 3-, and 6-month delay conditions. After introduction of the verbal labels, the number of 16-month-olds evidencing the pattern indicative of recall of the individual target actions of the events also was reliable in the 12-month delay condition. In terms of the number of pairs of actions produced in the target order, for the 13-month-olds, prior to introduction of the verbal reminders, the numbers of children whose levels of performance on old event sequences were greater than on new event sequences were greater than chance in the 1- and 3-month delay conditions. After introduction of the verbal labels, the effect was above chance in the 1-month delay condition and approached significance in the 3-month delay condition. For the 16-month-olds, prior to reminding, the numbers of children whose levels of performance on old event sequences were greater than on new event sequences were greater than chance in the 1- and 3-month delay conditions; in the 6-month delay condition, the effect approached significance. With the aid of verbal reminders, the number of 16-month-olds evidencing recall was greater than chance in the 1-, 3-, and 6-month delay conditions. Thus, among the 16-month-olds the size of the difference between performance on previously experienced event sequences and on new events did not reach statistical significance in the 6-month delay condition. Nevertheless, the number of children whose performance on previously experienced events was larger than on new events was reliably greater than chance. In contrast, for the 13-month-olds, neither the sizes of the differences between performance on old and new event sequences nor the number of children exhibiting greater performance on old than on new events was indicative of ordered recall beyond 3 months.

Third, for children tested on three-step sequences, prior to introduction of the verbal reminders of the events, there were reliable age differences in children's absolute levels of production of the individual target actions of the old event sequences (but not on ordered pairs of actions). For events previously only watched, the age effects were observed even when differential levels of problem-solving ability were controlled. For events that the children had been permitted to imitate, even with differential levels of initial learning, differential levels of problem-solving ability, or both, controlled, the effect was observed for all but the mixed event sequences in the 6-month delay condition. After introduction of the verbal reminders of the event sequences, as they had for the children tested on four-step event sequences, for children tested on three-step event sequences, age effects diminished, such that they were apparent only in the 1-month delay condition.

With the exception of the age effect in the 1-month delay condition, the findings for the children tested on three-step event sequences are consistent with those for the children tested on four-step event sequences. In both cases, when the children were prompted by the event-related props alone, age effects were apparent, even when potentially confounding differential levels of initial learning and problem solving were controlled. When the children were prompted by the props and by the verbal labels for the event sequences, age effects were less obvious. For the children tested on four-step event sequences, they were most apparent on measures of children's ordered recall and they were more obvious at the longer, relative to the shorter, retention intervals. Likewise, for the children tested on three-step event sequences, age effects were most obvious in terms of the reliability of ordered recall: Whereas the number of 16-month-olds who produced nominally higher numbers of ordered pairs of actions on old events relative to new events was greater than chance after 1, 3, and 6 months, it was only in the 1-month (both prior to and after verbal labels) and 3-month (prior to verbal labels only) delay conditions that the pattern obtained for 13-month-olds.

The results of regression analyses are consistent with the suggestion that age-related effects on recall are especially evident at longer retention intervals. They also suggest that age-related effects are more apparent on children's ordered recall than on their recall of the individual target actions of event sequences. Specifically, in step-wise regression analyses, age emerged as a significant, and in some cases, as the sole, predictor of children's post-reminder performance at the longer retention intervals of 6, 9, and 12 months. Age was a more consistent predictor of children's ordered recall performance than of their production of the individual target actions of the event sequences. This finding complements the results of the analyses of the numbers of children in each age and step-length group for whom post-reminder performance on previously experienced events was greater than performance on new events. As summarized above, for temporally ordered recall, (a) the numbers of 20-month-old children who demonstrated the pattern were reliably different from chance at all retention intervals, (b) the numbers of 16-month-old children who demonstrated the pattern were reliable at the 1-, 3-, and 6-month retention intervals (observed among the children tested on three-step and four-step event sequences), and (c) the number of 13-month-old children who demonstrated the pattern was reliable only in the 1-month delay condition; in the 3-month delay condition, the effect approached significance. In contrast, there were not marked differences in the reliability with which recall of the individual target actions of the event sequences was observed among the younger and the older children in each step-length group.

EFFECTS OF SEQUENCE TYPE

The effects of the temporal structure of the to-be-remembered event sequences on children's delayed recall were different for the four-step compared with the three-step event sequences. For the children tested on four-step event sequences, the most striking finding was the virtual absence of sequence type effects on children's ordered recall. Prior to introduction of the verbal reminders for the event sequences, there were no effects of sequence type on ordered recall. After provision of the verbal reminders, the children tested on four-step event sequences produced a larger number of ordered pairs of actions on event sequences wholly constrained by enabling relations, relative to event sequences partially constrained by enabling relations. However, with the variance associated with differential initial learning of the event sequences controlled, the effect was apparent only in the 6-month delay condition, and then only among the 20-month-olds. Thus, even after only a 1-month delay, the children did not show what has become a common pattern in ordered recall performance when children are tested immediately or after a short delay (e.g., 1 week), namely, superior ordered recall of event sequences constrained by enabling relations, relative to event sequences that are arbitrarily ordered (see, for example, Barr & Hayne, 1996; Bauer & Dow, 1994; Bauer & Hertsgaard, 1993; Bauer, Hertsgaard, et al., 1998; Bauer & Travis, 1993). Although in contrast to the pattern observed when recall is tested after short delays, this pattern is consistent with that observed in Bauer et al. (1994), in which we found that after 8 months, sequence type effects were greatly diminished, even though they had been robust over the short term (i.e., at immediate and 1 week delayed testing).

Whereas sequence type was not observed to affect ordered recall by the children tested on four-step event sequences, there was some differential recall of the individual target actions of the different sequence types. The most consistent finding was of higher levels of production of the individual target actions of the arbitrarily ordered event sequences, relative to the sequences that were wholly or partially constrained by enabling relations; levels of production of the individual target actions of enabling and mixed event sequences did not differ. Even though higher levels of delayed recall of the individual target actions of the arbitrarily ordered event sequences, relative to the sequences with enabling relations, was not predicted, it was not unexpected. In previous related research, patterns of *ordered* recall have consistently favored event sequences the temporal orders of which were constrained by enabling relations. However, there has been no consistent pattern of relative levels of recall of the individual target actions of events with and without enabling relations. In some previous research, production of individual target actions has been higher on events with arbitrary temporal relations, relative to enabling event sequences (e.g., Bauer, 1992, Experiment 1; Bauer & Travis, 1993, Experiment 1; de Haan et al., 2000); in some previous research production of individual target actions has been higher on events with enabling relations, relative to arbitrarily ordered event sequences (e.g., Bauer & Hertsgaard, 1993, Experiment 2; Bauer, Hertsgaard, et al., 1998; Bauer et al., 1995, Experiments 1 and 2); and in some previous research, production of individual target actions on events with and without enabling relations has not differed reliably (e.g., Bauer & Hertsgaard, 1993, Experiment 1; Bauer & Mandler, 1989; Bauer & Travis, 1993, Experiment 2). Indeed, it appears that in a study of sufficient size (i.e., with a number of different groups, all tested on the same event sequences), the pattern of relative levels of production of the individual target actions of different types of event sequences is not even necessarily internally consistent: In the present case, in some delay conditions but not others, the children produced more of the individual target actions of the arbitrarily ordered event sequences relative to the enabling event sequences; in some delay conditions but not others, the children produced more of the individual target actions of the arbitrarily ordered event sequences relative to the mixed events.

For the children tested on three-step event sequences, the pattern of ordered recall performance was consistent with that observed in previous related research: Children produced a larger number of pairs of actions in the target order on sequences constrained by enabling relations than on sequences that were arbitrarily ordered. This pattern was observed even though in the 1- and 3-month delay conditions, the number of individual target actions that the children produced did not differ on the

arbitrary and enabling event sequences. For the girls in the sample, ordered recall performance on mixed event sequences was intermediate and
did not differ from that on either enabling or arbitrarily ordered event
sequences. In contrast, as had the 13-month-olds at immediate testing,
after the delays, the boys in the sample treated the mixed event sequences as arbitrary. That is, the boys' ordered recall performance on the
mixed event sequences was lower than on enabling event sequences and
did not differ from arbitrarily ordered events. For the boys, ordered recall performance on the mixed event sequences was so low that it did not
differ from the level of performance on new event sequences either before or after provision of the verbal reminders for the events (see Appendix C). Moreover, in general, the children produced a smaller number of
the individual target actions of the mixed event sequences, relative to the
enabling events. The 13-month-olds also produced a smaller number of
the individual target actions of the mixed event sequences, relative to
arbitrarily ordered sequences.

Because the present study is the first in which mixed structure sequences have been used, we cannot at this time determine whether either
the boys' low levels of ordered recall on mixed event sequences or the
general pattern of low levels of production of individual target actions on
the mixed event sequences are replicable effects. Inspection of the error
patterns on the three-step mixed event sequences provides some insight
into the source of the effects, however. The structure of the mixed event
sequences was such that Step 2 could be executed either before or after
Step 1, with no impact on the final product of the sequence of actions.
For example, in the three-step mixed event sequence *Dumptruck*, the experimenter modeled putting a truck bed on a base, placing some blocks
into the truck bed, and tipping the truck bed, thereby dumping out the
blocks. A reasonable alternative order was to perform Step 2, placing blocks
into the truck bed, before Step 1, putting the truck bed onto the base.
Beginning the sequence with Step 2, rather than the modeled order, was
typical among the children tested on three-step event sequences. In some
cases the children went on to produce Steps 1 and 3 but in others, they
either produced Step 2 alone or produced Step 2 followed by Step 3,
without "backtracking" to produced Step 1. The result was a lower level
of ordered recall (particularly apparent among the boys in the sample),
as well as a lower level of production of the individual target actions of
the mixed event sequences. Again, we caution that because this is the
first study in which mixed structure sequences have been used, we cannot
determine whether the effects apparently associated with this hybrid sequence type are reliable, or not.

Another curiosity in the patterns of performance on the different
sequence types is why effects of enabling relations on ordered recall

diminished more rapidly on four-step event sequences than on three-step event sequences. One possibility is that the specific four-step sequences used did not lend themselves to the organizational advantage typically associated with enabling relations in events, whereas the three-step sequences did. This explanation seems unlikely, given the prominent effects of enabling relations observed at immediate testing. Prior to imposition of the delays, the extent to which the children adhered to the temporal order in which the events were modeled was a linear function of the number of enabling relations in the sequences: Recall of sequences wholly constrained by enabling relations was greater than of partially constrained sequences, which in turn was greater than of arbitrarily ordered sequences. This finding contradicts the suggestion that the four-step event sequences were not coherent in their organization, whereas the three-step sequences were.

Children's apparent inability to maintain the organizational advantage for sequences constrained by enabling relations, on the heels of their well-ordered immediate recall of the enabling and mixed event sequences, is reminiscent of the pattern of immediate and delayed recall of arbitrarily ordered events observed among 22-month-olds in Bauer, Hertsgaard et al. (1998). Specifically, 22-month-old children reproduced arbitrarily ordered three-step event sequences immediately after seeing them modeled, but they did not maintain order information over a 2-week delay. In contrast, 28-month-old children evinced accurate immediate as well as delayed recall of sequences of the same length. We attributed the age-related differences in children's maintenance of well-organized representations of arbitrarily ordered event sequences over a delay to cross-domain changes in the ability to store and retrieve ever larger input patterns (see, for example, Bates, Thal, & Marchman, 1991, and Shore, 1986, for related arguments). It is possible that the four-step sequences on which the children were tested in the present research were of a level of complexity that simply exceeded the children's information processing capacities. Consistent with this suggestion, in research undertaken since the inception of the present study, we have established that it is not until 24 months of age that the majority of children are able to accurately recall entire four-step sequences immediately after seeing them modeled one time (Schwade, 1999). In the present research, repeated experience of the sequences likely made it possible for the majority of 16-month-olds and 20-month-olds to recall the four-step enabling and mixed sequences immediately (see Bauer, Hertsgaard et al., 1998, for a similar effect on 16-month-olds' recall of arbitrarily ordered event sequences). It apparently was not sufficient, however, to permit maintenance over time of the highly organized event representations that typically are associated with the presence of enabling relations.

EFFECTS OF MODE OF EXPERIENCE

For the children tested on four-step event sequences, neither conclusions regarding whether the children remembered the individual target actions of the event sequences nor children's relative levels of performance on the to-be-remembered events was affected by whether the children had been permitted to imitate the events prior to imposition of the delays. That is, the children remembered the individual target actions of the events that they had been given the opportunity to imitate and the events that they had only watched; the number of individual target actions that the children produced on events that they had been permitted to imitate and on events previously only watched did not differ. There were some effects of mode of experience on children's ordered recall. However, they were opposite those that might be expected. Rather than on events previously imitated, children's performance was more consistent on event sequences previously only watched: (a) prior to provision of verbal reminders, in the 9- and 12-month delay conditions, the children showed evidence of ordered recall of events watched but not of events imitated, and (b) after provision of verbal reminders, in the 9-month delay condition, the children showed evidence of ordered recall of events watched but not of events imitated. Nevertheless, there were two cells of the design in which the opportunity to imitate did have facilitating effects. Specifically, prior to provision of verbal reminders, 20-month-old girls in the 1- and 3-month delay conditions produced a larger number of pairs of actions in the target order on the events that they previously had been permitted to imitate than on the events that they previously had only watched. The effect was not observed at the longer retention intervals, among the 16-month-old girls, or among either the 16-month-old or the 20-month-old boys. Moreover, performance after provision of the verbal reminders was not affected by the mode of experience manipulation (see Appendix C).

With one exception, the mode of experience of the three-step event sequences prior to imposition of the delay had no effect on conclusions regarding whether or not the children remembered the events. The one exception was that even after provision of the verbal reminders, 13-month-old and 16-month-old girls tested on three-step event sequences did not recall the temporal order of the enabling events that they had only watched: Girls' performance on enabling event sequences previously only watched was not different from that on enabling event sequences new to them at Session 4. Across gender groups, prior to introduction of the verbal reminders of the event sequences, the children produced a larger number of the individual target actions of the enabling event sequences that they had been provided the opportunity to imitate, relative to those that they had only watched. However, analyses for gender effects revealed this pattern only among the girls. In any case, once the verbal reminders for the event sequences were provided, the effect was not apparent for either gender group (see Appendix C).

EFFECTS OF VERBAL REMINDERS

With two exceptions, across all age and step-length groups, delay conditions, sequence types, and modes of experience, children's performance after the delays was facilitated by provision of verbal reminders. That is, in virtually all cells of the design, children's performance when prompted by the event-related props and verbal reminders was greater than their performance when prompted by the event-related props alone. The exceptions to the pervasive effects of reminding were (a) for the children in the four-step group, ordered recall of mixed sequences was not facilitated by the verbal labels for the events, and (b) for the 16-month-olds in the three-step group, in the 3-month delay condition, ordered recall of enabling event sequences was not facilitated by provision of verbal reminders. With these exceptions aside, verbal reminding was effective in increasing the amount of event-related information recalled by even the youngest children in the sample. This result is consistent with that of Bauer, Hertsgaard et al. (1998), in which we found that the effects of verbal reminding were not age or sequence type dependent but instead were linked to how well the mental representation of the event was organized.

EFFECTS OF THE LENGTH OF THE TO-BE-REMEMBERED EVENT SEQUENCES

We included in this research two groups of 16-month-olds: one group was tested on four-step event sequences and the other was tested on three-step event sequences. Contrary to the reasonable expectation that the two groups would show evidence of recall over delay intervals of similar lengths, there were striking differences in the lengths of time over which the two groups of 16-month-olds appeared to remember. Specifically, whereas even after 12 months, the 16-month-olds tested on four-step event sequences showed evidence of recall of some of the individual target actions as well as some of the pairs of actions of the sequences to which they had been exposed, the 16-month-olds tested on three-step event sequences showed evidence of recall of the individual actions of the events for only 6 months and of the order of the actions of the events for only 3 months.

We suggest that the apparent differences between the step-length groups be attributed to higher levels of discovery of the individual target actions and the order of actions of the new three-step event sequences compared with the new four-step event sequences. Concern that at the longer delay intervals, the children would be able to deduce and infer substantial portions of event sequences that were new to them, thereby obscuring mnemonic effects, was precisely what prompted us to include in the research design the group of 16-month-olds tested on four-step event sequences. Research initiated after the inception of the current study has demonstrated that children make great strides in problem solving and planning ability between the ages of 21 and 27 months of age (Bauer et al., 1999). It is entirely reasonable then that children 25 and 28 months of age (the approximate ages of 16-month-olds after 9- and 12-month delays, respectively) would be able to deduce and infer portions of three-step event sequences.

Consistent with the suggestion that higher levels of performance on new event sequences obscured evidence of memory in the 16-month-olds tested on three-step event sequences were analyses of children's performance on the new event sequences prior to demonstration of them at Session 4: The analyses revealed differences between the groups of children tested on three-step and four-step sequences. With the exception of the 6-month delay condition, in which the pre-verbal-suggestion performance of the step-length groups did not differ, the 16-month-olds tested on three-step event sequences spontaneously generated a larger proportion of the individual target actions of the new event sequences, relative to their peers tested on four-step event sequences. In all delay conditions, the children tested on three-step event sequences spontaneously generated a larger proportion of ordered pairs of actions, relative to their four-step peers. Since whether children remembered the individual target actions and the order of actions of the event sequences was determined by differences between performance on previously experienced and on new event sequences, relatively higher levels of performance on new events makes detection of a reliable difference more difficult.

Additional evidence that relatively high levels of performance on new event sequences, rather than low levels of performance on previously experienced event sequences, contributed to the appearance of more rapid forgetting on the part of 16-month-olds tested on three-step event sequences compared with 16-month-olds tested on four-step event sequences comes from analyses of children's long-term recall performance. Specifically, the proportions of individual target actions and pairs of actions of the to-be-remembered event sequences produced by the 16-month-olds tested on three-step events in most cases were greater than, and never were less than, the proportions produced by the 16-month-olds tested on four-step events. Finally, there were similarities in the reliability with which recall was observed among the two groups of 16-month-olds. For both step-length groups, when the children were prompted by the event-related props and by verbal labels for the event sequences, the number of children showing evidence of recall of the individual target actions of the events was reliably greater than chance in the 1-, 3-, 6-, and 12-month delay conditions; the number of children showing evidence of ordered recall was reliably greater than chance in the 1-, 3-, and 6-month delay conditions. Together, these patterns indicate that differences in the long-term recall performances of the 16-month-olds in the two different step-length groups were more apparent than real.

VIII. IMPLICATIONS OF THE FINDINGS AND CONCLUSIONS

IMPLICATIONS OF THE FINDINGS

Informing the Specific Issues Motivating the Research

Two major issues provided the motivation and rationale for the research reported in this monograph. The first major issue was whether in the pre-preschool years, there are systematic age-related changes in the length of time over which children are able to recall specific past events. The second major issue was whether factors known to affect recall over the short and intermediate terms of hours to weeks also affect recall over longer retention intervals. We discuss each of these issues in turn.

Age-Related Differences in Long-Term Recall

For children of preschool age and older, the question of whether there are age-related differences in the amount of information that can be retained over time has been addressed empirically and answered affirmatively: When tested after a delay, older children remember more than younger children (see Howe & O'Sullivan, 1997, for a review). The effect is observed even when levels of initial learning are controlled (e.g., Brainerd & Reyna, 1995). At the inception of the present research, the question had not been addressed in the literature on younger children's recall. Since then, there have been a small number of studies, the results of which are contradictory (compare, for example, the results of Bauer et al., 1994, and Meltzoff, 1995, with Howe & Courage, 1997b, and Sheffield & Hudson, 1994). The literature also contains evidence of retention by very young children over intervals longer than those seemingly tolerated by children much older (contrast, for example, Mandler & McDonough, 1995, and McDonough & Mandler, 1994, with Hudson & Sheffield, 1998, and Sheffield & Hudson, 1994). Moreover, in most cases, the scales of the investigations of long-term recall in young children had been small, no more than two age groups had been compared in any single experiment, and the same age group had not been examined over different retention intervals. Finally, because address of the question had to be "pieced together" across a patchwork of different laboratories, different experiments, and thereby, different procedures, it was not clear which differences were real and which were only apparent.

The present research provides clear evidence that age-related differences in long-term recall extend to children younger than preschool age. For both step-length groups, when differences in children's initial learning and in their problem-solving abilities were not controlled, age-related differences in children's levels of performance were apparent, both prior to and after introduction of the verbal reminders of the event sequences; the effects were obtained across modes of experience. That is, the older children in the samples produced more of the individual target actions of the event sequences (both step-length groups) and more ordered pairs of actions of the event sequences (four-step group only), relative to the younger children. Even with these sources of variance controlled, age-related differences in long-term recall were observed (a) when the children were prompted by the event-related props alone (for both step-length groups, apparent on events previously imitated and events previously only watched), (b) after verbal reminding, on event sequences that the children had only watched (children tested on four-step event sequences), and (c) at the longer retention intervals of 9 and 12 months (children tested on four-step event sequences). Thus, even though, within step-length groups, both age groups of children showed evidence of memory for the event sequences over the same retention intervals, under conditions of greater cognitive demand (i.e., prompted by event-related props alone, no prior opportunity to imitate the event sequence, longer retention intervals), the older children showed more robust memory, relative to the younger children. Moreover, in each step-length group, at the longer retention intervals, ordered recall was more reliably observed among the older relative to the younger children. These results suggest both that age-related developments become more apparent at longer retention intervals and that they play a more prominent role in children's temporally ordered recall than in recall of the individual target actions of event sequences (see Chapter VII for elaboration of these patterns).

The results of regression analyses also indicate that age-related changes are more apparent at longer retention intervals and that they are a more significant source of variance in children's temporally ordered recall than in recall of the individual target actions of event sequences. Specifically, in step-wise regression analyses, age emerged as a significant, and in some cases, as the sole, predictor of children's performance at the longer retention intervals of 6, 9, and 12 months. Age was a more consistent predictor of children's ordered recall performance than of their production of the individual target actions of the event sequences. Rather than age, the factor that emerged as the most consistent, and in some cases, the only significant predictor of children's recall of the individual target actions of the event sequences was their level of initial learning of them (as measured by immediate recall).

That children's levels of initial learning of the event sequences proved such an important predictor of their subsequent long-term recall has important implications for interpretation of existing studies as well as for the design of future studies of long-term recall by children in the second and into the third years of life. In the world outside the laboratory, age-related differences in the comprehension of events, with resulting differences in mastery of them, abound. Moreover, the results of research with children of preschool age suggest that younger preschoolers may focus on, and therefore likely master, different features of events, relative to older preschoolers. For example, younger preschoolers focus on the more routine aspects of events (e.g., that when camping, one sleeps), rather than on the more distinctive features of them (i.e., that when camping, one sleeps in a tent; e.g., Fivush & Hamond, 1990). The results of the present research strongly imply that differential mastery of to-be-remembered events is one source of observed age effects in long-term memory performance.

Precisely because differential initial learning is a fact of developmental life, it is imperative that we understand its influence. Unfortunately, in most of the existing literature, the extent to which this source of variance has affected conclusions regarding developments in long-term recall ability cannot be established because either levels of initial learning were not measured (true of any study in which the opportunity for imitation is deferred until the long-term recall test; e.g., Meltzoff, 1995) or their influence simply was not evaluated (e.g., Bauer et al., 1994). In future research, levels of initial learning should be evaluated and their effects controlled. Ideally, the findings from studies employing statistical controls, such as used in the present research, would be complemented by those from studies employing criterion designs, in which differences in initial mastery of the to-be-remembered material are eliminated (e.g., Howe & Courage, 1997b). Both approaches are necessary because neither is without its drawbacks. Principally, in the case of fixed-trial designs, differences in initial learning can be controlled statistically but they cannot reliably be eliminated. In the case of criterion designs, the demand for multiple trials to a set criterion can, as noted by Howe and Courage (1997b), test the tolerance of young participants' attention and cooperation. In addition, such designs introduce ambiguity of their own: It is not clear what to say about the level of mastery of a child who accurately reproduces an event on one, but not on two consecutive, trials. Because neither approach is ideal, multiple perspectives on the question, provided by multiple converging measures, are most desirable.

In the present research, even with differences in initial learning (as well as problem-solving ability) controlled, age-related differences in children's mnemonic performance were apparent under conditions of greater cognitive demand and lesser environmental support for recall. Specifically, age-related differences were more readily observed when the children were prompted by the event-related props alone and on measures of their recall of the temporal order of the actions in the event sequences, as opposed to the more heavily cued individual target actions of the events. This pattern is not surprising. The existing literature makes clear that age effects emerge along a continuum of support: They are strongest under conditions of less support and diminish as more support for recall is provided (e.g., Price & Goodman, 1992). Indeed, in the case of recognition testing, when mnemonic supports are greatest, age effects all but disappear (see Brainerd et al., 1985, and Brainerd & Reyna, 1995, for reviews).

The results of the present research can be used to inform the question of why in some studies, age-related differences in long-term recall are apparent whereas in others, they are not. Specifically, Bauer et al. (1994) and Meltzoff (1995) suggest that children 13, 16, and 20 months of age all remember over an interval of 8 months, and both 14- and 16-month-olds remember over intervals of 2 and 4 months, respectively. In contrast, Sheffield and Hudson (1994) reported longer retention by 18-month-olds (10 weeks) than by 14-month-olds (8 weeks). The results of Howe and Courage (1997b) likewise suggest that over a 3-month delay, 15-month-olds forget more than 18-month-olds (Experiment 1) and 12-month-olds forget more than 15-month-olds (Experiment 2). In the present research, age effects were particularly apparent in children's recall of the order in which the actions of the target sequences unfolded. In both Howe and Courage (1997b) and Sheffield and Hudson (1994), the scoring criteria required that children perform two- and three-step sequences of action in order to succeed on the tasks presented to them. In Experiment 1 of Bauer et al. (1994), although children who had been 13 and 16 months of age at the time of experience of event sequences both showed evidence of memory for them 8 months later, ordered recall performance was greater among the older than the younger children. In contrast, age-related effects were not observed in Meltzoff (1995), wherein children were required to remember single object-specific actions (e.g., separating the two ends of a dumbbell-shaped toy). Likewise, in Bauer et al. (1994), age was not observed to affect children's production of the

150

individual target actions of the event sequences. That age effects will be more apparent in children's recall of temporal order information also is consistent with the results of de Haan, Bauer, Georgieff, and Nelson (2000), in which we found the variable of correctly ordered pairs of actions recalled to be sensitive to potential developmental delay associated with preterm birth.

What the present research cannot resolve is why in some studies, very young children are shown to recall information over delays longer than those seemingly tolerated by children much older. For example, Mandler and McDonough (1995) found that children 11 months of age were able to recall event sequences after a delay interval of 12 weeks, whereas in Sheffield and Hudson (1994), children 14 and 18 months of age were shown to recall for intervals of only 8 and 10 weeks, respectively. Rather than resolving the issue, the present research makes clear why it will remain: Outcomes are multiply determined. In the present case, children's age and the delay interval over which they were tested were only two of a number of factors that affected children's recall. Also important were the level of initial mastery of the to-be-remembered material, the complexity of the material, children's problem-solving abilities, and in some cases, even their level of productive vocabulary at the time of exposure to the event sequences. Moreover, the factors that predicted children's recall differed across the different delay conditions; in no case were we able to predict all of the variance in children's recall. Our point here is that attempts to determine "growth chart"–type functions of the lengths of time over which children of various ages are able to recall can hope to meet with success only within the confines of a single experiment or perhaps, paradigm (Hartshorn et al., 1998). Attempts to compare absolute lengths of retention intervals across experiments seem to us to be doomed, due to the myriad factors that affect children's performance.

On a related note, we point out that the lengths of time over which the children in the present research were shown to recall should not be taken as absolute. For example, that 13-month-olds provided evidence of memory for some of the individual target actions of the event sequences for 6 months but not longer does not imply that it is impossible for children so young to remember event-related information for longer than 6 months. Indeed, the results of Bauer et al. (1994) indicate that under certain circumstances, children as young as 13 months at the time of exposure to events remember them for at least 8 months (see also McDonough & Mandler, 1994). This finding does, however, imply that the circumstances under which such young children are able to retain information over long periods of time might be somewhat limited and that, in the present research, those conditions were not met. The bulk of evidence suggests that one of the changes that occurs with age is an increase in the reliability with which children evince recall, particularly at longer retention intervals.

Factors Affecting Long-Term Recall

The second major issue that provided motivation and rationale for the present research was whether factors known to affect recall over the short and intermediate terms of hours to weeks also affect recall over longer retention intervals. We were particularly interested in three factors that have emerged as major determinants of young children's recall: the nature of the temporal relations inherent in events, active participation in events, and the availability of verbal reminders of to-be-remembered events (see Bauer, 1996, for a review). (A fourth factor, namely, the number of experiences of an event, has been found to affect young children's recall memory but was not varied in the present research.)

Event structure. Over the short to intermediate term, enabling relations in event sequences have been shown to exert a significant and robust facilitating effect on children's ordered recall (e.g., Barr & Hayne, 1996; Bauer, Hertsgaard et al., 1998; Mandler & McDonough, 1995). In contrast, prior to this research, the only investigation that had permitted a test of the effects of enabling relations on recall over the extended term indicated that recall of two-step event sequences was not affected by the nature of the temporal relations inherent in the events whereas that of three-step event sequences was affected (Bauer et al., 1994). We also entertained the possibility that there would be an interaction between age and the effects of the structure of to-be-remembered material on recall over extended intervals with younger children failing to remember event sequences wholly or partially unconstrained by enabling relations and older children demonstrating greater facility with them.

The findings from the present research suggest that with few exceptions, with increasing delay, the effects of sequence type diminished, for all groups of children. At immediate testing, consistent with previous research (e.g., Barr & Hayne, 1996; Bauer & Dow, 1994; Bauer & Travis, 1993), there were clear effects of sequence type: in both step-length groups, ordered recall of event sequences with enabling relations was greater than ordered recall of sequences that were arbitrarily ordered. The relative levels of performance on the sequences that contained a mixture of enabling and arbitrary temporal relations differed across the age groups. For the 20-month-olds and the 16-month-olds (both those tested on four-step and those tested on three-step event sequences) ordered recall of mixed event sequences was lower than of sequences completely constrained by enabling relations, yet was greater than of arbitrarily ordered sequences. There was a linear relation then between the number of enabling relations in the event sequences and the accuracy of ordered recall of them. In contrast, for 13-month-olds, ordered recall of mixed event sequences was less than that of sequences wholly constrained by enabling relations and not different from that of arbitrarily ordered events. That reduction in the internal coherence of the event sequences had a particularly detrimental effect on the younger children's performance is consistent with the existing literature on developments in reliable temporal sequencing of arbitrarily ordered events. It is not until approximately 22 months of age that children's immediate ordered recall of arbitrarily ordered event sequences is reliably greater than chance (e.g., Bauer, Hertsgaard et al., 1998; Bauer & Thal, 1990; Wenner & Bauer, 1999) and not until approximately 28 months of age that children reliably reproduce arbitrarily ordered event sequences after a delay (Bauer, Hertsgaard et al., 1998). Although 16-month-olds' facility with arbitrary temporal relations can be facilitated by repeated experience (Bauer, Hertsgaard et al., 1998), it is possible that 13-month-olds' either cannot be, or that more than three exposures would be necessary.

As time passed, the advantage associated with enabling relations in events diminished. For the children tested on four-step event sequences, prior to introduction of the verbal reminders of the event sequences, there were no effects of sequence type on children's long-term ordered recall in any of the delay conditions. After provision of the verbal reminders, the children tested on four-step event sequences showed higher levels of temporally ordered recall on event sequences wholly constrained by enabling relations, relative to event sequences only partially constrained by enabling relations. However, with the variance associated with differential initial learning of the event sequences controlled, the effect was apparent only among 20-month-olds in the 6-month delay condition. Children's production of individual target actions was similarly relatively unaffected by sequence type: With a few exceptions, the children produced roughly equivalent numbers of the individual target actions of the enabling, mixed, and arbitrarily ordered event sequences.

The long-term recall patterns observed among the children tested on three-step event sequences was more similar to that obtained in studies of the effects of sequence type at short to intermediate delays. That is, ordered recall by the 13-month-olds and the 16-month-olds tested on three-step event sequences was greater for event sequences wholly constrained by enabling relations, relative to event sequences that were arbitrarily ordered; mixed event sequences were recalled at levels that did not differ from arbitrarily ordered events. Because the children tested on three-step event sequences did not show evidence of recall of the temporal order of any of the event types for intervals longer than 3 months, it is not possible to determine whether effects of sequence type on ordered recall would have been apparent at delays of more than 3 months. In general, the children tested on three-step event sequences produced a smaller number of the individual target actions of the mixed event sequences, relative to the enabling event sequences.

An important implication of the findings of the effects (and lack thereof) of sequence type is that, even for children in the second year of life, neither recall of the individual target actions of multistep event sequences nor recall of the temporal order of actions in sequences is dependent upon the constraints imposed by enabling relations. This implies that the ability to recall is quite general: it extends to events of varying temporal structures. A second important implication is that the benefits typically associated with certain event structures will not necessarily be available to support recall over the long term. In the present research, we attributed the absence of sequence type effects on long-term ordered recall by the children tested on four-step event sequences to the level of challenge posed by the events. Simply stated, maintenance and later retrieval of four-step sequences may have exceeded the information processing capabilities of the 20-month-olds and 16-month-olds whom we charged to remember. The general implication of this argument is that long-term retention and subsequent retrieval of event-related information will be dependent in part on a "match" between the information processing abilities of the child and the demands imposed by the to-be-remembered material. Children will not benefit from the internal coherence in events if appreciation of that coherence requires resources that exceed those currently available to them. Such an effect recently was observed in preschoolers' recall of orally presented narratives. The children showed the benefits of goal-based organization in their recall of a standard length narrative, but not in their recall of a substantially longer version of the same narrative (Wenner, 1999).

Active participation. Active participation in to-be-remembered events also has been shown to have significant facilitating effects on recall over the relatively short term; its effects on long-term recall were less apparent. For example, after a 1-month delay, 14-month-olds who had been permitted to imitate event sequences prior to imposition of the delay recalled more than did children who had only been permitted to watch (Bauer et al., 1995). In contrast, after delays of 2 and 4 months, recall by 14-month-olds and 16-month-olds was comparable for children who had been and had not been permitted to imitate prior to imposition of the delays (Meltzoff, 1995). In the present research, the children were given the opportunity to imitate the event sequences one time prior to imposition of the delays. Although children's pre-delay performance on the event sequences was not perfect, levels of participation in the opportunity to imitate were quite high. Indeed, the children produced one or more of the individual target actions on fully 99% of the event sequences available for imitation (i.e., 1,426 of the 1,440 event sequences: 360 children × 3 imitate event sequences per child). Nevertheless, the effects of the mode-of-participation manipulation were clear: Conclusions regarding whether the children remembered the individual target actions of the event sequences were not affected by the mode of experience of the events. There were some effects of the mode of experience on children's ordered recall: even after provision of verbal reminders (a) in the 9-month delay condition, the children tested on four-step event sequences failed to show evidence of ordered recall of events imitated; and (b) across the 1- and 3-month delay conditions, the children tested on three-step event sequences failed to show evidence of ordered recall of enabling event sequences that they had only watched. In the balance of the cells of the design, conclusions regarding temporally ordered recall were not affected by whether the children had been permitted the opportunity to imitate prior to imposition of the delays.

The present findings of long-term recall of events imitated and of events only watched extends those of Meltzoff (1995), in which it was shown that children 14 and 16 months of age at the time of exposure to single object-specific actions were able to recall them 2 and 4 months later, whether or not they had been permitted imitation of them prior to the delay. It makes clear that acquisition and long-term retention of event-related material are not dependent on the child's own motor action, even when the to-be-remembered event is a complex, multistep action sequence. This outcome has important implications for arguments about the nature of the memory representation upon which subsequent performance is based. Some have argued that, when children are permitted to produce an elicited imitation response prior to imposition of a delay, they establish a "motor memory" and that any subsequent reproduction is of their own actions, rather than of the actions or sequences of actions that they observed (see, for example, Meltzoff, 1990, for discussion). The opportunity to imitate prior to imposition of a delay is thereby equated with formation of a procedural, as opposed to a declarative, memory representation.

What the present results make clear is that mnemonic performance on events previously imitated one time and on events only watched does not differ. Given that in other contexts procedural and declarative memories have been shown to be affected quite differently (e.g., to be context dependent versus independent, respectively), it seems reasonable to conclude that the opportunity to imitate a to-be-remembered event prior to imposition of a delay does not fundamentally alter the nature of the representation underlying it. As has been pointed out elsewhere (e.g., Carver & Bauer, 1999), procedural tasks such as, for example, serial reaction time require 200 to 400 interactive trials to be learned (e.g., Knopman & Nissen, 1987). With a single imitation opportunity, it is highly unlikely that a procedural memory would be formed. Indeed, we are not aware of a single example in the literature wherein a single opportunity (or even small number of opportunities) to produce a multistep sequence of actions resulted in a nondeclarative memory representation. Such conditions simply are not conducive to procedural learning. In any case, logic aside, the present results make clear that children 13, 16, and 20 months of age are able to remember both the individual target actions and the temporal order of actions of event sequences that they have been permitted to imitate and event sequences that they have only watched.

Whereas it is clear from the present research that even after long delays, recall is not dependent on the opportunity to imitate, there were some instances of better recall for event sequences that the children had imitated relative to those that they had only watched. Specifically, among 20-month-old girls in the 1- and 3-month delay conditions, prior to provision of verbal reminders, ordered recall performance was facilitated by the opportunity to imitate. In addition, when they were prompted by the event-related props alone, the girls tested on three-step event sequences produced a larger number of the individual target actions of the enabling event sequences that they had been provided the opportunity to imitate. In both cases, once the verbal reminders for the event sequences were provided, the effects no longer were apparent (see Appendix C).

We already have argued that any benefits associated with the opportunity to imitate prior to imposition of a delay should not be attributed to formation of a qualitatively different type of memory resulting from motor practice. A more parsimonious explanation for the observed facilitation of recall by a single opportunity to imitate is that which would be provided were the effect to be observed in an older child or an adult, namely, that active participation in a to-be-remembered event affords more elaborative encoding of it. Even if no benefit was derived from the act of imitation per se (indeed, in one case noted above, imitation actually had a detrimental effect on performance; detrimental effects could result from interference associated with inaccurate imitation), it could derive from the greater attention that children often paid to the model at the third exposure session. Once they realized that they *finally* would be permitted to participate in some of the interesting events that they there-to-fore had only watched, the children often visibly "sat up and took notice," if not literally, then figuratively.

Availability of verbal reminders. The third determinant of children's short and intermediate term recall that we investigated in this research was the availability of verbal reminders of events. With two exceptions, across all age and step-length groups, delay conditions, sequence types, and modes of experience, children's performance after the delays was facilitated by the verbal labels provided as reminders of the previously experienced event sequences. The exceptions to the ubiquitous facilitating effects of verbal reminders were on ordered recall of mixed event sequences by the children tested on four-step event sequences and on 16-month-olds' tested on three-step sequences ordered recall of enabling events. With these two exceptions, consistent with prior research (e.g., Bauer et al., 1995), children's performance when prompted by the event-related props and verbal reminders was greater than their performance when prompted by the event-related props alone. Verbal reminding was effective in increasing the amount of event-related information recalled for even the youngest children in the sample.

That the performance of even the youngest children in the sample was affected by verbal reminding is notable for two reasons. First, reminding seems to work to ameliorate forgetting of events the representations of which are well organized. As such, we thought that older children, who could be expected to form better organized event representations, would experience a larger facilitating effect. Moreover, we also anticipated that the efficacy of verbal reminding might diminish as the memory trace decayed. Given reason to expect more rapid decay of mnemonic traces in younger children, we expected age-related differences in the efficacy of verbal reminding. Another reason to expect age-related differences in the efficacy of verbal reminding is that its effects may reasonably be expected to depend upon children's level of command of language: Children with less facility with language could be expected to benefit less from the availability of verbal reminders. Given the rapid strides in language development that take place over the 2nd and 3rd years of life, we expected to see age-related changes in the strength of verbal reminding effects. That verbal reminding had such a uniformly positive effect on children's recall is remarkable, considering that at the time of exposure to the test events, children in the present sample had productive vocabularies ranging from 0 to 651 words and that, at the time of delayed recall testing, the children ranged in age from 14 to 32 months.

One possible alternative interpretation of the effects of verbal reminders is that the changes in performance we attributed to the reminders themselves actually should be attributed to the greater amount of time that the children had to manipulate the event-related props once the verbal reminders were delivered. That is, the verbal reminders always were provided only after the children had had a period of recall prompted by

157

the event-related props alone. Thus, provision of the verbal reminders was confounded with time. It is possible then that what appear to be effects of verbal reminders could be effects of a greater amount of time permitted for recall.

Because of the fixed order of the phases of delayed recall testing, we cannot absolutely eliminate the possibility that the effects of verbal reminding are attributable to increased time alone. Nevertheless, we deem this possibility unlikely. First, as demonstrated by the analyses of the lengths of time that the children manipulated the event-related props (see Appendix B), children's levels of performance were not related to the lengths of the response periods. For example, baseline manipulation periods were longer than immediate recall periods yet children produced more individual target actions and more pairs of actions in the target order in immediate recall than in baseline. Second, in Experiment 1 of Bauer et al. (1995), the behavior of children in a "no reminder" group (i.e., the children were presented with the event-related props alone) was compared to that of children in a verbal reminder condition in which the reminder was provided immediately upon presentation of the event-related props. Although the time available to manipulate the event-related props did not differ between the groups, the performance of the verbal reminder group was facilitated relative to the no reminder group. Third, Experiment 3 of Bauer et al. (1995) featured a within-subjects replication of the conditions of testing in Experiment 1; effects of reminding were apparent. These findings strongly indicate that the amount of time that children spend manipulating event-related props is not the major determinant of their performance. Moreover, effects of verbal reminding are apparent even when they are provided at the beginning of a response period. We conclude, therefore, that the facilitating effects of verbal reminding observed in the present research were the result of exposure to the specific verbal cues.

Implications for Early Memory Development and Its Assessment

The results of the present research have implications for issues and questions beyond those that provided the immediate motivation and rationale for it. One of the major issues faced by researchers interested in the early development of the ability to recall has been a methodological one: How is one to "extract" from a pre- or early-verbal child evidence of recall of a specific past event? The elicited imitation paradigm has proven quite useful in this regard. It has permitted examination of behavior that increasingly is recognized as indicative of recall, in children too young to participate in verbal recall paradigms. In the present research, we witnessed both the utility and some of the limitations of the paradigm. Since we hope that by this point, the utility of the paradigm is apparent, we focus here on its limitations.

A notable limitation of the use of objects to enact event sequences in the elicited imitation paradigm is that, as children get older and thus, more savvy in the ways of the world and the materials that occupy it, they become increasingly able to detect the affordances of the materials used to produce test sequences, to infer the likely combination of materials, or both. As a result, they are more likely to spontaneously generate the target events. Children's high level of generation of target event sequences makes it increasingly difficult to detect evidence of memory as delay interval and thus, age, increases. Indeed, we attribute the absence of evidence of memory for the three-step event sequences by the 16-month-olds at delay intervals of longer than 6 months to precisely this phenomenon.

Fortunately, just as children's increased deductive and inferential abilities seem to present insurmountable challenges, another ability reaches a point at which it can be exploited to aid in determination of whether or not children remember past events. As discussed in Bauer and Wewerka (1995, 1997), at the time their delayed recall was tested, some of the children in the present sample used their newly developing language skills to talk about the materials in front of them and the events that the materials could be used to produce. In a number of cases sufficient to compel formal examination, the children's comments were indicative of memory for the event sequences that they had experienced 1 to 12 months previously. That the children spontaneously made verbal mnemonic comments after delays of as many as 12 months provides evidence that converges with the nonverbal indices in the present research, thereby strengthening the conclusion that even in the longest delay condition, the older children remembered aspects of the events to which they had been exposed. Children's verbal mnemonic comments also suggest that a likely productive avenue for future research is the combination of elicited imitation and verbal recall paradigms to test recall over extended periods of time. In Bauer, Kroupina, Schwade, Dropik, and Wewerka (1998), we combined these methods in an investigation of the later verbal accessibility of children's memories for the event sequences used in this research. We found that at 3 years of age, some of the children were able to verbally describe the events that they had first experienced at the ages of 16 and 20 months (children who had been 13 months at the time of experience of the events were not included in the report). Later verbal accessibility of memories of the event sequences used in the present research is one more indication that they were derived from declarative rather than nondeclarative mnemonic representations (i.e., nondeclarative memories are, by definition, not verbally accessible).

159

The second broad implication of this research concerns the time course of development of the ability to recall over the long term. In the introduction to this report, we summarized behavioral evidence (a) that by the second half of the 1st year of life, the ability to recall is evident (e.g., Barr et al., 1996; Meltzoff, 1988b), (b) that the ability to recall for a period as long as 1 month is evident by late in the 1st year (Carver & Bauer, 1999), and (c) that during the 2nd year, long-term recall ability consolidates and becomes reliable (e.g., Bauer & Hertsgaard, 1993; Bauer et al., 1995). The present research provides additional evidence consistent with the suggestion that important developments in long-term recall occur during the 2nd year of life. The first indication was in terms of the lengths of time over which the youngest compared with the oldest children were able to recall. Whereas the 13-month-olds remembered some of the individual target actions of the event sequences for 6 months, the 20-month-olds showed evidence of memory for some of the event-related actions for as many as 12 months.

Age-related differences in children's ordered recall were even more pronounced: 13-month-olds showed evidence of memory for the temporal order of some of the actions of the event sequences for only 3 months; 20-month-olds showed evidence of memory for the temporal order of some of the actions of the event sequences for 12 months. Moreover, even at the longest delay, the number of 20-month-olds whose pattern of performance was indicative of temporally ordered recall was reliably greater than the number that would be expected by chance. The number of 13-month-olds evincing the pattern was greater than chance only in the 1-month delay condition (before and after verbal labels) and the 3-month delay condition (before verbal labels only). These findings are clear indications of age-related differences in the reliability with which long-term recall is observed.

The second indication of important developments during the second year was in terms of the amount of event-related information recall. The 20-month-olds and 16-month-olds tested on four-step event sequences remembered both the individual target actions of the events and their temporal order over the same length of time. Nevertheless, even with the variance associated with differential initial learning (events imitated) and differential problem-solving ability (events imitated and events only watched) controlled, the older children had higher levels of performance (a) on events only watched, both before and after provision of verbal reminders, (b) on events that they had been given the opportunity to imitate, before provision of verbal reminders, and (c) on events that they had been permitted to imitate, after provision of verbal reminders, at the longer retention intervals of 9 and 12 months. Thus, on event sequences presumably less elaborately encoded, with fewer contextual supports, and at the longer delay intervals, the older children retrieved a greater amount of event-related information, relative to the younger children. Among the children tested on three-step event sequences, prior to provision of the verbal reminders, the 16-month-old children produced a larger number of the individual target actions of the event sequences, relative to the 13-month-old children.

Changes in long-term recall performance during the 2nd year of life are consistent with our current understanding of the time course of development of the neural correlates that support the ability. As summarized in the introduction, the capacity for long-term recall of an event that happened in the past is thought to depend upon a cortico-limbic-diencephalic circuit involving medial temporal lobe structures as well as higher cortical association areas (Mishkin & Appenzeller, 1987; Squire & Zola-Morgan, 1991), including the prefrontal cortex. Whereas medial temporal lobe structures are necessary for consolidation of new memories, neocortical associate areas serve as the storage sites for long-term memories (Squire, 1992; Zola-Morgan & Squire, 1993); prefrontal cortex most likely serves the function of retrieval of declarative memory representations (Tulving et al., 1994). In contrast to the medial temporal lobe components that, for the most part, are functional at an early age (see C. A. Nelson, 1995, for discussion), the neocortical components and the reciprocal connections between the medial temporal lobe structures and the neocortex appear to develop slowly (e.g., Bachevalier et al., 1993; Webster et al., 1991). As summarized in Carver (1998), the period of 8 months to 2 years is a time of marked neuroanatomical (e.g., Huttenlocher, 1990; Koenderink, Uylings, & Mrzljak, 1994) and neurophysiological (e.g., Chugani, Phelps, & Mazziotta, 1986) changes in prefrontal cortex. Behaviorally, we would expect such changes to be apparent in increased reliability of the functions served by this brain region. In this vein it is particularly noteworthy that age-related changes in the reliability with which long-term recall memory was observed were most apparent in children's recall of the temporal order of the event sequences on which they were tested: Recall of the order in which two or more actions occurred likely poses greater retrieval demands than recall of an individual target action. Moreover, in adults, damage to prefrontal regions is associated with deficits in recall of temporal order information (e.g., Shimamura, Janowsky, & Squire, 1991).

A third broad implication of this research concerns the complement of remembering, namely, forgetting. In light of traditional assumptions of mnemonically incompetent preschoolers and, by extension, younger children, researchers' focus on children's abilities to remember material over long delay intervals is reasonable and appropriate. Indeed, the major purpose of the present research was to test children's powers of remembering.

161

What is absolutely obvious, however, is that even as they remembered, the children in this research forgot. In fact, among the children tested on four-step event sequences there was evidence of significant forgetting both of the individual target actions and of the temporal order of actions even in the 1-month delay condition; by 3 months, both step-length groups showed evidence of forgetting. The 20-month-olds provide an illustrative example. At immediate testing, across delay conditions, the 20-month-olds produced an average of 97% of the individual target actions and 71% of the pairs of actions in the target order (see Table 2 for relevant means). After delays of 1 and 3 months, they produced an average of 83% and 67% of possible individual target actions, respectively, and 52% and 36% of possible pairs of actions in the target order, respectively (see Table 3 for relevant means). Thus, whereas the children were retaining a sufficient amount of information to yield a reliable difference between levels of performance on events previously experienced and events that were new at Session 4, the 20-month-olds nevertheless were performing at levels significantly below those attained at the beginning of the retention period. This was true even though, as indexed by both dependent measures, the children showed high levels of initial mastery of the to-be-remembered events.

It is, of course, not surprising that young children forget and that they forget proportionally more as time passes: Older children and adults also forget. Our point in making the observation is to encourage attention to the apparently profound changes that mnemonic traces undergo during the first several days and weeks following exposure to to-be-remembered material. Indeed, recent research in our laboratory makes clear that for children as old as 20 months of age, significant forgetting already has occurred after as few as 48 hours have passed between exposure to and testing for retention of specific event sequences (Bauer, Van Abbema, & de Haan, 1999). Now that it is increasingly clear that children in the 2nd year of life remember specific past events over long periods, it seems reasonable and appropriate to begin to document the changes that make mnemonic traces unavailable over these same spaces of time.

We take the opportunity of readers' focus on forgetting to make another point about interpretation of the results of the present research. We used differences in children's levels of performance on previously experienced event sequences and on new event sequences as our means of establishing whether or not they remembered the target events. The comparison is a strong criterion that adequately controls for maturational and experiential changes in children's problem-solving abilities across the broad intervals of time represented in this research. Unfortunately, the comparison also invites calculations of differences between the levels of performance on old event sequences (likely supported by both memory and problem solving) and the levels of performance on new event sequences (supported exclusively by problem solving) and attributions of the differences to memory. By this interpretation, the children in the present research not only forgot relatively quickly, but they forgot relatively completely. For example, across modes of experience, when they were prompted by both the event-related props and by verbal reminders, after 12 months, the children tested on four-step event sequences produced 52% of total possible individual target actions. That the same children spontaneously generated 42% of possible individual target actions of the event sequences that were new to them leaves a 10% residual to be attributed to memory. Such a low figure steals some of the thunder from conclusions that the children remembered aspects of the test events for as many as 12 months.

Whereas we see the logic in the "memory residuals" argument, we caution against it. It is essential to keep in mind that just because, in the case of new events, the children earned 100% of their 1.67 target actions by problem solving, does not mean that in the case of old events, the children earned 1.67 of their 2.07 target actions by problem solving, and that they therefore only remembered 0.40 individual target actions (values for performance on four-step events by children in the 12-month delay condition). Performance on new event sequences establishes the *maximum* that children can achieve through problem solving. On old event sequences, anything above the level of performance on new event sequences can with confidence be attributed to memory. It would be a mistake, though, to assume that because we know what proportion of variance is accounted for by a given process when only that process is available, that we also know what proportion of variance is accounted for by that process when it is only one of two available. Consider that in the present research, in step-wise regression analyses, performance on new event sequences contributed unique variance to predictions of levels of production of the individual target actions of events in three delay conditions (1 month, 6 month, and 9 month) and it contributed unique variance to predictions of ordered recall in two delay conditions (1 month and 9 month). However, once the variance associated with all of the other potential predictor variables had been removed, performance on new event sequences contributed unique variance only once: to production of individual target actions in the 9-month delay condition.

The above example makes clear that the predictive utility of a given variable is not a constant. It varies as a function of the power of the other variables in the equation. The example also contains a strong suggestion that in the case of old event sequences, the children did not make full use of the 1.67 target actions that they could have achieved through problem solving: If the majority of children's long-term recall

163

"credit" actually was earned through problem solving, then measures of problem solving (i.e., performance on new event sequences) should have been more predictive of performance after the delays. Moreover, measures of problem solving should have increased in predictive utility with the passage of time. Contrary to these expectations, performance on new event sequences was not especially predictive of children's performance after the delays and its predictive utility did not increase over time. These patterns contraindicate the suggestion that, in delayed recall, the majority of children's performance was supported by problem solving, rather than memory.

By cautioning against underestimations of the amount that the children in the present research actually remembered about the specific event sequences, we do not mean to deflect attention away from the fact that the children forgot substantial amounts of what they once knew about the events. On the contrary, we already have documented the progressive loss of accessibility of memories once demonstrated to have been encoded and retained over some period of time. Such exercises are important in their own right. The data derived from such investigations also likely will play a key role in explanations as to the source of infantile or childhood amnesia. Traditional explanations of the amnesia shared the perspective that over the course of development, recall processes change qualitatively (e.g., Freud, 1905/1953; Neisser, 1988; Wetzler & Sweeney, 1986). Before the change, children were thought incapable of forming memories that would endure and later be accessible.

Prior to the present research, the existing literature already contained evidence inconsistent with notions of qualitative change in basic mnemonic processes. As reviewed in Bauer (1996), the mnemonic processes of young children had been shown to be affected by some of the same factors, in the same fashion, as those of older children and even adults (see also Howe & Courage, 1997a). Specifically, over short retention intervals, like older children, young children benefit from verbal reminders, repeated experience with events, the presence of causal or enabling relations in events, and active participation in events (e.g., Bauer et al., 1995). The results of the present research make clear that, with one possible exception, these factors do not place limitations on young children's abilities to remember over long delays. Young children's recall is not limited to events in which they have been active participants or to events with certain temporal structure; even after long retention intervals, verbal reminding has a significant facilitating effect. The only one of these four factors that we did not investigate in this research was repeated experience: The children experienced the event sequences at each of three exposure sessions. We have no way of knowing then whether the patterns of recall observed in this research would be apparent for events experienced only one time. What we do know is that if an event is adequately encoded, then children are able to remember it over extended delays. Moreover, the results of Bauer and Wewerka (1995, 1997) and Bauer, Kroupina et al. (1998) make clear that, under conditions of considerable contextual support (i.e., testing in the same laboratory, using the same props, by the same experimenter), 3-year-olds are able to demonstrate verbally accessible memories of events that they experienced in the second year of life and that likely were encoded without the benefit of language.

That under certain circumstances preschoolers are able to talk about the events for which they here provided nonverbal evidence of memory still does not address the question of whether they later are able to provide autobiographical accounts of them. Autobiographical or personal memories (Brewer, 1986), involve recollection of specific episodes, accompanied by a sense of personal involvement. In other words, they are memories of specific past events in which the subject was an involved participant; they constitute one's life story or personal past. It is the relative paucity among adults of these types of memories from early in life that characterizes the phenomenon of infantile amnesia.

It is likely that until young children can be made to speak in complete sentences and verbally describe their experiences in narrative form, an answer to the question of whether early memory is at all autobiographical will elude us. This is because, for adults, recollections of a unique episode from one's past usually include the same categories as are included in a full narrative, namely, the *who, what, where, when, why,* and *how* of an event (K. Nelson, 1993). This has led to the suggestion that, developmentally, the emergence of autobiographical memory is linked with the acquisition of narrative form to use as a frame for structuring and remembering experience (see, e.g., K. Nelson, 1993; Pillemer & White, 1989). Conversely, the absence of narrative form is considered to differentiate early memories of specific events from later, more adult-like, autobiographical memories. A number of authors describe the development of narrative form, and thus of autobiographical memory, as a product of social construction, established in the context of talking about and sharing past experiences (see, e.g., Fivush, 1988; K. Nelson, 1993; Pillemer, 1989; Pillemer & White, 1989; for further discussion). Critically, whereas there is no doubt that use of conventional narrative form to report on past experiences makes it easier to detect the presence of accessible, personally relevant memories from early in life, its unavailability should not be taken as evidence of the absence of such memories (see Bauer, 1993, for further discussion). Traditionally, a child's inability to provide a verbal report of an experience was equated with an inability to remember the experience. In essence, early memory was defined out of existence. Equating the onset of autobiographical memory with the development of narrative form, with verbal expression of personal relevance, or both, carries with it the same potential.

In addition to a lack of availability of a reporting medium for auto-biographical memories, there is another quality that our young children may have lacked that perhaps would have limited their capability to construct personally meaningful memories. Howe and Courage (1993, 1997a), for example (see also Fivush, 1988), have suggested that memories, be they of potentially self-relevant experiences or not, cannot take on personal significance in the absence of a cognitive self or concept of "me" as an object of knowledge. In other words, in the absence of a self for whom experiences are relevant, there can be no "auto" in the "biography." Eighteen to 24 months of age, a time by which the majority of infants recognize themselves in the mirror, has been suggested as the youngest age at which experiences might be encoded as being personally relevant and therefore, potentially autobiographical (Howe & Courage, 1993, 1997a). By this metric, many of our 13-month-old to 20-month-old children would not have been capable of forming autobiographical memories because they would not have had a sufficiently well-developed cognitive self.

In summary, whereas the results of the current research have important implications for theories as to the source of infantile amnesia, they cannot unravel its mystery. On the basis of the available data, we do not know whether the children in our sample coded as personally relevant or meaningful the experiences that they had in our laboratory, or even whether they had a sense of "person" to which to relate them. Moreover, we do not know whether the children would have remembered their experiences for comparable lengths of time had they had only a single visit to the laboratory and thus, only one exposure to the to-be-remembered events. Importantly, what the present research makes clear is that the absence of verbally accessible memories from the second and third years of life cannot be attributed to failure to encode specific events into memory or to retain them in an accessible form over an extended period of time. The children in this study amply demonstrated their abilities to perform these functions.

CONCLUSIONS

In the present research, children 13, 16, and 20 months of age at the time of exposure to specific multistep event sequences demonstrated their ability to encode, maintain, and later retrieve information about the individual target actions of event sequences as well as the temporal order of the actions of the events over substantial delays. Whereas the longest interval over which the youngest children in the sample evidenced recall of sequence-relevant information was 6 months, children in the older age groups demonstrated recall of some of the individual target actions of the event sequences as well as some information about their temporal order for as many as 12 months. Even with differences in children's initial mastery of the event sequences and their problem-solving abilities controlled, age-related differences in long-term recall were observed (a) on event sequences that the children only watched, (b) when the children were prompted by the event-related props alone (event previously imitated), (c) at longer retention intervals, and (d) on measures of children's ordered recall. Age-related differences were apparent in terms of the robustness of children's memories: 20-month-olds recalled both a larger number of individual target actions and a larger number of pairs of actions in the target order, relative to 16-month-olds tested on four-step event sequences. Likewise, at the longer delay intervals of 9 and 12 months for the children tested on four-step event sequences, and 3 and 6 months for the children tested on three-step event sequences, age-related differences in the reliability with which temporally ordered recall was observed also were apparent. Children's levels of initial mastery of the event sequences were predictive of their production of the individual target actions of the events in the 1-, 6-, and 9-month delay conditions; age emerged as a significant, and in some cases, as a unique, predictor of children's ordered recall in the 6-, 9-, and 12-month delay conditions. Thus, measures of children's abilities to maintain information about the temporal order of event sequences were particularly sensitive to age-related changes in long-term recall ability.

Continuities in recall processes across the age range tested in this research were apparent in children's responses to the variables that we manipulated. In each case, the variables functioned similarly in the three age groups. Effects of sequence type, so pronounced at immediate testing, dissipated as the retention intervals increased. Even in the youngest age group, children's long-term recall of the event sequences was not dependent on the opportunity to imitate the to-be-remembered events prior to imposition of the delays. Infrequently observed differences in the amount of information recalled about events previously imitated and previously only watched suggested that in some circumstances, the opportunity to imitate provided for more elaborative encoding of the event sequence. For virtually all delay intervals, age groups, sequence types, and experience conditions, children benefited from verbal reminders of the to-be-remembered event sequences. The results of this research not only informed the questions that motivated it, they also contributed to our understanding of developments in long-term recall ability that occur during the 2nd year of life, and they provide motivation for research on the complement of remembering, namely, forgetting.

Presented here are descriptions of the three-step and four-step event sequences used in the present research. Materials necessary to produce the event sequences are included in parentheses.

THREE-STEP EVENT SEQUENCES

Enabling Event Sequences

1. *Rattle* (two halves of a small barrel, wooden block). The experimenter modeled putting the block in one barrel half, putting the two halves together, and shaking the barrel (thereby causing it to rattle).

2. *Gong* (base with two posts, bar hinged to one of the posts, metal plate with a lip to fit over the bar, small plastic mallet). The experimenter modeled putting the bar across the posts (to form a crosspiece), hanging the plate from the bar, and hitting the plate with the mallet (thereby causing it to ring).

3. *Tools* (wooden rectangular base with two hinged doors attached to the sides and clear plastic knobs attached to each door, wooden rectangular peg board with a peg placed in one of the holes of the board, wooden hammer). The experimenter modeled pulling open the doors of the base, placing the board on top of the opened base, and pounding the nail (thereby causing the nail to disappear).

4. *Horse ride* (plastic rectangular box with small hole at top, knob attached to a rod running through the length of the box, plastic stick, plastic horse with hole through its middle). The experimenter modeled putting the stick into the hole in the box, placing the horse on the stick, and pulling the knob (thereby causing the horse to "take a ride," moving from side to side).

Mixed Event Sequences

1. *Dumptruck* (wooden base with wheels, plastic truck bed, two small wooden blocks). The experimenter modeled putting the truck bed on the base, placing the blocks in the truck bed, and tipping the truck bed (thereby dumping out the blocks).

2. *Popper* (clear plastic cylinder mounted to a base, small entrance tube attached to the top of the cylinder and an exit tube attached underneath the cylinder and to one side of the tube, plunger with knob running through the cylinder, small plastic ball). The experimenter modeled pulling out the plunger, placing the ball into the entrance hole, and pushing in the plunger (thereby causing the ball to roll out the exit tube).

3. *Jumper* (rectangular box with a small hole at top, string on side of box, stick, cone sized to fit on top of the stick). The experimenter modeled putting the stick into the hole in the box, placing the cone on the top of the stick, and pulling the string (thereby causing the stick and cone to "jump" up and down).

4. *Sled ride* (wooden block, wooden ramp, wooden sled with wheels on one end, pair of wheels with Velcro™ backing). The experimenter modeled attaching the ramp to the block, attaching the wheels to the sled, and rolling the sled down the ramp.

Arbitrarily Ordered Event Sequences

1. *Windmill* (rectangular hollow base, clear square tube connected to the base, plastic ball, rectangular block with thin wooden stick, a spinner attached to the top of the stick). The experimenter modeled putting the block into the hollow base, dropping the ball into the tube, and hitting the spinner (thereby causing it to spin around).

2. *House* (wooden house with felt roof, door, plastic saw, paintbrush). The experimenter modeled putting on the door (attaching it to the house with Velcro), sawing the house, and painting the roof.

3. *Party hat* (cloth-covered head-band, plastic cone with round base and hole at the top, pom-pom connected to a stick, small sticker). The experimenter modeled putting the band around the base of the cone, putting the pom-pom into the top of the cone, and putting the sticker on the front of the cone.

4. *Bunny* (wooden bunny head with ears attached by a hinge to the back of the head, plastic eyes with magnetic backing, plastic carrot). The experimenter modeled putting up the bunny's ears, putting on the bunny's eyes, and "feeding" the bunny the carrot (making "yum yum" noises while holding the carrot at the location of the mouth).

FOUR-STEP EVENT SEQUENCES

Enabling Event Sequences

1. *Popper* (clear plastic tube with plunger hinged at its midsection and folded in half, small plastic ball). The experimenter modeled unfolding the tube, pulling out the plunger, putting the ball into the tube, and pushing in the plunger (thereby causing the ball to "pop" out).

2. *Gong* (base with two posts, small wooden cup attached to one post, wooden bar sitting in the cup, metal plate with a lip, small plastic mallet). The experimenter modeled lifting the bar from the cup, putting the bar across the posts (to form a crosspiece), hanging the plate from the bar, and hitting the plate with the mallet (thereby causing it to ring).

3. *Jumper* (wooden rectangular base with a metal lever extending from its side, wooden wedge with a circular cutout, clear plastic globe with a small hole at its top and a larger hole at its base, small plastic ball held by three prongs inside the top of the globe). The experimenter modeled fitting the wedge onto the base, putting the globe onto the wedge, inserting her finger through the hole to push the ball out of the globe, and pushing the lever up and down (thereby causing the ball to "jump").

4. *Duck walk* (wooden base with wheels, plastic plate on a wooden wedge, small posts attached to each corner of the plate, plastic ring, rubber duck). The experimenter modeled attaching the wedge onto the wooden base (with Velcro™), placing the ring between the four posts, placing the duck inside the ring, and moving the base back and forth (thereby causing the duck to "walk" back and forth in the ring).

Mixed Event Sequences

1. *Tools* (wooden rectangular base with two hinged doors attached to sides and clear plastic knobs attached to each door, wooden rectangular peg board with a peg placed in one of the holes of the board, wooden hammer head and stick). The experimenter modeled pulling open the doors of the base, placing the board on top of the opened base, putting the hammer head on the stick, and pounding the nail (thereby causing the nail to disappear).

2. *Clowns* (square base with two holes on the top and a knob on the side of the base, plastic acrylic wall sitting on the base perpendicular to it, painted wooden clown, small plastic shaft attached to a circular piece with Velcro™ on its outer surface). The experimenter modeled attaching the circular piece to the bottom of the clown, inserting the shaft into the hole on the base, removing the wall, and turning the knob (thereby causing the clown to spin).

3. *Dumptruck* (wooden base with wheels, wooden top for base, plastic truck bed, two small wooden blocks). The experimenter modeled putting the top on the base, putting the truck bed on the top, placing the blocks in the truck bed, and tipping the truck bed (thereby causing the blocks to dump out).

4. *Sled ride* (wooden block, plastic ramp hinged at its midsection and folded in half, wooden sled with wheels on one end, pair of wheels with Velcro™ backing). The experimenter modeled unfolding the ramp, attaching the ramp to the block, attaching the wheels to the sled, and rolling the sled down the ramp.

Arbitrarily Ordered Event Sequences

1. *Windmill* (rectangular hollow base, clear square tube connected to the base, plastic ball, rectangular block with thin wooden stick, a spinner attached to the top of the stick, small wooden sticker). The experimenter modeled putting the block into the hollow base, dropping the ball into the tube, attaching the sticker to the front of the tube, and hitting the spinner (thereby causing it to spin around).

2. *House* (wooden house with felt roof, door, wooden block with sandpaper glued to one side, plastic saw, paintbrush). The experimenter modeled putting on the door (attaching it to the house with Velcro™), sanding the house, sawing the house, and painting the roof.

3. *Bus ride* (commercially available plastic school bus cut in half horizontally into a top [the bus] and a base [the wheels], plastic dog, plastic headlights, plastic stop sign hinged to the side of the bus). The experimenter modeled putting the top on the base, putting on the headlights (attaching them to the front of the bus), putting the dog in the bus, and opening the stop sign.

4. *Bunny* (wooden bunny head with ears attached by a hinge to the back of the head, plastic eyes with magnetic backing, wooden peg nose, plastic carrot). The experimenter modeled putting up the bunny's ears, putting on the bunny's eyes, putting in the bunny's nose, and "feeding" the bunny the carrot (making "yum yum" noises while holding the carrot at the location of the mouth).

APPENDIX B

POTENTIAL EFFECTS ON CHILDREN'S PERFORMANCE OF FEATURES OF THE RESEARCH DESIGN

In addition to the variables of interest in this research (namely, age, delay, sequence type, mode of experience, and verbal reminders), children's performance may have been affected by a number of features of the research design. This Appendix is a report of the results of analyses of three potential influences on the children's performance. First, we examined the possibility that the particular experimenter who conducted the session might have affected the children's performance. Second, we examined the possibility that conclusions regarding children's recall of the event sequences were qualified by specific event sequence effects. Third, we examined the possibility that differences in the lengths of the child-controlled response periods might account for the patterns of effects observed. Although in each case some effects obtained, in no case did the findings present substantive qualifications to the major patterns described in the body of the text.

EXPERIMENTER

As described in Chapter II (Method and Analytic Strategy), the 1,440 testing sessions represented in this *Monograph* were conducted by two experimenters. Because the experimenters did not test an equivalent number of participants in each delay condition, we are precluded from conducting an analysis to determine possible effects of experimenter on children's performance after the delay. We can, however, examine possible experimenter effects on baseline and immediate recall performance. Because the effects of the other variables already have been discussed, only main effects and interactions involving experimenter are described.

As noted below, there were some experimenter-associated effects on children's baseline performance. However, neither baseline levels of performance nor the specific experimenter by which the children were tested accounted for unique variance in predictions of children's long-term recall (see Chapter VI: Predictions of Long-Term Mnemonic Performance). Moreover, there were no experimenter-associated effects on children's learning of the event sequences.

Baseline

To investigate possible experimenter effects on baseline levels of performance, for each step-length group, we conducted 2 (experimenter: PLD, SSW) × 2 (age: younger children, older children) × 3 (sequence type: enabling, mixed, arbitrary) × 2 (experience: imitate, watch) mixed analyses of variance on both the number of individual target actions produced and the number of pairs of actions produced in the target order. For the 20-month-olds and the 16-month-olds tested on four-step event sequences, across cells of the design, the children tested by PLD produced a larger number of individual target actions than did the children tested by SSW: $F(1,176) = 6.29$, $p < .02$, $MSE = 0.89$ [$Ms = 0.88$ and 0.73 ($SDs = 0.77$ and 0.81), respectively]. There were no other reliable effects associated with experimenter.

For the 13-month-olds and the 16-month-olds tested on three-step event sequences, prior to exposure to the event sequences, the children tested by PLD produced a larger number of individual target actions than did the children tested by SSW: $F(1,176) = 5.56$, $p < .02$, $MSE = 0.78$ [$Ms = 0.77$ and 0.64 ($SDs = 0.79$ and 0.76), respectively]. Although the main effect of experimenter was not significant on the variable of pairs of actions in the target order, the interaction of Experimenter × Age × Sequence type was reliable: $F(2,352) = 4.55$, $p < .02$, $MSE = 0.11$. For the 13-month-olds, the main effect of experimenter indicated greater spontaneous production of pairs of actions in the target order among children tested by PLD ($M = 0.10$, $SD = 0.32$) than among children tested by SSW ($M = 0.05$, $SD = 0.23$). For the 16-month-olds, analysis of the Experimenter × Sequence type interaction, $F(2,176) = 3.98$, $p < .02$, $MSE = 0.15$, revealed that on enabling event sequences, the 16-month-olds tested by PLD spontaneously produced fewer pairs of actions in the target order ($M = 0.09$, $SD = 0.33$) than did the same-age children tested by SSW ($M = 0.24$, $SD = 0.52$). On mixed and arbitrarily ordered event sequences, there were no reliable differences in spontaneous levels of production of pairs of actions in the target order among the children tested by PLD and SSW.

Immediate Recall

Separate 2 (experimenter) × 2 (age) × 3 (sequence type) mixed analyses of variance for both dependent measures revealed no significant main effects of or interactions involving experimenter for either step-length group, for either dependent variable. Thus, although in both step-length groups there were some experimenter-associated effects in the baseline period, once the children were exposed to the target event sequences, effects no longer were apparent.

ITEM-SPECIFIC EFFECTS

As described in Chapter II (Method and Analytic Strategy), for each step-length group, there were four different event sequences of each type (i.e., enabling, mixed, arbitrary). At the outset of the investigation, the specific sequences of each type were counterbalanced across the 20 cells of the design (4 groups × 5 delay conditions per group). However, due to unanticipated attrition, participants later excluded in order to provide equal cell frequencies, and occasional procedural errors, in the end, counterbalancing was only approximate. This raises the possibility that uncontrolled differences across the different sequences of each type could affect the pattern of results obtained. Because, on average, only four or five children per age and delay condition were tested on each sequence in each experience condition (i.e., 18 children per cell divided by 4 different sequences per type), it was not reasonable to conduct a full analysis of children's performance with specific sequence as a variable. Instead, we focused on the two potential sequence-specific effects that might qualify the general conclusions: (a) Did the children learn each of the event sequences as a result of exposure to them (conducted on event sequences in the imitate experience condition only) and (b) At all delays over which the children showed evidence of memory, was the evidence apparent across sequences of a given type?

Initial Learning of Specific Event Sequences

There were some item-specific effects in the baseline assessment period [e.g., the children tested on four-step event sequences spontaneously produced a larger number of individual target actions on the event sequence *Popper* ($M = 1.20$, $SD = 1.10$) than on the event sequences *Jumper* and *Duck walk* [$Ms = 0.72$ and 0.64 ($SDs = 0.81$ and 0.74), respectively; details on this and other baseline differences are available from PJB]. Nevertheless, for each step-length group and each sequence type (i.e., enabling, mixed, arbitrary), 2 (age) × 2 (modeling condition: pre-modeling, post-modeling) × 4 (specific event sequence) mixed analyses of variance revealed that for all sequences, there were reliable pre-modeling to post-modeling increases in children's performance, on both dependent measures (the analyses were conducted across delay conditions, in order to provide sufficient cell frequencies; details of the analyses are available from PJB). Thus, in each step-length group, both the younger and the older children learned both the individual target actions and the temporal order of actions of each of the four event sequences of each sequence type.

Delayed Recall of Specific Event Sequences

It was not advisable to use straightforward parametric tests to examine possible item-specific qualifications on conclusions regarding the delays over which the children showed evidence of memory. First, the number of children on which the comparisons would have been based would have been prohibitively small. To determine whether the children recalled the event sequences, for each sequence type, to children's performance on one event sequence that was new to them at Session 4, we compared their performance on one event sequence that they had been permitted to imitate and on one event sequence that they had only watched. Each sequence was used approximately equally often in the imitate, watch, and new experience conditions. The result was a design in which for each sequence type, there were 12 different old-versus-new pairings (i.e., each of four event sequences paired with each of the three other sequences of the same type); one to two children per age and delay experienced each pair as their imitate-new comparison and one to two children per age and delay experienced each pair as their watch-new comparison, for a total of two to four children per pair per age and delay condition. For children tested on four-step event sequences, because there was evidence of memory of the events in all delay conditions, a total of approximately 15 children who received each old-new pair could have been included in each analysis. However, for children tested on three-step event sequences, there was evidence of memory for the individual target actions in three delay conditions (i.e., 1, 3, and 6 months) and of the temporal order of actions in only two delay conditions (i.e., 1 and 3 months). As a result, only approximately nine children would have been included in the analyses of production of individual target actions and only approximately six children would have been included in the analyses of production of pairs of actions in the target order.

Second, a full parametric examination would have entailed 36 analyses of children's production of the individual target actions of the event sequences (i.e., 12 old-new pairs for each of 3 sequence types) and 36 analyses of children's production of pairs of actions in the target order, for a total of 72 analyses per step-length group. Particularly in the case of atheoretical analyses based on small cell frequencies, separating the wheat from the chaff in a field of 144 analyses would have been a difficult endeavor. Third, a substantial number of the cells for children's performance on new event sequences had means of 0 (e.g., for the 13-month-olds, on arbitrarily ordered event sequences, 9 of the 12 comparisons of the number of pairs of actions produced in the target order featured new performance of 0). As a result, assumptions underlying analyses of variance could not be met.

Rather than parametric tests, we conducted sign tests of the number of old-new contrasts on which the children's performance on the old event sequences was nominally greater than their performance on the new event sequences. We conducted the analyses in two ways: across sequence types and separately for each sequence type. Conducting the analyses across sequence types required a total of eight tests (i.e., 4 groups × 2 dependent measures per group). All eight of the tests were statistically reliable (i.e., sign tests for related samples $ps < .003$; one-tailed). In terms of the numbers of individual target actions produced, the numbers of old-new pairs that were in the expected direction (of 36 for each group: 12 old-new pairs for each of 3 sequence types) were 34, 31, 31, and 27, for the 20-month-olds, 16-month-olds tested on four-step event sequences, 16-month-olds tested on three-step event sequences, and 13-month-olds, respectively. In terms of the number of pairs of actions produced in the target order, the numbers of old-new pairs that were in the expected direction were 31, 35, 32, and 28, for the 20-month-olds, 16-month-olds tested on four-step event sequences, 16-month-olds tested on three-step event sequences, and 13-month-olds, respectively. These analyses indicate that the pattern of higher levels of performance on previously experienced event sequences relative to new event sequences was not attributable to a small number of specific sequences but was observed across a number of different event sequences.

Conducting the analyses separately for each sequence type required a total of 24 tests (i.e., 4 groups × 2 dependent measures per group × 3 different sequence types). Twenty-two of the 24 tests were statistically reliable (i.e., sign tests for related samples $ps < .003$; one-tailed). The two exceptions were among the 13-month-olds on mixed event sequences: for both dependent measures, only 5 of the 12 comparisons were in the expected direction. The only mixed event sequence on which the 13-month-olds performed well consistently was *Jumper*. Possible reasons for the low levels of performance on mixed event sequences are discussed in Chapter VII (Summary and Interpretation of Major Findings).

LENGTH OF RESPONSE PERIODS

As described in Chapter II (Method and Analytic Strategy), the baseline, immediate, and delayed recall response periods were child controlled. They ended when the children pushed the props away, or engaged in repetitive exploratory behaviors, such as banging or mouthing the objects, or engaged in other off-task behaviors, such as throwing the props on the floor. Because the timing of the response periods was not experimenter controlled, they could be expected to vary in length. It is possible that differences in the time allowed to manipulate the props varied systematically by delay, age, sequence type, or experience condition, and that the variability could account for the observed effects of these variables.

The possibility that uncontrolled differences in the lengths of response periods could account for patterns of performance is rarely explored in research on children's long-term memory. In studies with infants and very young children, some researchers impose absolute upper limits on the amount of time participants are permitted to interact with the event-related prop(s) (e.g., 90 s in Hayne, MacDonald, & Barr, 1997). However, no assessment is made of whether infant-imposed differences in the amount of time spent actually engaged with a prop or props are systematically related to individual differences in performance. In research with children of preschool age, effects of time to supply mnemonic responses have not been evaluated, even in paradigms like that employed in the present research, in which props are used to support recall (e.g., Boyer et al., 1994; Fivush & Hamond, 1989; Price & Goodman, 1990). Although differences in the lengths of response periods have not been a source of concern, we deemed it reasonable and appropriate to examine their possible effects in at least a subset of the sample. Accordingly, we timed and analyzed the lengths of the response periods for 25% of the participants (i.e., 90 children). A sample of 90 was estimated to provide sufficient power to test the possibility that the observed effects could be attributed to differences in the lengths of the child-controlled response periods. The sample was the same as that on which we calculated reliability of coding. As such, the participants whose sessions were timed were approximately evenly divided across all cells of the design. As described below, although the analyses yielded some significant effects, they were in directions opposite those required to account for the patterns of findings associated with the variables of interest.

Children Tested on Four-Step Event Sequences

The sample of children on which we evaluated the length of the child-controlled response periods totaled 40. There were nineteen 16-month-olds and twenty-one 20-month-olds. Because of the small frequencies in each Delay × Age cell, we could not conduct analyses that included both age and delay condition. Therefore, for each response period, we conducted two separate analyses: one that included age as a variable and another that included delay condition as a variable.

Baseline

To determine whether there were systematic differences in the lengths of the baseline manipulation periods, we conducted a 2 (age: 16-month-old, 20-month-old) × 3 (sequence type: enabling, mixed, arbitrary) × 2 (experience condition: imitate, watch) mixed analysis of variance. None of the main effects or interactions was reliable. Thus, the amount of time provided to manipulate the props did not differ for the 16-month-olds and the 20-month-olds [Ms = 81.83 and 72.01 (SDs = 35.38 and 28.54), respectively]; the amount of time to manipulate the props did not differ for sequences that the children subsequently would be permitted to imitate and the sequences that they subsequently would be permitted only to watch [Ms = 77.04 and 76.31 (SDs = 32.07 and 32.62), respectively]; the amount of time to manipulate the props did not differ across sequence types [Ms = 75.73, 78.10, and 76.20 (SDs = 41.06, 26.71, and 27.38), for enabling, mixed, and arbitrary, respectively]. The Delay × Sequence type × Experience analysis of variance revealed no effects of delay condition: The time permitted for baseline manipulation of the event-related props did not differ across delay conditions (see Table B-1, Panel A, for relevant means).

Initial Learning

To determine whether (a) longer response periods for the 20-month-olds compared with the 16-month-olds could account for the older children's higher levels of performance, (b) pre- to post-modeling differences in children's performance could be due to a greater amount of time allotted after, relative to before, modeling, or (c) longer response periods for some sequence types could account for higher levels of production of individual target actions or pairs of actions in the target order, we conducted a 2 (modeling condition: pre-modeling, post-modeling) × 2 (age) × 3 (sequence type) mixed analysis of variance on the amount of time that the children manipulated the props.

Main effects indicated that the lengths of the response periods differed as a function of modeling condition and age: $F(1,38)$ = 21.90, $p <$ .0001, MSE = 1155.83, and $F(1,38)$ = 18.39, $p <$ .0001, MSE = 1722.75,

TABLE B-1

AMOUNT OF TIME ALLOTTED FOR MANIPULATION OF EVENT-RELATED
PROPS DURING CHILD-CONTROLLED RESPONSE PERIODS

Response Period (time in seconds)	Delay Condition				
	1 Month	3 Month	6 Month	9 Month	12 Month
Panel A. Children tested on 4-step event sequences					
Baseline					
Mean	87.76	78.17	77.22	80.75	64.27
SD	47.23	34.72	24.78	26.28	24.38
Immediate Recall					
Mean	71.00	69.47	67.46	70.23	58.80
SD	42.17	49.60	40.38	34.07	36.19
Delayed Recall					
Mean	63.41	79.20	81.43	86.68	75.92
SD	27.41	30.84	26.16	33.74	20.75
Panel B. Children tested on 3-step event sequences					
Baseline					
Mean	76.52	68.73	72.89	73.45	58.14
SD	34.43	26.59	28.55	31.72	20.49
Initial Learning					
Mean	63.30	62.87	57.64	73.10	46.68
SD	40.96	35.19	36.30	41.93	24.98
Delayed Recall					
Mean	61.27	70.17	72.41	79.87	71.73
SD	31.81	35.35	25.91	45.87	31.51

respectively. The differences could not, however, account for the observed effects. Specifically, pre-modeling response periods ($M = 77.04$, $SD = 32.07$) were longer than post-modeling response periods ($M = 56.50$, $SD = 44.44$); the 16-month-olds ($M = 78.85$, $SD = 42.00$) spent more time manipulating the props, relative to the 20-month-olds ($M = 55.84$, $SD = 34.83$). Analysis of the Modeling condition × Age interaction, $F(1,38) = 20.74$, $p < .0001$, $MSE = 1155.83$, revealed that whereas the pre- and post-modeling response periods differed for the 20-month-olds, $F(1,20) = 59.55$, $p < .0001$, $MSE = 827.66$ [$Ms = 75.62$ and 36.06 ($SDs = 32.01$ and 25.02), respectively], they did not differ for the 16-month-olds [$Ms = 78.61$ and 79.09 ($SDs = 32.35$ and 50.14), for pre- and post-modeling, respectively]. The amount of time to manipulate the props did not differ across sequence types [$Ms = 67.98$, 65.80, and 66.54 ($SDs = 45.19$, 36.08, and 38.69), for enabling, mixed, and arbitrary, respectively]. The Modeling condition × Delay × Sequence type analysis of variance revealed no effect of delay condition (see Table B-1, Panel A, for relevant means).

Delayed Recall

To determine whether (a) longer response periods for the 20-month-olds compared with the 16-month-olds could account for the older children's higher levels of delayed recall, (b) differences in children's performance on events previously experienced compared with new events could be due to a greater amount of time allotted for events previously imitated and previously only watched, relative to new events, or (c) longer response periods for some sequence types could account for higher levels of production of individual target actions, we conducted a 2 (age) × 3 (sequence type) × 2 (experience condition: imitate, watch, new at Session 4) mixed analysis of variance on the amount of time that the children were permitted to manipulate the props.

Neither the main effect of age nor the main effect of experience condition was reliable. Thus, the amount of time provided to manipulate the props did not differ for the 16-month-olds and the 20-month-olds [Ms = 78.46 and 76.85 (SDs = 25.24 and 31.16), respectively]; the amount of time to manipulate the props did not differ for sequences that the children previously had been permitted the opportunity to imitate, the sequences that they previously had been permitted only to watch, and the sequences that were new to the children at Session 4 [Ms = 81.02, 75.88, and 75.96 (SDs = 29.98, 28.12, and 27.19), respectively].

Whereas the main effect of sequence type was not reliable, the interaction of Age × Sequence type was significant: $F(2,76) = 4.73$, $p < .02$, $MSE = 659.05$. Separate analyses for each age group revealed that the length of time that the 20-month-olds manipulated the props did not differ across sequence types [Ms = 72.37, 84.13, and 74.06 (SDs = 32.97, 28.62, and 30.93), for enabling, mixed, and arbitrary, respectively]. The 16-month-olds manipulated the props for the arbitrarily ordered event sequences (M = 86.04, SD = 30.27) longer than they did those for the enabling event sequences (M = 73.67, SD = 25.03); they manipulated the props for the mixed event sequences (M = 75.68, SD = 17.35) for an amount of time that was intermediate between that for the arbitrary and enabling events, and which did not differ from them. Finally, the Delay × Sequence type × Experience analysis of variance revealed a main effect of delay condition: $F(4,35) = 3.47$, $p < .02$, $MSE = 1455.33$. The amount of time that the children manipulated the props was shorter in the 1-month delay condition than in the 9-month delay condition (see Table B-1, Panel A, for relevant means); there were no other reliable differences between delay conditions. Given that children's levels of performance were higher in the 1-month delay condition than in the 9-month delay condition, this difference is inconsequential.

Children Tested on Three-Step Event Sequences

The sample of children on which we evaluated the length of the child-controlled response periods totaled 50. There were twenty-four 13-month-olds and twenty-six 16-month-olds. As we did for the children tested on four-step event sequences, for each response period, we conducted two separate analyses: one that included age as a variable and another that included delay condition as a variable.

Baseline

A 2 (age: 13-month-old, 16-month-old) × 3 (sequence type) × 2 (experience) mixed analysis of variance on the lengths of the baseline manipulation periods revealed no reliable main effects. Thus, the amount of time that the 13-month-olds and the 16-month-olds manipulated the props did not differ [*Ms* = 72.72 and 66.89 (*SDs* = 30.91 and 27.16), respectively]. The amount of time to manipulate the props did not differ for sequences that the children subsequently would be permitted to imitate and the sequences that they subsequently would be permitted only to watch [*Ms* = 70.56 and 68.82 (*SDs* = 32.45 and 25.44), respectively]. The amount of time that the children manipulated the props for the enabling, mixed, and arbitrarily ordered event sequences did not differ [*Ms* = 68.59, 66.36, and 74.12 (*SDs* = 26.45, 26.58, and 33.50), respectively]. The Delay × Sequence type × Experience analysis of variance revealed no effect of delay condition: The time permitted for baseline manipulation of the event-related props did not differ across delay conditions (see Table B-1, Panel B, for relevant means).

Initial Learning

Main effects indicated that the lengths of the response periods differed as a function of modeling condition and age: $F(1,48) = 35.73$, $p < .0001$, $MSE = 993.42$, and $F(1,48) = 18.98$, $p < .0001$, $MSE = 1671.91$, respectively. As had been the case for the children tested on four-step event sequences, the differences could not, however, account for the observed effects. Specifically, the pre-modeling response periods ($M = 70.56$, $SD = 32.45$) were longer than post-modeling response periods ($M = 48.81$, $SD = 37.40$); 13-month-olds ($M = 70.39$, $SD = 37.18$) spent more time manipulating the props than the 16-month-olds ($M = 49.80$, $SD = 33.26$). Analysis of the Modeling condition × Age interaction, $F(1,48) = 15.69$, $p < .0002$, $MSE = 993.42$, revealed that whereas the pre-modeling and post-modeling response periods differed for the 16-month-olds, $F(1,25) = 85.64$, $p < .0001$,

181

MSE = 577.24 [Ms = 67.60 and 32.00 (SDs = 28.91 and 27.37), respectively], they did not differ for the 13-month-olds [Ms = 73.76 and 67.01 (SDs = 35.82 and 38.44), for pre- and post-modeling, respectively].

The amount of time to manipulate the props differed across sequence types: $F(2,96)$ = 6.15, $p < .004$, MSE = 956.75. The children spent more time manipulating the props for the arbitrarily ordered event sequences (M = 68.19, SD = 40.73) than for the enabling event sequences (M = 53.29, SD = 33.31) and the mixed event sequences (M = 57.57, SD = 34.08); the amount of time that the children spent manipulating the props for the enabling and mixed event sequences did not differ. The Modeling condition × Delay × Sequence type analysis of variance revealed no effect of delay condition (see Table B-1, Panel B, for relevant means).

Delayed Recall

We conducted a 2 (age) × 3 (sequence type) × 2 (experience condition) mixed analysis of variance on the amount of time that the children manipulated the props at the time delayed recall was tested. The main effect for age was reliable: $F(1,48)$ = 5.20, $p < .03$, MSE = 2451.67. The 13-month-olds (M = 75.95, SD = 34.41) manipulated the props for longer periods of time than did the 16-month-olds (M = 65.29, SD = 32.83). The effect was, however, qualified by the interaction of Age × Sequence type: $F(2,96)$ = 3.34, $p < .04$, MSE = 838.66. Separate analyses for each sequence type revealed age effects only on mixed event sequences: $F(1,48)$ = 8.64, $p < .005$, MSE = 1679.40 [Ms = 82.15 and 62.46 (SDs = 40.28 and 27.72), for 13- and 16-month-olds, respectively]. On enabling and arbitrarily ordered event sequences, the length of time that the children spent manipulating the event-related props did not differ reliably [Ms for enabling event sequences = 72.25 and 62.42 (SDs = 30.30 and 39.18), for 13- and 16-month-olds, respectively; Ms for arbitrarily ordered event sequences = 73.44 and 70.99 (SDs = 31.39 and 30.15), for 13- and 16-month-olds, respectively].

The amount of time that the children spent manipulating the props did not differ for sequences that they previously had been permitted the opportunity to imitate, the sequences that they previously had only watched, and the sequences that were new to the children at Session 4 [Ms = 74.32, 69.47, and 67.43 (SDs = 39.21, 34.90, and 26.43), respectively]. The main effect of sequence type also was not reliable. Thus, the amount of time that the children spent manipulating the props for the enabling, mixed, and arbitrarily ordered event sequences did not differ reliably [Ms = 67.14, 71.91, and 72.17 (SDs = 35.43, 35.61, and 30.67), respectively]. Finally, the Delay × Sequence type × Experience analysis of variance revealed no main effect of delay but an interaction of Delay × Sequence type: $F(8,90)$ = 2.43, $p < .02$, MSE = 786.67. Separate analyses for each sequence type revealed no delay condition effects for enabling or arbitrarily ordered event sequences. For mixed event sequences, children in the 1-month delay condition ($M = 61.09$, $SD = 28.19$) spent less time manipulating the props than did children in the 9-month delay condition ($M = 97.48$, $SD = 62.06$); there were no other differences between cell means. Because children in the 1-month delay condition showed evidence of memory for the event sequences, whereas the children in the 9-month delay condition did not, this difference is inconsequential.

POTENTIAL EFFECTS ON CHILDREN'S PERFORMANCE OF CHILD LANGUAGE AND GENDER

In addition to the variables manipulated in this research, children's performance may have been affected by individual and group differences among the participants. This Appendix is a report of analyses of two child variables that might have influenced their performance. First, to determine whether initial differences in facility with language by children in the different delay conditions may have influenced the patterns obtained, we compared children's levels of productive vocabulary at the time of enrollment in the study. Second, we report analyses designed to determine whether there were any differences in performance associated with child gender. Although with regard to child gender, some effects obtained, in no case did the findings present substantive qualifications to the major patterns described in the body of the text.

PRODUCTIVE VOCABULARY

At the time of enrollment in the study, using the MacArthur Productive Vocabulary checklist for toddlers (20-month-olds) or infants (13-month-olds and 16-month-olds), we collected from the parents of the majority of the participants information on their children's productive vocabularies. As described in Chapter II (Method and Analytic Strategy), we had completed inventories for 336 of our 360 participants (93.3% of the sample). In Chapter V, we reported the results of analyses of the inventories for the two groups of 16-month-olds. We found neither step-length group differences (i.e., differences between the 16-month-old randomly assigned to be tested on three-step event sequences and the 16-month-olds assigned to be tested on four-step event sequences) nor delay condition differences (i.e., differences between the children randomly assigned to the 1-, 3-, 6-, 9-, and 12-month delay conditions).

To address the possibility that random assignment to delay conditions might inadvertently have resulted in delay-group differences among the 13-month-olds, the 20-month-olds, or both, we conducted one-way analyses of variance with five levels of delay for each of the age groups separately, with reported productive vocabulary at the time of enrollment as the dependent variable. The 20-month-olds had an average reported productive vocabulary of 172 words ($SD = 161.53$); the 13-month-olds had an average reported productive vocabulary of 12 words ($SD = 15.67$). In neither age group was there evidence of a delay condition effect. There was no suggestion, then, that preexisting differences in children's levels of productive vocabulary contributed to differential performance across delay conditions.

GENDER

In order to examine the possible influence of potential gender differences on the results obtained, we conducted separate analyses of baseline, immediate recall, and delayed recall performance, as well as of the factors affecting delayed recall. Because the effects of the other variables already were discussed in the main body of the text, only main effects and interactions involving gender are described. As will become apparent, there were several gender-related effects. However, because (a) we had neither conceptually motivated nor empirically motivated hypotheses regarding gender effects, (b) gender-related effects typically were based on small numbers of children per cell, and (c) gender-related effects accounted for no significant variance in children's delayed-recall performance (see Chapter VI: Predictions of Long-Term Mnemonic Performance), we do not expend significant energy interpreting the findings obtained. For present purposes, the effects are of interest only to the extent that they qualify conclusions based on the sample as a whole. In the interest of space, details of some analyses are omitted. In all cases where they were conducted, separate analyses at each level of a variable were indicated by higher-order interactions. Details are available from PJB.

Children Tested on Four-Step Event Sequences

Baseline

To investigate the possible influence of gender on baseline levels of performance, we conducted separate 2 (gender: girls, boys) × 5 (delay: 1 month, 3 month, 6 month, 9 month, 12 month) × 2 (age: 16-month-olds, 20-month-olds) × 3 (sequence type: enabling, mixed, arbitrary) ×

2 (experience: imitate, watch) mixed analyses of variance for each dependent measure. Girls' and boys' baseline levels of production of the individual target actions of the events did not differ. Although the Gender × Delay × Experience interaction was reliable ($p < .03$), follow-up analyses revealed no reliable differences between girls and boys.

For the variable of production of pairs of actions in the target order, the interaction of Gender × Delay × Experience was reliable: $F(4,160) = 2.80$, $p < .03$, $MSE = 0.11$. Separate analyses at each delay revealed an effect in the 9-month delay condition only: Girls produced a smaller number of pairs of actions in the target order than did boys [$Ms = 0.04$ and 0.12 ($SDs = 0.19$ and 0.35), respectively]: $F(1,34) = 6.01$, $p < .02$, $MSE = 0.06$. The participation of experience condition in the interaction was revealed only with separate analyses for each gender group. For girls, analysis of the Delay × Experience condition interaction, $F(4,89) = 3.32$, $p < .02$, $MSE = 0.08$, revealed that in the 3-month delay condition, girls produced more pairs of actions in the target order on events that they subsequently would be permitted to imitate ($M = 0.24$, $SD = 0.43$), relative to on events that they subsequently would be permitted only to watch ($M = 0.04$, $SD = 0.19$). There were no other reliable effects. The patterns were not altered when, in analysis of covariance, we controlled for the number of individual target actions produced. Given the low levels of spontaneous production of pairs of actions in the target order, the psychological significance of the observed effects is questionable.

Immediate Recall

Analyses of effects of gender on children's immediate recall were conducted only on events in the imitate condition. Accordingly, we conducted separate 2 (gender) × 5 (delay) × 2 (age) × 3 (sequence type) analyses for each dependent measure. On neither measure were girls and boys found to differ. However, analysis of covariance with the number of component actions produced controlled indicated that the girls' and boys' levels of immediate recall of the temporal order of the event sequences differed reliably [$Ms = 1.91$ and 1.78 ($SDs = 0.86$ and 0.83), respectively]: $F(1,160) = 4.41$, $p < .04$, $MSE = 0.56$. There were no interaction effects. Thus, girls and boys entered the delay interval with small yet statistically reliable differences in levels of initial mastery of the temporal order of the to-be-remembered material.

Delayed Recall

To evaluate possible gender-differential patterns of long-term recall, we conducted 2 (gender) × 5 (delay) × 2 (age) × 3 (sequence type) ×

3 (experience: imitate, watch, new at Session 4) mixed analyses of variance for both dependent measures, both prior to and after introduction of the verbal labels for the events. Because we are interested in whether there were gender-related qualifications on conclusions regarding children's event memories, we focus on potential interactions involving both gender and experience. The analyses revealed gender-differential effects when the children were prompted by the event-related props alone but not when they were prompted by both the props and the verbal labels for the events. Specifically, prior to introduction of the verbal reminders, interactions of Gender × Delay × Experience suggested gender-associated differential patterns of delayed recall of both the individual target actions and the temporal order of actions of the event sequences: $Fs(16,320)$ = 8.47 and 7.64, $ps < .0001$, $MSEs$ = 0.87 and 0.36, respectively. Separate analyses for each gender group revealed interactions of Delay × Experience for both girls and boys, on both dependent measures: $Fs(8,178)$ > 10.75, $ps < .0001$, $MSEs < 0.90$, for girls, for individual target actions and pairs of actions in target order; $Fs(8,162) > 3.95$, $ps < .0003$, $MSEs < 1.00$, for boys, for individual target actions and pairs of actions in target order.

Analyses of the interactions revealed that when the girls were prompted by the props alone, in the 1-, 3-, and 6-month delay conditions they showed evidence of memory for the individual target actions of event sequences imitated and only watched; in the 12-month delay condition, they showed evidence of memory for the individual target actions of events watched [$Fs(2,34) > 3.35$, $ps < .05$, $MSEs < 1.45$]; the girls evidenced memory for the temporal order of actions in the 1-, 3-, and 6-month delay conditions (events imitated and events watched) [$Fs(2,34) > 3.50$, $ps < .04$, $MSEs <$ 0.70]. When the boys were prompted by the props alone, they showed evidence of memory for the individual target actions and order of actions in all but the 12-month delay condition (6-month ordered recall of events imitated only; all other effects for events watched as well as imitated) [$Fs(2,34) > 3.05$, $ps < .05$, $MSEs < 1.20$]. Critically, once they were prompted by both the event-related props and the verbal labels for the event sequences, there were no effects involving gender and experience. Thus, although there were some gender-specific patterns of performance when the children were prompted by the props alone, after provision of the verbal labels for the event sequences, there were none.

Factors Affecting Delayed Recall

Effects of delay, age, sequence type, and mode of experience. The above analyses revealed that both gender groups recalled the event sequences over the delays. As will become apparent, with some exceptions, the girls and boys also were similarly affected by the variables of delay, age, sequence type, and mode of experience. To determine whether there were differential gender effects, we conducted separate 2 (gender) × 5 (delay) × 2 (age) × 3 (sequence type) × 2 (experience: imitate, watch) mixed analyses of variance for each dependent variable; we conducted parallel analyses for performance before and after introduction of the verbal reminders of the event sequences. Gender-related effects were associated with the variables of sequence type and mode of experience.

Both prior to and after provision of the verbal reminders, the girls were more likely to show sequence type effects, relative to the boys. Prior to introduction of the verbal reminders, the girls showed consistently higher levels of production of the individual target actions of the arbitrarily ordered event sequences relative to the mixed event sequences: $Fs(2,34-36) > 3.45$, $ps < .05$, $MSEs < 1.05$. In contrast, boys showed sequence type effects only in the 3-, 6-, and 9-month delay conditions: (a) in the 3-month delay condition, boys' performance on arbitrarily ordered event sequences was greater than performance on enabling event sequences [$F(2,34) = 4.56$, $p < .02$, $MSE = 0.92$], (b) in the 6-month delay condition, boys' performance on arbitrarily ordered event sequences was greater than performance on both enabling and mixed event sequences [$F(2,32) = 7.69$, $p < .002$, $MSE = 0.87$], and (c) in the 9-month delay condition, boys' performance on enabling event sequences was greater than performance on both mixed and arbitrarily ordered event sequences [$F(2,34) = 6.66$, $p < .004$, $MSE = 0.74$].

After provision of the verbal labels for the event sequences, the girls produced a greater number of the individual target actions of the arbitrarily ordered event sequences, relative to both the enabling and mixed event sequences, which did not differ from one another: $F(2,178) = 16.70$, $p < .0001$, $MSE = 1.05$. Boys' performance was affected by sequence type only in the 6- and 9-month delay conditions: $F(2,32) = 7.82$, $p < .002$, $MSE = 0.55$, 6-month delay condition; and $F(2,34) = 8.55$, $p < .001$, $MSE = 0.79$, 9-month delay condition. In the 6-month delay condition, boys' performance on arbitrarily ordered events was greater than on mixed events. In the 9-month delay condition, boys' performance on enabling event sequences was greater than performance on both arbitrarily ordered and mixed event sequences. There were no differential effects of sequence type on girls' and boys' ordered recall.

In two cells of the design, the recall performance of girls and boys was differentially affected by the opportunity to imitate the events prior to imposition of the delay. In the 1- and 3-month delay conditions, when the children were prompted by the event-related props alone, 20-month-old girls showed higher levels of ordered recall of event sequences previously imitated compared with event sequences previously only watched: $Fs(1,8) > 9.65$, $ps < .02$, $MSEs < 0.50$. There were no mode of experience effects on 20-month-old girls' ordered recall in the 6-, 9-, or 12-month delay conditions, and there were no mode of experience effects for the 16-month-old girls or for the boys of either age group. After provision of the verbal reminders, mode of experience effects were not observed for either gender group of either age.

Effects of verbal reminders. To determine whether girls and boys were similarly affected by the verbal reminders provided, as in the main analyses reported in Chapter III, we created scores reflective of the difference in levels of performance prior to and after exposure to the verbal reminders. We then subjected the difference scores to separate 2 (gender) × 5 (delay) × 2 (age) × 3 (sequence type) × 2 (experience condition) mixed analyses of variance for (a) the difference in production of individual target actions before and after verbal reminding, and (b) the difference in production of ordered pairs of actions before and after verbal reminding. Gender × Sequence type interactions emerged in both analyses: $Fs(4,320)$ = 4.47 and 4.41, $ps < .002$, $MSEs$ = 0.60 and 0.25, for target actions and pairs of actions, respectively. In each case, the smallest difference score was for girls on mixed event sequences. Even for this cell, however, t tests indicated that the sizes of the differences were greater than zero. The absence of any other interactions involving gender and reminding condition indicates that both girls' and boys' performance was facilitated by verbal reminders.

Summary. Analyses examining possible effects of gender group revealed two types of qualifications of the patterns observed in the sample as a whole. First, sequence type affected girls' performance more than it did boys'. Both prior to and after introduction of the verbal reminders, the girls showed higher levels of production of the individual target actions of the arbitrarily ordered event sequences relative to the mixed event sequences. In addition, after provision of the verbal reminders, girls' levels of production of the individual target actions of the arbitrarily ordered event sequences were higher than their production of the individual target actions of the enabling event sequences. In contrast to the relatively consistent sequence type effects on the girls' recall of the individual target actions of the event sequences, boys' performance was affected by sequence type in some but not all delay conditions and the effects were not consistent from one delay condition to the next. Moreover, only 20-month-old girls' ordered recall was affected by sequence type. Second, in the 1- and 3-month delay conditions, when they were prompted by the event-related props alone, 20-month-old girls' ordered recall performance was affected by whether or not they had been permitted the opportunity to imitate the event sequences prior to imposition of the delay.

Mode of experience effects were not observed among 16-month-old girls or among boys of either age. Nor were they observed after provision of verbal reminders. The analyses of potential gender effects revealed no qualifications to the patterns of results observed to be associated with the variables of delay interval, age at the time of exposure to the event sequences, or the availability of verbal reminders.

Children Tested on Three-Step Event Sequences

Baseline

We conducted separate 2 (gender) × 5 (delay) × 2 (age: 13-month-olds, 16-month-olds) × 3 (sequence type) × 2 (experience) mixed analyses of variance for both dependent measures. For the variable of production of individual target actions, the interaction of Gender × Experience was reliable: $F(1,160) = 4.81$, $p < .03$, $MSE = 0.55$. Separate analyses for each experience condition revealed that on event sequences that the children subsequently would be permitted to imitate, girls' and boys' performance did not differ. On event sequences that they subsequently would be permitted only to watch, girls produced a smaller number of individual target actions than did boys: $F(1,178) = 4.00$, $p < .05$, $MSE = 0.64$ [$Ms = 0.64$ and 0.78 ($SDs = 0.76$ and 0.78), respectively]. The girls' and boys' levels of production of pairs of actions in the target order did not differ significantly. The patterns were not altered when, in analysis of covariance, we controlled for the number of individual target actions produced.

Immediate Recall

We conducted separate 2 (gender) × 5 (delay) × 2 (age) × 3 (sequence type) analyses of variance for each dependent measure. On neither measure were girls and boys found to differ. There were no interaction effects. No effects emerged when, in analysis of covariance, we controlled for the number of individual target actions produced.

Delayed Recall

To evaluate possible gender-related differential patterns of production of the individual target actions of the event sequences, we conducted 2 (gender) × 3 (delay: 1 month, 3 month, 6 month) × 2 (age) × 3 (sequence type) × 3 (experience) mixed analyses of variance, both prior to and after exposure to the verbal labels for the event sequences. Prior to introduction of the verbal labels, the five-way interaction of the variables was statistically significant: $F(16,384) = 1.88$, $p < .03$, $MSE = 0.74$. For the

190

girls, we pursued the significant four-way interaction, $F(8,192) = 2.24$, $p <$ .03, $MSE = 0.77$, with separate analyses for each age group; both analyses yielded Sequence type × Experience interactions: $Fs(4,96) > 2.45$, $ps <$ .05, $MSEs < 1.00$. For the boys, we pursued the resulting Sequence type × Experience interaction [$F(4,192) = 2.41$, $p = .05$, $MSE = 0.71$] and the Delay × Experience interaction [$F(4,96) = 3.41$, $p < .02$, $MSE = 0.83$] with separate analyses by sequence type and delay, respectively.

Analyses of the interactions revealed that when the 16-month-old girls were prompted by the props alone, they showed evidence of memory of the individual target actions of the event sequences that they previously had been permitted to imitate, and for the target actions of the mixed and arbitrarily ordered event sequences that they previously had only watched. They did not show evidence of memory of the individual target actions of the enabling event sequences that they had only watched [$Fs(2,52) > 5.70$, $ps < .006$, $MSEs < 1.35$, for enabling, mixed, and arbitrarily ordered event sequences]. The 13-month-old girls remembered the individual target actions of the enabling and arbitrarily ordered event sequences, regardless of their mode of experience of them: $Fs(2,52) >$ 5.90, $ps < .005$, $MSEs < 0.70$, for enabling and arbitrarily ordered event sequences. They did not show evidence of memory of the individual target actions of the mixed event sequences. When the boys were prompted by the props alone, they showed evidence of memory for the individual target actions of the enabling and arbitrarily ordered event sequences, regardless of their mode of experience of them: $Fs(2,106) > 6.10$, $ps <$ .003, $MSEs < 0.85$, for enabling and arbitrarily ordered events. The boys remembered the mixed event sequences that they had imitated, but not those that they had only watched [overall $p > .10$; Dunnett's $p < .05$, for events imitated]. Across sequence types, the boys in the 1-month delay condition remembered the individual target actions of the event sequences that they had been permitted to imitate and that they had only watched [$F(2,34) = 23.50$, $p < .0001$, $MSE = 0.78$]; the boys in the 3-month delay condition remembered the target actions of the event sequences that they had only watched, but not of those that they had been given the opportunity to imitate [$F(2,34) = 3.47$, $p < .05$, $MSE = 1.15$]; the boys in the 6-month delay condition remembered the target actions of the event sequences that they had been permitted to imitate, but not those that they had only watched [overall $p > .10$; Dunnett's $p < .05$ for events imitated].

Once they were prompted by both the event-related props and the verbal labels for the event sequences, both the girls and the boys showed evidence of memory for the individual target actions of the event sequences in the 1-, 3-, and 6-month delay conditions. Thus, just as for the children tested on four-step event sequences, although there were some gender-specific patterns of performance when the children were prompted by the props alone, once the verbal labels for the event sequences were introduced, gender-specific patterns no longer were apparent.

To investigate possible gender-related effects on children's ordered recall, we conducted 2 (gender) × 2 (delay: 1 month, 3 month) × 2 (age) × 3 (sequence type) × 3 (experience) mixed analyses of variance both before and after provision of the verbal labels for the events. Prior to verbal labeling, the interaction of Gender × Age × Sequence type × Experience was reliable: $F(8, 256) = 2.83$, $p < .005$, $MSE = 0.24$; after provision of the verbal labels, the interaction of Gender × Sequence type × Experience was reliable: $F(4, 256) = 2.75$, $p < .03$, $MSE = 0.31$. In each case, we pursued the interactions with separate analyses for each gender group.

Analyses of the interactions revealed the same pattern for the girls before and after the verbal labels. Specifically, in both cases, there were interactions of Sequence type × Experience: $F(4, 136) = 3.96$, $p < .005$, $MSE = 0.26$, before verbal labels; $F(4, 140) = 2.71$, $p < .04$, $MSE = 0.29$, after verbal labels. Separate analyses for each sequence type revealed that, whereas the girls showed evidence of memory of the temporal order of the actions of the mixed and arbitrarily ordered event sequences that they had watched and that they had been permitted to imitate, they remembered the temporal order of the enabling event sequences that they had been permitted to imitate, but not of those they had only watched [before verbal labels: $Fs(2, 70) > 5.00$, $ps < .009$, $MSEs < 0.40$; after verbal labels: $Fs(2, 70) > 5.05$, $ps < .009$, $MSEs < 0.45$].

For boys, before the verbal labels for the events, the interaction of Age × Sequence type × Experience was reliable: $F(4, 136) = 3.62$, $p < .008$, $MSE = 0.24$. Separate analyses for each age group revealed Sequence type × Experience interactions: $Fs(4, 68) > 4.25$, $ps < .004$, $MSEs < 0.35$, for 16-month-olds and 13-month-olds. Separate analyses for each sequence type revealed that both age groups of boys remembered the temporal order of the actions of the enabling event sequences that they had been permitted to imitate; the older boys also showed ordered recall of the event sequences that they had only watched: $Fs(2, 34) > 6.40$, $ps < .005$, $MSEs < 0.55$, for 16-month-olds and 13-month-olds. For mixed event sequences, neither age group showed evidence of temporally ordered recall. For arbitrarily ordered event sequences, the older boys showed evidence of ordered recall of the sequences that they had been given the opportunity to imitate, but not of those that they had only watched: $F(2, 34) = 7.00$, $p < .003$, $MSE = 0.34$. Analysis of the boys' performance when they were prompted both by the event-related props and by the verbal labels for the event sequences yielded the interaction of Sequence type × Experience: $F(4, 140) = 3.38$, $p < .02$, $MSE = 0.35$. Separate analyses for each sequence type showed evidence of memory for the temporal order of enabling and arbitrarily ordered event sequences in both the imitate and the watch experience conditions: $Fs(2,70) > 4.50$, $ps < .02$, $MSEs < 0.55$; the boys did not show evidence of temporally ordered recall of the mixed event sequences, regardless of the mode of experience of them. In their indication of variability in children's retention of temporal order information over time, these analyses are consistent with those of the sample as a whole. Together, they suggest that for children 13 and 16 months of age, there is greater fragility in the ability to maintain and retrieve temporal order information over time, relative to information about the individual target actions of to-be-remembered events.

Factors Affecting Delayed Recall

Effects of delay, age, sequence type, and mode of experience. To determine whether there were differential gender effects on children's production of the individual target actions of the event sequences as a function of the variables of delay, age, sequence type, and experience condition, we conducted mixed analyses of variance with three levels of delay (1 month, 3 month, 6 month); for the variable of pairs of actions in the target order, the analyses included only two levels of delay (1 month, 3 month). For each dependent measure, we conducted parallel analyses for performance before and after introduction of the verbal reminders of the event sequences. Gender-related effects were associated with each of the variables.

Prior to introduction of the verbal reminders, there were no gender-related effects of delay condition. After introduction of the verbal reminders, the 16-month-old boys exhibited a sharper decline in production of the individual target actions of the event sequences, relative to the 13-month-old boys and the girls. [We pursued the interaction of Gender × Delay × Age × Experience with separate analyses by gender; for boys, we pursued the interaction of Delay × Age × Experience with separate analyses by age.] That is, for the older boys, production of the individual target actions of the event sequences was lower after 3 months and 6 months than after only 1 month. For the younger boys and both age groups of girls, production of the individual target actions of the event sequences was lower after 6 months than after 1 month; performance in the 3-month delay condition was intermediate and did not differ from that in the shorter or the longer delay conditions. There were no gender-related effects of delay on children's ordered recall, either before or after provision of the verbal reminders.

When the children were prompted by the event-related props alone, gender-related effects of age were apparent on ordered recall. [Specifically, we pursued the interaction of Gender × Age × Sequence type × Experience with separate analyses for each gender group.] For girls, there was no age effect. The older boys produced a larger number of pairs of actions in the target order, relative to the younger boys: $F(1,34) = 22.41$, $p < .0001$, $MSE = 0.71$. There were no gender-related effects of age in children's post-reminder performance. Neither were there any effects on children's production of the individual target actions of the events.

There were gender-related effects of sequence type both on children's production of the individual target actions of the event sequences and on their production of ordered pairs of actions. Before introduction of the verbal reminders, both girls and boys produced larger numbers of individual target actions of the arbitrarily ordered relative to the mixed event sequences. The boys also produced larger numbers of individual target actions of the enabling relative to the mixed event sequences. For the girls, production of the individual target actions of the enabling events was intermediate and did not differ from the other two sequence types [$Fs(2,106) = 5.07$ and 15.05, $ps < .008$, $MSEs = 0.77$ and 0.77, for girls and boys, respectively]. After introduction of the verbal reminders, the girls and boys exhibited the same patterns of recall.

Both prior to and after exposure to the verbal reminders, girls' ordered recall of the enabling event sequences was higher than that of the arbitrarily ordered events. Ordered recall performance on the mixed event sequences was intermediate and did not differ from that on the other two sequence types [before verbal reminders: $F(2,68) = 3.46$, $p < .04$, $MSE = 0.37$; after verbal reminders: $F(2,70) = 5.34$, $p < .007$, $MSE = 0.27$]. For the boys, ordered recall of the enabling event sequences was greater than that of both the arbitrarily ordered and the mixed event sequences, both prior to and after exposure to the verbal labels for the events [before verbal reminders: $F(2,68) = 20.32$, $p < .0001$, $MSE = 0.33$; after verbal reminders: $F(2,70) = 13.52$, $p < .0001$, $MSE = 0.42$].

Finally, on the enabling event sequences, prior to provision of the verbal labels for the event sequences, the performance of the girls and the boys was differentially affected by the opportunity to imitate the event sequences prior to imposition of the delays. Specifically, the girls produced both more individual target actions [$F(1,53) = 22.53$, $p < .0001$, $MSE = 0.56$] and more pairs of actions in the target order [$F(1,35) = 9.70$, $p < .004$, $MSE = 0.41$] of the enabling event sequences that they had been permitted to imitate, relative to the enabling event sequences that they had only watched. The effect was not apparent on the other two sequence types; the effect was not apparent for the boys for any sequence type. After provision of the verbal reminders, mode of experience effects were not observed for either gender group.

Effects of verbal reminders. To determine whether girls and boys were similarly affected by the verbal reminders, we conducted analyses parallel to those described for the children tested on four-step event sequences. For children's production of the individual actions of the sequences, interactions of Gender × Experience [$F(2,96) = 5.56$, $p < .006$, $MSE = 0.36$] and of Gender × Delay × Age [$F(4,96) = 4.27$, $p < .004$, $MSE = 0.32$] were observed. In both cases, the smallest difference scores were for boys: for the Gender × Experience effect, the difference scores were the smallest for boys on events previously imitated; for the Gender × Delay × Age effect, the difference scores were the smallest for the 16-month-old boys in the 1-month delay condition. Even in these cells, however, t tests indicated that the sizes of the differences were greater than zero. There were no effects of gender in the analysis of children's ordered recall performance. Thus, girls and boys were similarly affected by the availability of verbal reminders of the events.

Summary. The analyses examining possible effects of gender group revealed several specific effects. With one exception, the effects were observed when the children were prompted by the event-related props alone; once verbal labels for the event sequences were introduced, the effects diminished. First, and in exception to the pattern just noted, after introduction of the verbal labels for the event sequences, the girls and the 13-month-old boys exhibited more gradual decrements in production of the individual target actions of the event sequences, relative to the 16-month-old boys. Second, prior to provision of the verbal reminders for the event sequences, age effects on children's production of ordered pairs of actions were observed for boys but not for girls. Third, for girls, ordered recall performance on mixed event sequences was not significantly lower than on enabling event sequences, whereas for boys, the difference in ordered recall was reliable. Fourth, prior to provision of the verbal labels for the event sequences, girls' performance on enabling events was affected by the opportunity to imitate prior to imposition of the delays. Mode of experience effects were not apparent for boys on any sequence type. Neither were mode of experience effects apparent after provision of the verbal labels for the event sequences, for either gender group. Finally, girls and boys were similarly affected by provision of verbal reminders for the event sequences.

REFERENCES

Ashmead, D., & Perlmutter, M. (1980). Infant memory in everyday life. In M. Perlmutter (Ed.), *New directions for child development: Children's memory.* San Francisco: Jossey-Bass.

Bachevalier, J. (1990). Ontogenetic development of habit and memory formation in primates. In A. Diamond (Ed.), *The development and neural bases of higher cognitive functions.* New York: New York Academy of Science.

Bachevalier, J. (1992). Cortical versus limbic immaturity: Relationship to infantile amnesia. In M. R. Gunnar & C. A. Nelson (Eds.), *Developmental behavioral neuroscience: The Minnesota Symposia on Child Psychology* (Vol. 24). Hillsdale, NJ: Erlbaum.

Bachevalier, J., Brickson, M., & Hagger, C. (1993). Limbic-dependent recognition memory in monkeys develops early in infancy. *Neuroreport,* **4,** 77–80.

Bachevalier, J., & Mishkin, M. (1994). Effects of selective neonatal temporal lobe lesions on visual recognition memory in rhesus monkeys. *The Journal of Neuroscience,* **14,** 2128–2139.

Baker-Ward, L., Hess, T. M., & Flannagen, D. A. (1990). The effects of involvement on children's memory for events. *Cognitive Development,* **5,** 55–70.

Barnat, S. B., Klein, P. J., & Meltzoff, A. N. (1996). Deferred imitation across changes in context and object: Memory and generalization in 14-month-old children. *Infant Behavior and Development,* **19,** 241–251.

Barr, R., Dowden, A., & Hayne, H. (1996). Developmental changes in deferred imitation by 6- to 24-month-old infants. *Infant Behavior and Development,* **19,** 159–170.

Barr, R., & Hayne, H. (1996). The effect of event structure on imitation in infancy: Practice makes perfect? *Infant Behavior and Development,* **19,** 253–257.

Bates, E., Thal, D. J., & Marchman, V. (1991). Symbols and syntax: A Darwinian approach to language development. In N. Krasnegor, D. Rumbaugh, R. Schiefelbusch, & M. Sutddert-Kennedy (Eds.), *Biological and behavioral determinants of language development.* Hillsdale, NJ: Lawrence Erlbaum Associates Inc.

Bauer, P. J. (1992). Holding it all together: How enabling relations facilitate young children's event recall. *Cognitive Development,* **7,** 1–28.

Bauer, P. J. (1993). Identifying subsystems of autobiographical memory: Commentary on Nelson. In C. A. Nelson (Ed.), *Memory and affect in development: The Minnesota Symposium on Child Psychology* (Vol. 26). Hillsdale, NJ: Erlbaum.

Bauer, P. J. (1995). Recalling past events: From infancy to early childhood. *Annals of Child Development,* **11,** 25–71.

Bauer, P. J. (1996). What do infants recall of their lives? Memory for specific events by 1- to 2-year-olds. *American Psychologist,* **51,** 29–41.

Bauer, P. J. (1997). Development of memory in early childhood. In N. Cowan (Ed.), *The development of memory in childhood.* Hove, East Sussex: Psychology Press.

Bauer, P. J., & Dow, G. A. A. (1994). Episodic memory in 16- and 20-month-old children: Specifics are generalized, but not forgotten. *Developmental Psychology*, **30**, 403–417.

Bauer, P. J., & Hertsgaard, L. A. (1993). Increasing steps in recall of events: Factors facilitating immediate and long-term memory in 13.5- and 16.5-month-old children. *Child Development*, **64**, 1204–1223.

Bauer, P. J., Hertsgaard, L. A., & Dow, G. A. (1994). After 8 months have passed: Long-term recall of events by 1- to 2-year-old children. *Memory*, **2**, 353–382.

Bauer, P. J., Hertsgaard, L. A., Dropik, P., & Daly, B. P. (1998). When even arbitrary order becomes important: Developments in reliable temporal sequencing of arbitrarily ordered events. *Memory*, **6**, 165–198.

Bauer, P. J., Hertsgaard, L. A., & Wewerka, S. S. (1995). Effects of experience and reminding on long-term recall in infancy: Remembering not to forget. *Journal of Experimental Child Psychology*, **59**, 260–298.

Bauer, P. J., Kroupina, M. G., Schwade, J. A., Dropik, P., & Wewerka, S. S. (1998). If memory serves, will language? Later verbal accessibility of early memories. *Development and Psychopathology*, **10**, 655–679.

Bauer, P. J., & Mandler, J. M. (1989). One thing follows another: Effects of temporal structure on 1- to 2-year-olds' recall of events. *Developmental Psychology*, **25**, 197–206.

Bauer, P. J., & Mandler, J. M. (1992). Putting the horse before the cart: The use of temporal order in recall of events by one-year-old children. *Developmental Psychology*, **28**, 441–452.

Bauer, P. J., Schwade, J. A., Wewerka, S. S., & Delaney, K. (1999). Planning ahead: Goal-directed problem solving by two-year-olds. *Developmental Psychology*, **35**, 1321–1337.

Bauer, P. J., & Shore, C. M. (1987). Making a memorable event: Effects of familiarity and organization on young children's recall of action sequences. *Cognitive Development*, **2**, 327–338.

Bauer, P. J., & Thal, D. J. (1990). Scripts or scraps: Reconsidering the development of sequential understanding. *Journal of Experimental Child Psychology*, **50**, 287–304.

Bauer, P. J., & Travis, L. L. (1993). The fabric of an event: Different sources of temporal invariance differentially affect 24-month-olds' recall. *Cognitive Development*, **8**, 319–341.

Bauer, P. J., Van Abbema, D. L., & de Haan, M. (1999). In for the short haul: Immediate and short-term remembering and forgetting by 20-month-old children. *Infant Behavior and Development*, **22**, 321–343.

Bauer, P. J., & Wewerka, S. S. (1995). One- to two-year-olds' recall of events: The more expressed, the more impressed. *Journal of Experimental Child Psychology*, **59**, 475–496.

Bauer, P. J., & Wewerka, S. S. (1997). Saying is revealing: Verbal expression of event memory in the transition from infancy to early childhood. In P. van den Broek, P. J. Bauer, & T. Bourg (Eds.), *Developmental spans in event comprehension and representation: Bridging fictional and actual events.* Mahwah, NJ: Erlbaum.

Bower, G. H. (1981). Mood and memory. *American Psychologist*, **36**, 129–148.

Boyer, M. E., Barron, K. L., & Farrar, M. J. (1994). Three-year-olds remember a novel event from 20 months: Evidence for long-term memory in children? *Memory*, **2**, 417–445.

Boyer, M. E., & Farrar, M. J. (1994). *Space and experience as determinants of 20-month-old children's event memory.* Unpublished manuscript.

Brainerd, C. J., Kingma, J., & Howe, M. L. (1985). On the development of forgetting. *Child Development*, **56**, 1103–1119.

Brainerd, C. J., & Reyna, V. F. (1995). Learning rate, learning opportunities, and the development of forgetting. *Developmental Psychology*, **31**, 251–262.

Brewer, W. F. (1986). What is autobiographical memory? In D. C. Rubin (Ed.), *Autobiographical memory.* New York: Cambridge University Press.

Carver, L. J. (1998). *The dawning of a past: The emergence of declarative memory in infancy.* Unpublished doctoral dissertation, University of Minnesota.

Carver, L. J., & Bauer, P. J. (1999). When the event is more than the sum of its parts: Nine-month-olds' long-term ordered recall. *Memory, 7,* 147–174.

Chugani, H. T., Phelps, M. E., & Mazziotta, J. C. (1986). Positron emission tomography study of human brain functional development. *Annals of Neurology, 22,* 487–497.

Cohen, N. J., & Squire, L. R. (1980). Preserved learning and retention of pattern analyzing skill in amnesia: Dissociation of knowing how and knowing that. *Science, 210,* 207–209.

DeCasper, A. J., & Spence, M. J. (1986). Prenatal maternal speech influences newborns' perceptions of speech sounds. *Infant Behavior and Development, 9,* 133–150.

de Haan, M., Bauer, P. J., Georgieff, M. K., & Nelson, C. A. (2000). Explicit memory in low-risk infants aged 19 months born between 27 and 42 weeks of gestation. *Developmental Medicine and Child Neurology, 42,* 304–312.

Diamond, A. (1985). Development of the ability to use recall to guide action as indicated by infants' performance on AB. *Child Development, 56,* 868–883.

Eacott, M. J., & Crawley, R. A. (1998). The offset of childhood amnesia: Memory for events that occurred before age 3. *Journal of Experimental Psychology: General, 127,* 22–33.

Fagan, J. F. (1970). Memory in the infant. *Journal of Experimental Child Psychology, 9,* 217–226.

Fagan, J. F. (1990). The paired-comparison paradigm and infant intelligence. In A. Diamond (Ed.), *The development and neural bases of higher cognitive functions.* New York: New York Academy of Science.

Fenson, L., Dale, P. S., Reznick, J. S., Bates, E., Thal, D. J., & Pethick, S. J. (1994). Variability in early communicative development. *Monographs of the Society for Research in Child Development, 59*(5, Serial No. 242).

Fivush, R. (1984). Learning about school: The development of kindergartners' school scripts. *Child Development, 55,* 1697–1709.

Fivush, R. (1988). The functions of event memory. In U. Neisser & E. Winograd (Eds.), *Remembering reconsidered: Ecological and traditional approaches to the study of memory.* New York: Cambridge University Press.

Fivush, R. (1997). Event memory in early childhood. In N. Cowan (Ed.), *The development of memory in childhood.* Hove, East Sussex: Psychology Press.

Fivush, R., Gray, J. T., & Fromhoff, F. A. (1987). Two-year-olds talk about the past. *Cognitive Development, 2,* 393–410.

Fivush, R., & Hamond, N. R. (1989). Time and again: Effects of repetition and retention interval on 2 year olds' event recall. *Journal of Experimental Child Psychology, 47,* 259–273.

Fivush, R., & Hamond, N. R. (1990). Autobiographical memory across the preschool years: Toward reconceptualizing childhood amnesia. In R. Fivush & J. A. Hudson (Eds.), *Knowing and remembering in young children.* New York: Cambridge University Press.

Fivush, R., Hudson, J. A., & Nelson, K. (1984). Children's long-term memory for a novel event: An exploratory study. *Merrill-Palmer Quarterly, 30,* 303–316.

Fivush, R., Kuebli, J., & Clubb, P. A. (1992). The structure of events and event representations: A developmental analysis. *Child Development, 63,* 188–201.

Fivush, R., & Slackman, E. (1986). The acquisition and development of scripts. In K. Nelson (Ed.), *Event knowledge: Structure and function in development.* Hillsdale, NJ: Erlbaum.

Fox, N., Kagan, J., & Weiskopf, S. (1979). The growth of memory during infancy. *Genetic Psychology Monographs, 99,* 91–130.

Freud, S. (1966). *Introductory lectures on psychoanalysis.* Translated and edited by J. Strachey. New York: Norton. (Original work published 1916–1917)

Freud, S. (1953). Three essays on the theory of sexuality. In J. Strachey (Ed.), *The standard edition of the complete psychological works of Sigmund Freud* (Vol. 7). London: Hogarth Press. (Original work published 1905)

Goodman, G. S., Rudy, L., Bottoms, B. L., & Aman, C. (1990). Children's concerns and memory: Issues of ecological validity in the study of children's eyewitness testimony. In R. Fivush & J. A. Hudson (Eds.), *Knowing and remembering in young children*. New York: Cambridge University Press.

Graf, P., Squire, L. R., & Mandler, G. (1984). The information that amnesic patients do not forget. *Journal of Experimental Psychology: Learning, Memory, and Cognition*, **10**, 164–178.

Greco, C., Rovee-Collier, C., Hayne, H., Griesler, P. & Earley, L. (1986). Ontogeny of early event memory: I. Forgetting and retrieval by 2- and 3-month-olds. *Infant Behavior and Development*, **9**, 441–460.

Hamond, N. R., & Fivush, R. (1991). Memories of Mickey Mouse: Young children recount their trip to Disneyworld. *Cognitive Development*, **6**, 433–448.

Hanna, E., & Meltzoff, A. N. (1993). Peer imitation by toddlers in laboratory, home, and day-care contexts: Implications for social learning and memory. *Developmental Psychology*, **29**, 702–710.

Hartshorn, K., Rovee-Collier, C., Gerhardstein, P., Bhatt, R. S., Wondoloski, T. L., Klein, P., Gilch, J., Wurtzel, N., & Campos-de-Carvalho, M. (1998). The ontogeny of long-term memory over the first year-and-a-half of life. *Developmental Psychobiology*, **32**, 69–89.

Hayne, H., MacDonald, S., & Barr, R. (1997). Developmental changes in the specificity of memory over the second year of life. *Infant Behavior and Development*, **20**, 233–245.

Heimann, M., & Meltzoff, A. N. (1996). Deferred imitation in 9- and 14-month-old infants: A longitudinal study of a Swedish sample. *British Journal of Developmental Psychology*, **14**, 55–64.

Hill, W. L., Borovsky, D., & Rovee-Collier, C. (1988). Continuities in infant memory development. *Developmental Psychobiology*, **21**, 43–62.

Howe, M. L., & Courage, M. L. (1993). On resolving the enigma of infantile amnesia. *Psychological Bulletin*, **113**, 305–326.

Howe, M. L., & Courage, M. L. (1997a). The emergence and early development of autobiographical memory. *Psychological Review*, **104(3)**, 499–523.

Howe, M. L., & Courage, M. L. (1997b). Independent paths in the development of infant learning and forgetting. *Journal of Experimental Child Psychology*, **67**, 131–163.

Howe, M. L., & O'Sullivan, J. T. (1997). What children's memories tell us about recalling our childhoods: A review of storage and retrieval processes in the development of long-term retention. *Developmental Review*, **17**, 148–204.

Hudson, J. A. (1986). Memories are made of this: General event knowledge and development of autobiographic memory. In K. Nelson (Ed.), *Event knowledge: Structure and function in development*. Hillsdale, NJ: Erlbaum.

Hudson, J. A. (1990). Constructive processing in children's event memory. *Developmental Psychology*, **26**, 180–187.

Hudson, J. A. (1993). Reminiscing with mothers and others: Autobiographical memory in young two-year-olds. *Journal of Narrative and Life History*, **3**, 1–32.

Hudson, J. A., & Fivush, R. (1991). As time goes by: Sixth graders remember a kindergarten experience. *Applied Cognitive Psychology*, **5**, 346–360.

Hudson, J. A., & Nelson, K. (1986). Repeated encounters of a similar kind: Effects of familiarity on children's autobiographical memory. *Cognitive Development*, **1**, 253–271.

Hudson, J. A., & Sheffield, E. G. (1998). Déjà vu all over again: Effects of reenactment on toddlers' event memory. *Child Development*, **69**, 51–67.

Huttenlocher, P. R. (1990). Morphometric study of human cerebral cortex development. *Neuropsychologia, 28*, 517–527.

Jackson, A., & Morton, J. (1984). Facilitation of auditory word recognition. *Memory and Cognition, 12*, 568–574.

Kagan, J., & Hamburg, M. (1981). The enhancement of memory in the first year. *Journal of Genetic Psychology, 138*, 3–14.

Klein, P. J., & Meltzoff, A. N. (1999). Long-term memory, forgetting, and deferred imitation in 12-month-old infants. *Developmental Science, 2*, 102–113.

Knopman, D. S., & Nissen, M. J. (1987). Implicit learning in patients with probable Alzheimer's disease. *Neurology, 5*, 784–788.

Koenderink, M. J. T., Uylings, H. B. M., & Mrzljak, L. (1994). Postnatal maturation of the layer III pyramidal neurons in the human prefrontal cortex: A quantitative Golgi study. *Brain Research, 653*, 173–182.

Mandler, J. M. (1984). Representation and recall in infancy. In M. Moscovitch (Ed.), *Infant memory: Its relation to normal and pathological memory in humans and other animals.* New York: Plenum.

Mandler, J. M. (1986). The development of event memory. In F. Klix & H. Hagendorf (Eds.), *Human memory and cognitive capabilities—Mechanisms and performance.* New York: Elsevier Science.

Mandler, J. M. (1988). How to build a baby: On the development of an accessible representational system. *Cognitive Development, 3*, 113–136.

Mandler, J. M. (1990). Recall of events by preverbal children. In A. Diamond (Ed.), *The development and neural bases of higher cognitive functions.* New York: New York Academy of Science.

Mandler, J. M. (1998). Representation. In D. Kuhn & R. Siegler (Eds.), *Cognition, perception, and language,* Vol. 2 of W. Damon (Ed.), *Handbook of child psychology.* New York: John Wiley and Sons.

Mandler, J. M., & McDonough, L. (1995). Long-term recall of event sequences in infancy. *Journal of Experimental Child Psychology, 59*, 457–474.

McDonough, L. (1991, April). *Infant recall of familiar actions with de-contextualized objects.* Poster presented at the biennial meetings of the Society for Research in Child Development, Seattle, WA.

McDonough, L., & Mandler, J. M. (1994). Very long-term recall in infants: Infantile amnesia reconsidered. *Memory, 2*, 339–352.

McDonough, L., Mandler, J. M., McKee, R. D., & Squire, L. R. (1995). The deferred imitation task as a nonverbal measure of declarative memory. *Proceedings of the National Academy of Sciences, 92*, 7580–7584.

McKee, R. D., & Squire, L. R. (1993). On the development of declarative memory. *Journal of Experimental Psychology: Learning, Memory, and Cognition, 19*, 397–404.

Meltzoff, A. N. (1985). Immediate and deferred imitation in fourteen- and twenty-four-month-old infants. *Child Development, 56*, 62–72.

Meltzoff, A. N. (1988a). Infant imitation after a 1-week delay: Long-term memory for novel acts and multiple stimuli. *Developmental Psychology, 24*, 470–476.

Meltzoff, A. N. (1988b). Infant imitation and memory: Nine-month-olds in immediate and deferred tests. *Child Development, 59*, 217–225.

Meltzoff, A. N. (1988c). Imitation of televised models by infants. *Child Development, 59*, 1221–1229.

Meltzoff, A. N. (1990a). Foundations for developing a concept of self: The role of imitation in relating self to other and the value of social mirroring, social modeling, and self practice in infancy. In D. Cicchetti & M. Beeghly (Eds.), *The self in transition: Infancy to childhood.* Chicago: The University of Chicago Press.

Meltzoff, A. N. (1990b). The implications of cross-modal matching and imitation for the development of representation and memory in infants. In A. Diamond (Ed.), *The development and neural bases of higher cognitive functions.* New York: New York Academy of Science.

Meltzoff, A. N. (1995). What infant memory tells us about infantile amnesia: Long-term recall and deferred imitation. *Journal of Experimental Child Psychology*, **59**, 497–515.

Mishkin, M., & Appenzeller, T. (1987). The anatomy of memory. *Scientific American*, **256**, 80–89.

Myers, N. A., Clifton, R. K., & Clarkson, M. G. (1987). When they were very young: Almost-threes remember two years ago. *Infant Behavior and Development*, **10**, 123–132.

Myers, N. A., Perris, E. E., & Speaker, C. J. (1994). Fifty months of memory: A longitudinal study in early childhood. *Memory*, **2**, 383–415.

Neisser, U. (1962). Cultural and cognitive discontinuity. In T. E. Gladwin & W. Sturtevant (Eds.), *Anthropology and human behavior.* Washington, DC: Anthropological Society of Washington.

Neisser, U. (1967). *Cognitive psychology.* Englewood Cliffs, NJ: Prentice-Hall.

Neisser, U. (1988). Five kinds of self-knowledge. *Philosophical Psychology*, **1**, 35–59.

Nelson, C. A. (1995). The ontogeny of human memory: A cognitive neuroscience perspective. *Developmental Psychology*, **31**, 723–738.

Nelson, C. A. (1997). The neurobiological basis of early memory development. In N. Cowan (Ed.), *The development of memory in childhood.* Hove, East Sussex: Psychology Press.

Nelson, K. (1986). *Event knowledge: Structure and function in development.* Hillsdale, NJ: Erlbaum.

Nelson, K. (1993). Events, narratives, memory: What develops? In C. A. Nelson (Ed.), *Memory and affect in development: The Minnesota Symposium on Child Psychology.* Hillsdale, NJ: Erlbaum.

Nelson, K. (1997). Event representations then, now, and next. In P. van den Broek, P. J. Bauer, & T. Bourg (Eds.), *Developmental spans in event comprehension and representation: Bridging fictional and actual events.* Mahwah, NJ: Erlbaum

Nelson, K., & Gruendel, J. (1981). Generalized event representations: Basic building blocks of cognitive development. In M. E. Lamb & A. L. Brown (Eds.), *Advances in developmental psychology* (Vol. 1). Hillsdale, NJ: Erlbaum.

Nelson, K., & Gruendel, J. (1986). Children's scripts. In K. Nelson (Ed.), *Event knowledge: Structure and function in development.* Hillsdale, NJ: Erlbaum.

Nelson, K., & Ross, G. (1980). The generalities and specifics of long-term memory in infants and young children. In M. Perlmutter (Ed.), *New directions for child development— Children's memory.* San Francisco: Jossey-Bass.

Parkin, A. J. (1997). The development of procedural and declarative memory. In N. Cowan (Ed.), *The development of memory in childhood.* Hove, East Sussex: Psychology Press.

Peterson, C., & Rideout, R. (1998). Memory for medical emergencies experienced by 1 and 2-year-olds. *Developmental Psychology*, **34**, 1059–1072.

Piaget, J. (1952). *The origins of intelligence in children.* New York: International Universities Press.

Piaget, J. (1962). *Play, dreams and imitation in childhood.* New York: W. W. Norton & Co.

Pillemer, D. B. (1998). *Momentous events, vivid memories.* Cambridge, MA: Harvard University Press.

Pillemer, D. B., & White, S. H. (1989). Childhood events recalled by children and adults. In H. W. Reese (Ed.), *Advances in child development and behavior* (Vol. 21). San Diego: Academic Press.

Price, D. W. W., & Goodman, G. S. (1990). Visiting the wizard: Children's memory for a recurring event. *Child Development*, **61**, 664–680.

Ratner, H. H. (1980). The role of social context in memory development. In M. Perlmutter (Ed.), *New directions for child development—Children's memory*. San Francisco: Jossey-Bass.

Ratner, H. H., Smith, B. S., & Dion, S. (1986). Development of memory for events. *Journal of Experimental Child Psychology*, **41**, 411–428.

Roediger, H. L., & Blaxton, T. A. (1987). Effects of varying modality, surface features, and retention interval on priming in word-fragment completion. *Memory and Cognition*, **15**, 379–388.

Rovee-Collier, C. (1997). Dissociations in infant memory: Rethinking the development of implicit and explicit memory. *Psychological Review*, **104**, 467–498.

Rovee-Collier, C., & Gerhardstein, P. (1997). The development of infant memory. In N. Cowan (Ed.), *The development of memory in childhood*. Hove, East Sussex: Psychology Press.

Rovee-Collier, C. K., & Fagen, J. W. (1981). The retrieval of memory in early infancy. In L. P. Lipsitt (Ed.), *Advances in infancy research* (Vol. 1). Norwood, NJ: Ablex.

Rovee-Collier, C. K., & Shyi, G. C. W. (1992). A functional and cognitive analysis of infant long-term retention. In M. L. Howe, C. J. Brainerd, & V. F. Reyna (Eds.), *The development of long-term retention*. New York: Springer-Verlag.

Rubin, D. C. (1982). On the retention function for autobiographical memory. *Journal of Verbal Learning and Verbal Behavior*, **21**, 21–38.

Schachtel, E. (1947). On memory and childhood amnesia. *Psychiatry*, **10**, 1–26.

Schacter, D. L. (1987). Implicit memory: History and current status. *Journal of Experimental Psychology: Learning, Memory, and Cognition*, **13**, 501–518.

Schacter, D. L. (1990). Perceptual representation systems and implicit memory. In A. Diamond (Ed.), *The development and neural bases of higher cognitive functions*. New York: New York Academy of Science.

Schacter, D. L., & Moscovitch, M. (1984). Infants, amnesics, and dissociable memory systems. In M. Moscovitch (Ed.), *Infant memory: Its relation to normal and pathological memory in humans and other animals*. New York: Plenum.

Schneider, W., & Pressley, M. (1997). *Memory development between two and twenty* (2nd ed.). Mahwah, NJ: Lawrence Erlbaum Associates.

Schwade, J. A. (1999). *You say tomato, we say food: Vocabulary and categorization in 16- to 32-month-olds*. Unpublished doctoral dissertation, University of Minnesota.

Sheffield, E. G., & Hudson, J. A. (1994). Reactivation of toddlers' event memory. *Memory*, **2**, 447–465.

Sheingold, K., & Tenney, Y. J. (1982). Memory for a salient childhood event. In U. Neisser (Ed.), *Memory observed*. San Francisco: Freeman.

Sherry, F., & Schacter, D. L. (1987). The evolution of multiple memory systems. *Psychological Review*, **94**, 439–454.

Shimamura, A. P., Janowsky, J. S., Squire, L. R. (1991). What is the role of frontal lobe damage in memory disorders? In H. D. Levin, H. M., Eisenberg, & A. L. Benton (Eds.), *Frontal lobe functioning and dysfunction*. New York: Oxford University Press.

Shore, C. M. (1986). Combinatorial play, conceptual development, and early multiword speech. *Developmental Psychology*, **22**, 184–190.

Slackman, E. A., Hudson, J. A., & Fivush, R. (1986). Actions, actors, links, and goals: The structure of children's event representations. In K. Nelson (Ed.), *Event knowledge: Structure and function in development*. Hillsdale, NJ: Erlbaum.

Slackman, E. A., & Nelson, K. (1984). Acquisition of an unfamiliar script in story form by young children. *Child Development*, **55**, 329–340.

Slater, A. (1995). Visual perception and memory at birth. In C. Rovee-Collier & L. P. Lipsitt (Eds.), *Advances in Infancy Research* (Vol. 9). Norwood, NJ: Ablex.

Smith, B. S., Ratner, H. H., & Hobart, C. J. (1987). The role of cueing and organization in children's memory for events. *Journal of Experimental Child Psychology, 4*, 1–24.

Spear, N. E. (1978). *The processing of memories: Forgetting and retention.* Hillsdale, NJ: Erlbaum.

Squire, L. R. (1992). Memory and the hippocampus: A synthesis from findings with rats, monkeys, and humans. *Psychological Review, 99*, 195–231.

Squire, L. R., Knowlton, B., & Musen, G. (1993). The structure and organization of memory. *Annual Review of Psychology, 44*, 453–495.

Squire, L. R., & Zola-Morgan, S. (1991). The medial temporal lobe memory system. *Science, 253*, 1380–1386.

Todd, C. M., & Perlmutter, M. (1980). Reality recalled by preschool children. In M. Perlmutter (Ed.), *New directions for child development—Children's memory.* San Francisco: Jossey-Bass.

Tulving, E. (1985). How many memory systems are there? *American Psychologist, 40*, 385–398.

Tulving, E., Kapur, S., Markowitsch, H. J., Craik, F. I. M., Habib, R., & Houle, S. (1994). Neuroanatomical correlates of retrieval in episodic memory: Auditory sentence recognition. *Proceedings of the National Academy of Science, USA, 91*, 2012–2015.

Usher, J. A., & Neisser, U. (1993). Childhood amnesia and the beginnings of memory for four early life events. *Journal of Experimental Psychology: General, 122*, 155–165.

Webster, M. J., Ungerleider, L. G., & Bachevalier, J. (1991). Connections of inferior temporal areas TE and TEO with medial temporal-lobe structures in infant and adult monkeys. *The Journal of Neuroscience, 11*, 1095–1116.

Wenner, J. A. (1999). *Panning for goals: Preschoolers' comprehension of goal structure in narratives.* Unpublished doctoral dissertation, University of Minnesota.

Wenner, J. A., & Bauer, P. J. (1999). Bringing order to the arbitrary: One- to two-year-olds' recall of event sequences. *Infant Behavior and Development, 22*, 585–590.

West, T. A., & Bauer, P. J. (1999). Assumptions of infantile amnesia: Are there differences between early and later memories? *Memory, 7*, 257–278

Wetzler, S. E., & Sweeney, J. A. (1986). Childhood amnesia: A conceptualization in cognitive-psychological terms. *Journal of the American Psychoanalytic Association, 34*, 663–685.

White, S. H., & Pillemer, D. B. (1979). Childhood amnesia and the development of a socially accessible memory system. In J. F. Kihlstrom & F. J. Evans (Eds.), *Functional disorders of memory.* Hillsdale, NJ: Erlbaum.

Winograd, E., & Killinger, W. A., Jr. (1983). Relating age at encoding in early childhood to adult recall: Development of flashbulb memories. *Journal of Experimental Psychology: General, 112*, 413–422.

Zola-Morgan, S., & Squire, L. R. (1990). The primate hippocampal formation: Evidence for a time-limited role in memory storage. *Science, 250*, 288–290.

Zola-Morgan, S., & Squire, L. R. (1993). Neuroanatomy of memory. *Annual Review of Neuroscience, 16*, 547–563.

ACKNOWLEDGMENTS

Financial support for data collection and preparation was provided by grants from the National Institutes of Child Health and Human Development (HD-28425), the Graduate School of the University of Minnesota, and a McKnight Land-Grant Professorship to Patricia J. Bauer. Additional support for manuscript preparation was provided by a Bush Sabbatical Supplement Award to Patricia J. Bauer.

We are grateful to a number of individuals who lent their support and energy throughout the long periods of collection and preparation of data for this report. In addition to the small army of undergraduate student volunteers who worked to film testing sessions and code data from them, we thank Kathleen Delaney, Deborah Johnson, Kari Kaiser, Jennifer Lee, Caren Lowe, and Karen Meadows, for scheduling all of the participants; Mervyn Bergman, for so expertly realizing our designs for stimuli for this research, and for his nothing-short-of-valiant efforts at keeping them in serviceable order throughout the four-and-a-half years and over 1,500 testing sessions required to see this project through to completion; Diane Bearman, Melissa Burch, Leslie Carver, Dana Van Abbema, Louise Hertsgaard, Jennifer Schwade, Maya Sen, Jennie Waters, and Tiffany West, for so generously contributing their time to the massive coding effort that permitted the data to be available for analysis sooner, rather than later; Julie Buckel of Academic and Distributed Computing Services, for getting us off to a good start with SAS; and Dr. Mark L. Howe and three anonymous reviewers for their stimulating comments on an earlier version of this *Monograph*. Our most sincere thanks to each of you.

We reserve a particular type of gratitude to the children and their parents who so generously gave of their time in order to participate in this research. The pool of potential research participants from which the families were drawn is strictly volunteer. The small tokens of appreciation that we provided for their efforts could never begin to repay the debt that we owe for their contributions. We are sincerely and deeply appreciative of the commitment that our participants made to this research and of their generous efforts to see it through to completion. We thank you one and all.

HISTORICAL AND FUTURE TRENDS IN STUDYING THE DEVELOPMENT
OF LONG-TERM RETENTION

Mark L. Howe

As I am sure many of the readers of this *Monograph* series are aware, the purpose of a commentary is not to reiterate, summarize, or necessarily critique the *Monograph* itself. The *Monograph* serves as its own best conspectus. Rather, a commentary can offer to put the main work in a larger context and by so doing, highlight the contributions of the *Monograph* as well as some of the questions that need to be addressed. In the present commentary I will attempt to do this in two ways. First, I begin by putting this work in a historical context in which I briefly consider why the development of retention has been important in developmental psychology, why there was very little research on retention relative to acquisition, and what the recent state of research on retention has wrought. Second, I discuss a number of issues that remain unresolved and how research in this *Monograph* may help set the agenda for yet another shift in the manner in which we study retention across the early years. Here, I take up a number of issues raised in the *Monograph* including the simple but critical observation that in order to study retention, we must first measure what has been learned and ensure that the target information is actually in memory before we attempt to measure its forgetting. In this context, I discuss memory strength, developmental confounds, and longitudinal research.

Historical Context

Let me begin by setting a larger context within which this *Monograph* belongs. For much of the history of developmental psychology, there have been two conflicting claims about the development of retention during childhood. On the one hand, there are those theorists who claimed that early experiences are somehow preferentially preserved relative to later experiences and that these "memories" serve a crucial role in an individual's overall development (e.g., Bowlby, 1960; Tinbergen, 1951). On the other hand, there are a number of theorists who have claimed that retention does not worsen across the childhood years but rather improves. Here, infantile amnesia is said to represent a severe form of rapid forgetting found early in life that eventually gives way to a progressive series of improvement in memory for life experiences up to the level of late childhood, early adolescence (e.g., Burton, 1970; Pillemer & White, 1989).

Despite the prevalence of these opposing points of view, empirical studies of the time had routinely produced only null age effects for retention (for a review, see Howe & Brainerd, 1989). For example, Fajnsztejn-Pollack (1973) examined retention across four age levels—5-year-olds, 7-year-olds, 10-year-olds, and young adults—using over 300 subjects at each age level. Subjects first studied a series of 280 pictures and were subsequently asked to recognize a different subset of 28 of those pictures at 2, 5, 10, 20, and 49 weeks. Although picture recognition scores declined across the 49-week retention interval, there were no age differences in the rate of decline. A number of other studies produced similar results with a variety of researchers coming to the conclusion that "information is not lost more rapidly by children than by adults. Forgetting rates . . . were invariant from childhood to young adulthood" (Lehman, Mikesell, & Doherty, 1985, p. 27). It would seem that, at least from the pattern of findings up to early 1985, neither theory concerning the development of retention was correct. That is, forgetting rates neither increase nor decrease with age across the childhood years but rather, simply remain developmentally invariant.

At about this same time 15 years ago, Brainerd, Kingma, and Howe (1985; also see Brainerd, Reyna, Howe, & Kingma, 1990; Howe & Brainerd, 1989) challenged the notion that there was nothing of interest to developmental psychologists in the study of children's retention. They pointed out a number of problems with the corpus of studies that led to this conclusion, the most important being that recognition tests served as the sole memory measure. The problem here is that such measures are known not to be developmentally sensitive to changes in children's memory. Indeed, as mentioned in this *Monograph*, recognition measures are perhaps the least developmentally sensitive index of changes in memory as they provide the most environmental support for memory performance. Because the ability to make contact with previously stored traces is an important source of developmental variation in retention performance, providing such support eliminates an important source of developmental variation from measurements of children's retention.

More recently, researchers interested in long-term retention have turned their attention from questions concerning recognition to ones concerning recall (free and cued). The overwhelming conclusion from this next wave of research has been that there exist age differences in retention and that developmentally, younger children retain less than older children. Although this research has produced a number of results like this, a new problem emerged, namely, how to control for age differences in initial encoding and storage. Despite the fact that it has long been known that younger children take longer to learn almost any information than older children, rarely were attempts made to equate initial acquisition of information before measures of forgetting were obtained. When such differences are not controlled, it cannot be unambiguously claimed that any age differences found at retention are due solely to age differences in forgetting rates as such differences may reflect residual age differences in what was originally learned. Simply put, because in most studies researchers administer only a fixed number of study opportunities at acquisition, usually only one, younger children will have less information in memory in the first place than older children. To then claim that younger children's lower retention scores on some subsequent test is due to more rapid forgetting than older children is simply not right because the lower score at retention may simply reflect poorer initial learning, not more rapid forgetting. A number of performance-based criterion measures have been discussed over the years and a variety of solutions have been proposed (e.g., Howe & Courage, 1997).

This issue was addressed in the current *Monograph* using one of these approaches. Specifically, Bauer and her colleagues used an analysis of covariance to eliminate age differences in initial acquisition performance from the retention data before it was analyzed. Although this is an admirable approach and one that I have used myself, there are a number of important caveats that need to be considered. In particular, there may exist a number of nonlinear influences that covary with variation in initial learning opportunities that are not reflected in the covariance analysis. For example, consider the effects of suggestibility and misinformation. It has frequently been argued that strength of the original trace is somehow (linearly) related to the strength of misinformation effects in children's recall. However, recent evidence does not confirm this intuition. Indeed, Powell, Roberts, Ceci, and Hembrooke (1999) found that relative to a single experience with a target event, young children who had repeated opportunities to experience an event exhibited considerably less suggestibility than children exposed to only a single experience with the target event. In a more extreme example, Marche (1999; also see Marche & Howe, 1995) found that there was no linear relationship between preschoolers' original learning (one exposure versus criterion learning) and their subsequent acceptance of misinformation. Thus, there may be no simple linear relationship between initial learning opportunities, age, and retention that can be wholly eliminated using analysis of covariance.

Importantly, variation in initial learning is critical to consider not only from a methodological and measurement perspective but also because it is likely to be a variable affecting the real-life autobiographical experiences that we expect children to testify about in court. Indeed, personally meaningful experiences are probably much better encoded and stored than more mundane, everyday events. Thus, much of what children testify about is very likely very well encoded and represented with considerable strength in memory due to its personal significance. Understanding the effects (linear and nonlinear) of initial learning on subsequent retention is, therefore, paramount both from a theoretical as well as a pragmatic perspective. At the very least, it can be argued that the study of variation in initial learning conditions has considerable "ecological validity."

Given these challenges and their potential solutions (see Howe, 2000a), the question remains, what have we learned about developmental differences in retention over the last 15 years? It is generally true, as illustrated in this *Monograph*, that when some form of recall is used as our measure, younger children forget more than older children. This holds regardless of whether younger-versus-older means 12-month-olds versus 18-month-olds (e.g., Bauer, 1996; Howe & Courage, 1997; Hudson & Sheffield, 1998; Meltzoff, 1995), preschoolers versus kindergartners (e.g., Howe, 2000b; Marche, 1999), or kindergartners versus Grade 2 children (e.g., Howe, Courage, Vernescu, & Hunt, in press). Many of these findings hold regardless of whether we are talking about memory as studied in the lab (see review by Howe & O'Sullivan, 1997) or memory as it occurs au naturel, traumatic or not (Howe, 2000a).

From the evidence accumulated to date, it is clear that retention is of interest to developmental psychologists, that there are clear age trends, and that these trends are not identical to those found at acquisition. Concerning this latter point, a number of studies in which storage and retrieval processes have been separated have found that age differences at acquisition are often the result of variation in retrieval skills, whereas age differences at retention are often the result of variation in long-term storage skills (for a review, see Howe & O'Sullivan, 1997). As well, variables can have different effects on children's performance at acquisition and at retention. For example, Brainerd et al. (1985) found that the effect of taxonomic relatedness on learning increased with age particularly for atypical exemplars. However, at retention, age increases were confined to the typical exemplars with atypical exemplars actually showing a decrease with age. Thus, although there may be across-age similarities in the development of acquisition skills and in the development of retention skills, acquisition development and retention development are not two sides of the same memory development coin.

Challenges for the Future

Over the past decade or so we have gained considerable insight into the development of retention during the early childhood years. Although we know that younger children forget more than older children, we do not know whether younger children actually forget faster than older children. There are really three issues at stake here—first, do children of different ages forget different amounts of information (the answer is apparently yes); second, do children of different ages forget different types of information (the answer here is also apparently yes—e.g., younger children forget peripheral information more often than older children—see Howe, 2000a); and third, for a given unit of information in memory, do younger children generally forget that information more rapidly than older children? Here, the answer is unclear. But it is unclear for some very good reasons. First, in order to compute the rate of decay of information from memory we first need to establish the original strength of that information in memory (see earlier discussion on initial learning confounds). Second, we must then estimate the decay of that information over a variety of intervals and determine what function best describes that decline (e.g., Rubin, Hinton, & Wenzel, 1999; Rubin & Wenzel, 1996). Unfortunately, this is not as easy a matter as it might seem (Roberts & Pashler, 2000; Rubin et al., 1999). The problem here is that any number of models serve as appropriate descriptions of decay functions and, as yet, we have not gathered the appropriate data with which we can discriminate these different models.

One solution to this last problem might be to switch tactics in the study of the development of children's long-term retention. One possibility, exemplified in this *Monograph*, is to use a longitudinal design. To date, much of the work on children's retention has relied on a cross-sectional approach. Although much can be and has been learned using this design, parameter estimation and model verification is often more easily accomplished using multiple measures across time for the same individuals rather than a single measure taken across different individuals at one point in time. Not only do longitudinal studies provide researchers with numerous measurements on the same individual across time, something that affords the researcher a more sensitive window into retention of specific events within the same individual, but also provides measures that are not subject to between subject variability. Indeed, by using outcomes from longitudinal studies, researchers can cross-validate their modeling efforts within as well as across individuals.

Of course, longitudinal designs present researchers with a whole new set of methodological concerns, particularly when the population of interest is very young and the skill sets under investigation, or the requisite subskills that subserve the skill being investigated, develop rapidly. Reminiscent of the initial learning confound already discussed, researchers must be cognizant of the kinds of ancillary abilities that are developing that contribute to the competence under investigation. The research in this *Monograph* provides an excellent case in point. Recall that in this *Monograph*, long-term retention was evaluated using a nonverbal response, one that included the reconstruction of events that occur in a specific canonical order. A serious concern is that the ordering within these events can be found in one's real-world experience and that it is the development of knowledge based on these latter experiences that is being measured longitudinally and not an individual's memory for a specific, previously experienced event. To control for this possibility, a very elaborate series of controls were instituted by Bauer and her colleagues, ones that measured the growth in this knowledge *independent* of the memory for the original events. Such measures are crucial to the interpretation of memory development generally, and the development of long-term retention specifically, as our measures of growth in this area are always contingent on some intermediary output medium, verbal or nonverbal. Even in the case of verbal output, we must be careful to isolate the contribution in the growth of language skills (the output medium) from any growth in memory and retention skills. For example, a more extensive verbal report of a memory at a later age than at an earlier age does not mean that the memory reported at that later age is any more elaborate than it was earlier. Rather, it could simply mean that the individual's ability to verbally describe that memory has improved independent of any changes in memory.

More generally, longitudinal designs afford us the opportunity to examine the initial state of memory for the to-be-retained information as well as estimate changes to that information as time proceeds. Because memory storage is dynamic, changing in response to new experiences, knowledge, organizational structure, and so forth, longitudinal designs in which multiple test opportunities are implemented permit an evaluation of how changes in the these variables influence existing memories. As pointed out very recently (e.g., Howe, 2000a), this is perhaps one of the most important areas for the future of research on the development of long-term retention. Again, as we are able to study younger and younger populations in which development proceeds on a number of interrelated fronts simultaneously, understanding the influence of these parallel growth functions is essential to our understanding of any one of these skills, in this case, retention.

Another important question raised in the present *Monograph* concerns how studies of children's retention inform more pragmatic issues in children's memory. More specifically, much of the research on children's long-term retention has been used to address issues concerning the age at which children can provide valid accounts of events that happened to them, ones that can be used in forensic settings. This *Monograph* is uniquely situated in that debate—the age span across which this study takes us is from predominantly nonverbal (at least in terms of outward expression) to the early development of the verbal skills necessary to report the contents of memory.

Two points are important here. First, as already noted, nonverbal measures of memory particularly in the age range studied here are essential. However, considerable controversy surrounds the nature of nonverbal memory measures especially in the context and ages used in this *Monograph* (e.g., Rovee-Collier, 1997). Considerable work remains to be done if we are to develop valid and reliable nonverbal mechanisms for reporting the contents of memory, ones that have a reliability akin to verbal reporting. The current *Monograph* also makes it clear that issues such as conscious versus unconscious, declarative versus nondeclarative, explicit versus implicit are worth grappling with and are critical to understanding the nature of early memory functioning. The resolution of such issues is particularly important if we are going to inform the judicial system about the memory and reporting capabilities of young children, especially those who may have been preverbal at the time they witnessed the event.

Second, studies like the one presented in this *Monograph* bridge an important gap between laboratory research and more naturalistic studies of (autobiographical) memory. Although what is found in laboratory-based studies normally translates well into the other "real world," laboratory-based studies afford us certain important controls that are not always available in naturalistic settings, ones that are necessary if we are to properly interpret outcomes. For example, in the current context additional controls were instituted in order to estimate growth in world knowledge that might have contaminated "pure" memory measures. Similarly, information was available that was used to estimate the state of initial learning of the to-be-retained information. This estimate was then used to partially eliminate initial learning as a confound prior to drawing conclusions about these children's retention skills. Issues of this sort have been raised not only in laboratory tasks but also in "real-life" tasks involving autobiographical memory (e.g., Ross, 1997). For example, it is very difficult to know what someone has forgotten about his or her life experiences unless one has an earlier *memory* record of what was initially encoded. Although one could compare a current recollection of an event to some other record (either someone else's recollection or some veridical record—for example,

211

a police record, videotape, and so on), such comparisons do not answer the question of whether that specific person's memory of the event is now any better or worse than at the time the event occurred. Again, what is needed is an initial record of what was encoded and stored by that particular individual as well as information about subsequent experiences that may have led to the modification of those initial memories.

Conclusion

This *Monograph* has much to offer, not only in the historical context about the nature of early retention and its development, but also about where we need to look in the future to fill in the missing pieces. From a historical perspective this *Monograph* like other recent work makes it abundantly clear that there are important and independent changes that occur in children's long-term retention, ones that should be of interest to developmental scientists. Equally important, the longitudinal approach exemplified here verifies our commonly held belief that older children tend to forget less than younger children not only when compared across different groups of children but also when the same children are tested across protracted time intervals. In terms of the future of retention development research, use of a longitudinal approach such as the one illustrated in this *Monograph* is critical if we are to articulate a more complete model of group- and individual-based retention development. Indeed, a longitudinal approach is essential if we are to track and understand how the "contents" of memory storage change with the acquisition of new information, organizational structures, and knowledge. Tracking parallel developments in abilities that directly influence memory (e.g., categorization skills) or that affect the expression of memory (e.g., language) are essential to deepening our understanding of the development of retention in childhood. We are at a point in the study of the development of long-term retention where progress will be marked by large-scale studies like the one in this *Monograph*. Future advances will be contingent on the use of carefully articulated methods that control for initial knowledge states, measurement of endogenous and exogenous changes brought about in these states, and examination of a variety of reporting strategies, verbal and nonverbal alike. With *Monographs* like this setting the stage for the next generation of studies in this field, the future of this area looks very bright, indeed.

References

Bauer, P. J. (1996). What do infants recall of their lives? Memory for specific events by one- and two-year-olds. *American Psychologist*, **51**, 29–41.

Bowlby, J. (1960). Grief and mourning in infancy and early childhood. *Psychoanalytic Study of the Child*, **15**, 9–52.

Brainerd, C. J., Kingma, J., & Howe, M. L. (1985). On the development of forgetting. *Child Development*, **56**, 1103–1119.

Brainerd, C. J., Reyna, V. F., Howe, M. L., & Kingma, J. (1990). Development of forgetting and reminiscence. *Monographs of the Society for Research in Child Development*, **55**(3–4, Serial No. 222).

Burton, R. V. (1970). Validity of retrospective reports assessed by the multitrait-multimethod analysis. *Developmental Psychology Monographs*, **3**(3, Pt. 2).

Fajnsztejn-Pollack, G. (1973). A developmental study of decay rate in long-term memory. *Journal of Experimental Child Psychology*, **16**, 225–235.

Howe, M. L. (2000a). *The fate of early memories: Developmental science and the retention of childhood experiences*. Washington, DC: American Psychological Association.

Howe, M. L. (2000b). *The role of intentional forgetting in reducing children's retroactive interference*. Manuscript submitted for publication.

Howe, M. L., & Brainerd, C. J. (1989). Development of children's long-term retention. *Developmental Review*, **9**, 301–340.

Howe, M. L., & Courage, M. L. (1997). Independent paths in the development of infant learning and forgetting. *Journal of Experimental Child Psychology*, **67**, 131–163.

Howe, M. L., Courage, M. L., Vernescu, R., & Hunt, M. (in press). Distinctiveness effects in children's long-term retention. *Developmental Psychology*.

Howe, M. L., & O'Sullivan, J. T. (1997). What children's memories tell us about recalling our childhoods: A review of storage and retrieval processes in the development of long-term retention. *Developmental Review*, **17**, 148–204.

Hudson, J. A., & Sheffield, E. G. (1998). Deja vu all over again: Effects of reenactment on toddlers' event memory. *Child Development*, **69**, 51–67.

Lehman, E. B., Mikesell, J. W., & Doherty, S. C. (1985). Long-term retention of information about presentation modality by children and adults. *Memory & Cognition*, **13**, 21–28.

Marche, T. A. (1999). Memory strength affects reporting of misinformation. *Journal of Experimental Child Psychology*, **73**, 45–71.

Marche, T. A., & Howe, M. L. (1995). Preschoolers report misinformation despite accurate memory. *Developmental Psychology*, **31**, 554–567.

Meltzoff, A. N. (1995). What infant memory tells us about infantile amnesia: Long-term recall and deferred imitation. *Journal of Experimental Child Psychology*, **59**, 497–515.

Pillemer, D. B., & White, S. H. (1989). Childhood events recalled by children and adults. In H. W. Reese (Ed.), *Advances in child development and behavior* (Vol. 21). New York: Academic Press.

Powell, M. B., Roberts, K. P., Ceci, S. J., & Hembrooke, H. (1999). The effects of repeated experience on children's suggestibility. *Developmental Psychology*, **35**, 1462–1477.

Roberts, S., & Pashler, H. (2000). How persuasive is a good fit? A comment on theory testing. *Psychological Review*, **107**, 358–367.

Ross, M. (1997). Validating memories. In N. L. Stein, P. A. Ornstein, B. Tversky, & C. J. Brainerd (Eds.), *Memory for everyday and emotional events*. Mahwah, NJ: Erlbaum.

Rovee-Collier, C. (1997). Dissociations in infant memory: Rethinking the development of implicit and explicit memory. *Psychological Review*, **104**, 467–498.

Rubin, D. C., Hinton, S., & Wenzel, A. (1999). The precise time course of retention. *Journal of Experimental Psychology: Learning, Memory, and Cognition*, **25**, 1161–1176.

Rubin, D. C., & Wenzel, A. (1996). One hundred years of forgetting: A quantitative description of retention. *Psychological Review*, **103**, 734–760.

Tinbergen, N. (1951). *The study of instinct*. London: Oxford University Press.

CONTRIBUTORS

Patricia J. Bauer (Ph.D., 1985, Miami University) is professor of child psychology at the Institute of Child Development, University of Minnesota, Minneapolis, Minnesota. She is Associate Editor of the *Journal of Cognition and Development*, and is on the editorial boards of the *Journal of Experimental Child Psychology* and the *Journal of Experimental Psychology: General*. Her research interests include early cognitive development in general, and early memory and conceptual development in particular.

Jennifer A. Wenner (Ph.D., 1999, Institute of Child Development, University of Minnesota) is an Assistant Professor in the Psychology Department at Augsburg College, Minneapolis, Minnesota. Her research interests include cognitive development in infants and preschoolers, with particular emphasis on text and narrative comprehension and their relations with early literacy.

Patricia L. Dropik (B.S., 1998, University of Minnesota) is a doctoral student in Communication Disorders, University of Minnesota, Minneapolis, Minnesota. Her research and clinical focus is in communicative intervention with young children who require augmentative or alternative means to speech. She is particularly interested in processes that facilitate transition from prelinguistic to symbolic communication for these children.

Sandi S. Wewerka (M.P.H., 2000, University of Minnesota) is a research coordinator at the Institute of Child Development, University of Minnesota, Minneapolis, Minnesota. Her research interests include developmental cognitive neuroscience as well as issues in maternal and child health during the prenatal and perinatal periods.

Mark L. Howe (Ph.D., 1982, University of Western Ontario) is Dean of Graduate Studies and Research and Professor of Psychology at Lakehead University, Thunder Bay, Ontario, Canada. His research interests include early cognitive development in general and early memory development, particularly autobiographical memory, the development of long-term retention, and the retention of traumatic and distinctive experiences specifically. A summary of this research can be found in his recent book, *The Fate of Early Memories: Developmental Science and the Retention of Childhood Experiences.*

STATEMENT OF EDITORIAL POLICY

The *Monographs* series is devoted to publishing developmental research that generates authoritative new findings and uses these to foster fresh, better integrated, or more coherent perspectives on major developmental issues, problems, and controversies. The significance of the work in extending developmental theory and contributing definitive empirical information in support of a major conceptual advance is the most critical editorial consideration. Along with advancing knowledge on specialized topics, the series aims to enhance cross-fertilization among developmental disciplines and developmental subfields. Therefore, clarity of the links between the specific issues under study and questions relating to general developmental processes is important. These links, as well as the manuscript as a whole, must be as clear to the general reader as to the specialist. The selection of manuscripts for editorial consideration and the shaping of manuscripts through reviews and revisions are processes dedicated to actualizing these ideals as closely as possible.

Typically *Monographs* entail programmatic large-scale investigations, sets of programmatic interlocking studies, or—in some cases—smaller studies with highly definitive and theoretically significant empirical findings. Multi-authored sets of studies that center on the same underlying question can also be appropriate; a critical requirement here is that all studies address common issues and that the contribution arising from the set as a whole be unique, substantial, and well integrated. The needs of integration preclude having individual chapters identified by individual authors. In general, irrespective of how it may be framed, any work that is judged to significantly extend developmental thinking will be taken under editorial consideration.

To be considered, submissions should meet the editorial goals of *Monographs* and should be no briefer than a minimum of 80 pages (including references and tables). There is an upper limit of 150–175 pages. Only in exceptional circumstances will this upper limit be modified. (Please submit four copies of the manuscript.) Because a *Monograph* is inevitably lengthy and usually substantively complex, it is particularly important that the text be well organized and written in clear, precise, and literate English. Note, however, that authors from non-English-speaking countries should not be put off by this stricture. In accordance with the general aims of SRCD, this series is actively interested in promoting international exchange of developmental research. Neither membership in the Society nor affiliation with the academic discipline of psychology are relevant in considering a *Monographs* submission.

The corresponding author for any manuscript must, in the submission letter, warrant that all coauthors are in agreement with the content of the manuscript. The corresponding author also is responsible for informing all coauthors, in a timely manner, of manuscript submission, editorial decisions, reviews received, and any revisions recommended. The corresponding author also must warrant in the submission letter that the study has been conducted according to the ethical guidelines of the SRCD.

Potential authors who may be unsure whether the manuscript they are planning would make an appropriate submission are invited to draft an outline of what they propose and send it to the Editor for assessment. This mechanism, as well as a more detailed description of all editorial policies, evaluation processes, and format requirements, can be found at the Editorial Office web site (http://astro.temple.edu/~overton/monosrcd.html) or can be obtained by contacting the Editor, Willis F. Overton, Temple University–Psychology, 1701 North 13th St., Rm. 567, Philadelphia, PA 19122-6085 (e-mail: monosrcd@blue.vm.temple.edu) (telephone: 215-204-7718).

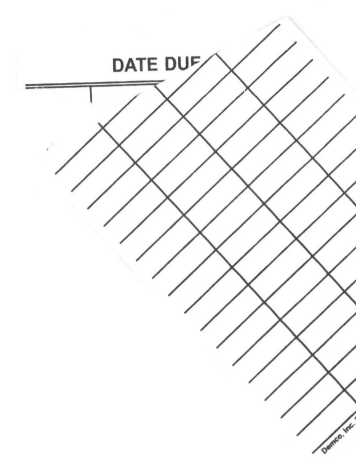

DATE DUE

Demco, Inc.